On Another Note

On Another Note

Making Music
at Head Start

Leah Wells

Foreword by Gabe Turow, Ed. M., Ed.D.

 Heliotrope Books

New York

Designed and Typeset by Heliotrope Books and AJJ Design
Cover Design by Naomi Rosenblatt, Anne Finkelstein, and Leah Wells
Cover photgraph by Judith Rosenblatt
Illustrations from public domain and by Naomi Rosenblatt

Dedicated to children growing up above 125th Street and below the poverty line, and to the hard workers who tend to preschoolers every day.

"Not the lofty, noble silvery vertical city but the vast, spread-out, sooty-gray and sooty-brown and sooty-red and sooty-pink horizontal city, the snarled-up and smoldering city, the old, polluted, betrayed, and sure-to-be torn-down-any-time-now city."

—Joseph Mitchell

"Tell me, where do the children play?"

—Cat Stevens

Author Note

In order to provide anonymity, the names of some characters and places described in this account have been changed.

TABLE OF CONTENTS

SONGS AND GAMES

SONGS AND GAMES (continued)

FOREWORD

With humor, dedication, and attitude, Leah Wells—a music teacher and gifted storyteller—takes readers to the South Bronx and her Head Start classrooms.

Her tender, insightful and sometimes tense accounts will be an asset to any music or art teacher, particularly specialists in early childhood education. Over and over again, Leah moves beyond bureaucratic hurdles to offer children inventive music and movement classes on the lowest budget possible.

Reading these accounts made me wonder why there is so little money for music and art classes these days, given the evidence that these courses have broad-based positive effects on children's thinking and cognition. Early childhood music education as Leah describes it—teaching students how to sing, dance, and play percussion in synchrony—can spur different brain areas to work together. In the last twenty years neurological studies have highlighted ways in which music engages children emotionally, verbally, physically, and in combination. Indeed, song is a first exposure to drama and poetry. From a neuroscience or cognitive psychology standpoint, music is an ideal vehicle for teaching and learning.

Listening to and singing songs is a potent form of mental stimulation, which makes Leah's work that much more vital to the growth of her students' minds. Through her lessons, children learn how to sing and play musical games with melody, rhythm, rhyme, and repetition. When those children learn to read, they will be asked to connect symbols on a page with sounds they have heard before, which is a musical task. Abstraction of sounds into discrete units is the basis of musical thinking, and this has clear overlaps with reading acquisition. In light of the cumulative abundance of research on music and the brain, music classes should be highly prized within schools—whereas it is actually the opposite. As school districts cut music programs, they end the very courses that have the most potential to activate students' brains.

Engaging a room full of children in song and movement is an art unto itself, and so the detailed lessons Leah presents here will be an invaluable resource for both teachers and parents. It is crucial for memoirs like this to be written and shared widely among classroom teachers so they can learn from each others' experiences, understand each other's roles, and work together better as an interdisciplinary community.

—Gabe Turow, Ed.M., Ed.D.

PROLOGUE

Over the years I've been employed as a visiting music and movement specialist in preschools, summer camps, and daycare centers in New York City. *On Another Note* is an account of my first year with Head Start, one of my steadiest employers. In 2003-2004 I found myself in neighborhoods I'd never known before—Marble Hill, Highbridge, and Castle Hill, in the Bronx—doing something I'd never dreamed I could—bringing music to preschoolers from diverse cultures and struggling families.

The Head Start Program is one facet of the larger war on poverty introduced during the Johnson administration. I was excited to learn that a family friend, social critic Dwight Macdonald, had helped inspire this program. I met Dwight when I was a kid and remember him as a white-haired, outspoken grown-up—someone to be admired. His writings about class in America bolstered President John F. Kennedy's efforts to attack poverty through instituting national programs that were designed to help the disadvantaged. Head Start was among the most popular of these programs as it served very young children, whom nobody could call "lazy" or "undeserving."

When Lyndon Johnson became president after Kennedy's assassination, he decided to carry forward Kennedy's uncompleted initiative. In his 1964 State of the Union Address, Johnson called on the nation to declare an "unconditional war on poverty." Launched in 1965, Head Start began as a catch-up summer school program. Its staff members were to help low-income children make a successful entry into elementary school.

Despite controversy over its effectiveness, Head Start continues to receive public support, serving over 22,000,000 low-income children. The initiative aims to provide comprehensive early childhood education, health, nutrition, and parent-involvement services to these children and their families. Its goals are threefold: (1) to foster stable family relationships and community; (2) to enhance children's physical and emotional wellbeing; and (3) to support development of children's strong cognitive skills. Clearly this was, and remains, a very ambitious program.

As a consultant for Head Start, I've seen strengths and shortcomings in its implementation, which I describe in this book. I've seen the centers provide nutritional meals for children who otherwise might not be well fed. I've seen the program provide companionship for children who otherwise might be socially isolated, and opportunity for their parents to take on jobs that upgrade a family's income. And I have been part of its effort to introduce children to the arts and culture, to help develop their cognitive, social, and motor coordination skills in creative and good-spirited ways.

At least at the time I describe, Head Start often followed no mandated arts or enrichment curriculum and employed uncertified consultants like me. Many of my original ideas for the music program came to me on a whim. Over time, my whims grew into a method. In this book, I share my process of designing music curriculum responsive to the needs of very young children, hoping that other teachers and caregivers may find my approach valuable—and fun.

Constructed as a "memoir with classroom exercises," On Another Note does not describe my young students in great detail, as in case studies. They were three- and four-year-olds, and I saw nearly a hundred of them on a given work-day. I was not their daily teacher, but a weekly visitor with a special mission: to help them sing and move. I describe only those children who touched me particularly. Therefore, the arc of growth presented in this memoir is mostly a record of my personal journey—how I faced the challenge of inventing fresh ideas for groups of preschoolers, how I gained confidence, worked with other adults around me, and learned about the neighborhoods where I taught.

I share my "slice of life" in its immediacy—local dialect and all. I have not attempted to conceal the colloquial speech I encountered in the Bronx. It is fair to assume that teachers throughout the United States speak with heavy accents and employ dialects common to their regions. What counts most with guardians of the very young is their vigilance and sensitivity.

High-quality early childhood programs are crucial to a society that calls itself civilized. Much of our character forms around the age of three; many of our interests and passions become alive then. We owe it to our children to nurture their creative spirits when they are so young and receptive. A recent piece in the New York Times Sunday Review by David L. Kirp reports long-term benefits for students who attended strong preschool programs like Head Start.

All of this said, however, a show is only as good as the folks who run it. In the hands of corrupt administrators, Head Start becomes as compromised as any utopian blueprint fallen to fools. While many staff members I met worked with valor and devotion, others disappointed me when they withheld teamwork that I sought from them in classrooms. Sadly, some staff members lacked empathy for the children and did not always serve their needs.

All social or educational programs need continual evaluation in order to improve. At Head Start, such testimony might be spoken not only by a professional inspector, but also by the guy who wields a mop, an administrative assistant, or even a middle-aged mother, like myself, who shows up for weekly music classes with a guitar on her back.

PART ONE

Facing the Music

Christmas break is over, and my guitar and I are back at the center in Castle Hill. Children rush to my legs, crying my name again and again like gulls calling above the surf: "Miss Leah, Miss Leah, Miss Leah!"

I put my instrument aside and stoop for hugs, noting how their bright eyes and small bodies have ever-so-slightly matured over the holiday—just a bit taller and more defined than when I'd seen them in December. I never perceive these changes in my own two sons, but wonder if their teachers will see a post-Christmas difference now.

"Move back, move back!" I command playfully. The children have clustered at my ankle boots, and I rise up, large as a grizzly bear as I strap my guitar over me, sending them to scoot backwards and giggle.

"Everybody, hands up high!" I'm pleased to see they remember this routine, and raise their arms as I do. "Okay...hands down low! Behind your back...where did they go?"

I look around, pantomiming confusion. The children delight in reassuring me that their hands have not disappeared behind their backs and jiggle them blissfully before me.

Strumming a D chord on the guitar, I prepare them to sing. There's a new activity up my sleeve, but I will first play a hearty round of "Jingle Bells" to unite the room in a familiar song before launching into new instructions. The holidays have passed, but winter songs still prevail.

My routine at this center is rigorous—six classes, five in a row before lunch. By the end of the morning I begin to crash, which makes it more challenging when my supervisor, Miss Catalina, accosts me on my way to the staffroom.

"We have to talk, Miss Leah." She tells me to meet her at her cubicle in back of the main office. Then she disappears through a classroom door carrying a stack of folders, and what can I do? Lunch in the staffroom will have to wait as I find my way to the stiff, plastic chair beside Miss Catalina's desk with nothing to fill my empty stomach but my own anxiety.

For a few minutes I sit listening to the secretaries take phone calls and then Miss Catalina swoops in. A Filipino woman of about sixty, she flashes me her most chilling smile. Once seated behind her desk she asks if I have had a nice vacation.

"Yes, thank you and how was yours?" I return as obediently as I have heard the children recite their daily grace.

She squeezes her eyes shut and nods. "Now that it is January, Miss Leah, I would like to know your intentions for our music program?"

I am too washed out to know in which direction to dodge. Is she going to tell me that, from now on, I am forbidden to bring in toys, trucks, and punching bags that make her classrooms too raucous, and that I must adhere to more conventional lesson plans? If that was the case, why had no one ever given me guidelines? As I hesitate, she prompts me. "For example, what did you prepare for us this morning?"

My mouth suddenly dry, I begin by saying that the children were all eager to tell me what they did over their vacation, "often all at the same time," I add, searching for her eyes behind the reflection of her glasses. But Miss Catalina isn't smiling. She rests her chin on her folded hands and I have no indication as to whether I am driving myself off a cliff. "I used this morning to review what we've been exploring in the weeks before Christmas," I go on. "We sang counting songs such as 'Eighteen Wheels on the Big Rig,' and took our ABCs to the next level with a spelling song called Ragg Mop.

"Oh, and I tried to sneak a few brain teasers into the mix. For example after we sang the days of the week I asked questions such as: 'What days make up the weekend? What days do I come and see you? I brought them a new song about children going to school all over the world." Sensing that I am babbling, I stop and shrug. "I thought it best to keep things light on our first day back together."

For a few terrible seconds she studies me. My head pounds and I hope she will release me before the cooks remove the trays of fish and potatoes from the staffroom. Finally she straightens her back like a cobra, announcing, "It is as I had thought. You are *deficient!*"

Deficient. My heart sinks.

"Have you not been told about the Extravaganzas? I am certain that your teachers informed you of the importance of our upcoming musical Extravaganzas. It is your chance for the children to show off what they have accomplished in all these weeks of music time...and here, you come to us unprepared." She smiles incongruously. "Clearly you have not even begun to think about what you will present."

I'd heard murmuring about an end-of-the-year event back in December. But we were so busy with Christmas then, and nobody had clarified exactly what the Extravaganza was supposed to be, or that I was under any kind of deadline to produce it.

"But we have until June, don't we?" I query weakly.

"Yes, but you are already deficient." That word again. "When Mr. Greg was with us he would begin preparing the children as early as October. Did you know that he would record the music himself and bring in such lovely CDs that the teacher could use to practice with their children?" she recalls, misting over.

What a blow, as I'm finally getting the hang of concocting successful activities—joyful ones that get the whole class spinning and singing, and present teaching opportunities—I am expected to sprout a whole additional skill-set and produce a musical revue for three- and four-year-olds.

I doubt I can succeed. I know how hard it is to gain the kids' cooperation, even with the fun of balls and balloons and an open-ended agenda. How can I get them to behave if I need them to sit still and memorize lyrics and practice routines?

Oh, what is wrong with just letting off steam, singing, dancing, playing games, and blowing bubbles? I had looked so forward to seeing the children's eyes when I surprised them with my parachute and new stack of colored scarves.

Over my thoughts, Miss Catalina explains that in the months to come I will be asked to contribute to other events such as Martin Luther King Day, an Earth Day show, and a spring assembly. Classroom teachers will lead most of these programs. The most important thing I must do in the months ahead, she emphasizes, is to prepare the children for the Extravaganza. "If this is to continue," she prefaces cryptically, I must pick a theme and craft a performance upon which my evaluation as a consultant will rest heavily.

"What is the budget for these Extravaganzas?" I ask, and she throws back her head and laughs. "We have noticed that you like to be very creative in your music classes with us, Miss Leah. Just use your creativity."

Trays of lunch are still on the staffroom table, but I've lost my appetite after my session in Miss Catalina's electric chair. I squeeze myself between the elbows of two teachers who speak Spanish and sit down with my throbbing head to ruminate. It isn't fair, with so much hanging on the success of these culminating events, that Head Start will not provide me with any money for props, costumes, or scenery. Miss Catalina's directive was clear: other than the long tubes of brown butcher paper that lay in the supply closets, I will be on my own. "Just use your creativity," she had sneered, making it sound like a gauntlet dropping.

"And don't forget to multiply this crisis by three because I have to pull off an Extravaganza for all three of my centers," I agonize to my husband Mark late that night, when our boys are asleep. I told him about being declared "deficient," and he knows this is not the first time Miss Catalina has put me in the hot seat.

"Why not kill three birds with one stone and recycle the same program for all three locations?" he suggests. Appreciating his point, I feel instantly less burdened; two thirds less burdened. "You always tell me that your classes feel too long," he continues, "that they drag on past their prime. Maybe rehearsing your bits for the Extravaganza could be just what you need to fill the time?"

For a moment I sit, marveling at the good sense he makes, and also at how fully he has listened to me.

"Hey, you know, you're not bad at this stuff," I say. " You've just given me more practical advice than all three of my so-called supervisors—you're a lot easier on the eyes, for that matter. Hmm, perhaps Brenda Keenan could find a center or two for you to run—"

But I should not have mentioned employment to Mark. A moody shadow crosses his features and in an instant he begins to pinch me.

"You are deficient!" he pipes.

"Ouch!" I cry. "That hurts!"

"You are deficient!" he repeats and tickles me until I dissolve into giggles. We both laugh so hard that at first we don't hear the faint wail that issues from behind the closed bedroom door. We had thought the boys were out cold, but suddenly our older son Haskell emerges from the darkness, sweet as Poo Bear in his pajamas with feet, rubbing his eyes and asking, "But Mommy, why does Miss Catalina hate you?"

Starting with Head Start: How it Began

Rewind five months: Long, stifling days roll August into September. My friend Janie calls to say that she and her husband are moving to California. "Thought I should let you know that Greg was doing music classes for Head Start last year. He says they're looking for someone to take over. Why don't you call them, Leah? Are you doing anything, are you working now?"

People who don't have kids are forever asking me if I'm "doing anything."

Janie doesn't understand that a tedious, blistering city summer of knotting water balloons and settling playground arguments has me longing for school to begin. The thought of packing my two sons, ages five and seven, off in the morning only to take a long subway ride and surround myself with legions of new four-year-olds feels overwhelming.

Still, times are tight because Mark has just lost his job.

"It's good money, Leah. You'd be surprised! You'd probably be doing what Greg was doing with the kids every day, just being yourself. Greg thinks you'd be really good at this. Come on, say something! You know, with your experience and skill-set you should at least give them a call. Here's the number. Ask for Brenda Keenan."

I had never thought of my hot-summer mothering days as comprising a "skill-set" or "experience" in the resume sense of the word. It's true that anything with strings on it—guitar, banjo, mandolin, fiddle—I can play. But does that count? In either of these two roles, as a mother and folk musician, people rarely want to pay me. Now Janie proposes I could be paid for the two of them put together. I'm warmed by how an enterprising friend fires up my own ambitions. Janie is a country and blues singer with whom I play banjo from time to time. A few years ago she married her lead guitarist, Greg, a hot jazz artist and arranger.

It is certainly telling that a musician as impressive as Greg must sing, "I'm A Little Teapot" all day long. Maybe the teapot is empty because now Greg and Janie are pulling up stakes to try their luck in the pressure-cooker of L.A. sunshine. Janie is bravely leaving her day job as an executive assistant. Then she really opens my bleary eyes by telling me that Greg is saying good-bye to a two hundred-dollar *per diem* rate, for what I assumed at the time was "musical babysitting."

And so, at Janie's insistence during the second muggy week of September 2003, I fax my resume to the Head Start office in the Bronx. Brenda Keenan, the staff coordinator, calls me right away. It's happening too fast. Thanks to a head lice infestation that my sons brought home from school—and Mark's insistence upon buzz-cutting the entire family (including my ample locks)—I now have a head as shiny as Mr. Clean's. But of course, I swathe it in bandannas and baseball caps, and sometimes even a wig. This does not strike me as job interview fare, but Brenda, with her husky alto, is encouraging. Over the phone she has a kind of gruff informality that makes me feel more like I'm getting slapped on the back by a teamster than scheduling an interview with an educational administrator.

The day I am to meet with her, I opt for a long, decorative Ukrainian babushka to shroud my baldness. Following Brenda's instructions, I board the Number 6 Train and am instantly sorry that I didn't bring something to read. I have nothing to calm my nerves as the subway winds us further north on this line than I've ever been. Although I was born in New York, nothing has ever summoned me to these heights, or should I say depths, because it is both. The train thunders through station after sooty station in the dark tunnel, and then climbs to daylight where we float over city blocks of low, pale-brick apartment buildings. When I disembark at the Castle Hill station my journey is far from complete.

At the foot of the elevated station, Castle Hill Avenue appears to be a long, bland strip of fast food restaurants and discount centers. None of the buildings are over two or three stories and their palette is unusually pastel for this city. As I make my way further from the station I pass residential buildings of clapboard and shingles, painted pink and turquoise, and the polluted breeze that hits my face is salted. Could we be close to a river or the ocean? Nobody I ask can confirm that I'm walking in the right direction for Metropolitan Avenue. Not one of the three people I've stopped speaks English.

When I finally arrive, I meet a statue of Jesus in the waiting room, unmistakable in his crown of thorns and red robes. I'm reminded that Head Start is partially funded by the Archdiocese of New York, and that its centers are hosted by Catholic schools. Before I meet Brenda, a secretary gives me a yellow application form that asks me to list experiences that prepare me for the teaching position. I don't have a baccalaureate degree—in fact, I have only a high school equivalency diploma. That was the best I could do with my severe dyslexia.

I'm in the middle of describing my square-dance calling and trying to up-grade the hassles of throwing my sons' birthday parties to "events planning," when a woman who I immediately assume is Brenda Keenan appears at the door with hands on her hips and a big smile for me. I follow her upstairs and through a hallway to her office. She's middle-aged, well preserved—pink and unwrinkled beneath her substantial weight and dyed brown hair.

"So how's Greg?" she asks in her low voice as we settle ourselves onto office chairs. We talk easily about his and Janie's move to California. I take the gamble of disclosing why I'm wearing the scarf, and she laughs and says they too have gone through many episodes of lice at different Head Start centers. I'm not necessarily glad to hear this, but I'm glad she's not thrown by my predicament. We've made a friendly bond, and as we continue speaking I sense that she's not even going to read what I've etched out on the application This woman has never heard my guitar playing or seen me interact with children. Yet I have a feeling that she likes me, and that the job is mine, in spite of my coming to the interview bald as Yul Brynner.

The walk back to the Castle Hill subway stop is lighthearted. For starters, I know where I'm going. What a relief not to have to stop and ask people for directions, people who regard me with suspicion and seem to speak no familiar language. I wonder if I've deceived myself about how well the interview went. Will I be hired? I don't want to leave the Bronx empty-handed, with no clear answer for the family. I know Mark is really worried; he was not given any kind of severance package from the digital printing house where he'd been night manager for years.

At the base of the elevated Castle Hill station a corner newsstand beckons. The trip back home will be long and I need some distraction from obsessing about whether I will be making this journey again with a guitar case strapped to my shoulders. I stand in line to drop my quarter for the daily paper—I have not yet learned how to throw it down for the clerk, like a time-hardened commuter.

Stalled in line, I turn my eyes to the display of glossy weeklies. Oh, to have a perky little turned-up nose and a peony pink bee-stung pout like these models on the covers! And should I have the thick slash of my unibrow plucked into those sassy, pencil-thin arches? Currently I have more hair in my eyebrows than on my head. All the lovelies this week are tilting their heads coyly and throw-ing these reckless, ecstatic smiles—perhaps the photogenic really do have more "phun."

Minutes later I huff up the long flight of iron stairs and board a southbound Number 6 Train that barrels up to the rickety platform, causing the concrete to tremble and sway like a buoy on the tide. When the doors close and the me-chanical woman's voice announces Parkchester as the next stop, I let myself sink, as much as possible, into the hard seat to enjoy the parade of exotic avenues, so new to my ears that I might as well have been visiting Estonia: St. Lawrence, Morrison-Soundview, Elder Avenue, Whitlock Avenue, Hunts Point Avenue, St. Mary's Street.

At some point while I was reading the paper, the train has re-entered sub-way darkness. "This is a Manhattan-bound Six Train. The next stop is Cypress Avenue." The female robot announces each station, which is also displayed in digitized red lights on screens at either end of the subway car. This announce-ment is followed, at intervals, by the ever-changing time, down to the minute. I must be a very important astronaut to be furnished with all these data, blinking at me from every direction! But while the high-tech Six Train rushes me into the future, the crumbling porcelain and the soot-blackened mosaic tiles of these ne-glected stations above 125th Street carry me back to Pompeii before the volcano.

Other than the shadowy old man, sitting like a slouched Van Gogh peasant at the far end of the car, the only other passengers are a pretty Hispanic mother, stroking the hair of a little girl whose head rests on her lap. We sit directly across from each other but avoid meeting eyes until the steel door at the end of the car slams open and a quintet of unruly teenagers erupts between us. The girls are wearing headphones and seem to be yelling at the boys over a soundtrack. Their voices are high-pitched and as piercing as car alarms. Every word they scream is "fuck" or "bitch."

The mother's hand that has been threading idly through her daughter's ponytail tightens and the little girl sits up. The teenagers push and shove each other; they wobble as the train bucks. Several times they almost step on me. Mother, daughter, and I have all stiffened in silent protest until the teenagers hurl themselves through the next door just as recklessly as they had surged into our car. The door slides shut with a loud crack and, in the abrupt silence, I final-ly meet eyes with the pretty mother who shakes her head.

"They gonna kill theysells," she says. I nod and raise my eyebrows. She looks away and shakes her head again. "Thasss it, I'm telling you. One day they all gonna kill theysells."

At the 125th Street station she and her daughter leave the train and, in a flutter of the most astonishing fingernails, she salutes me with a little wave. Her nails are lacquered fire-engine red, and so fiercely curled that they remind me of a long-horned sheep. Wow! How can you keyboard anything with a set of those? Maybe she doesn't have to. I will hope that for her.

It's late afternoon by the time I finally walk through my own door. As we agreed, my mother is watching the boys, and as usual the boys are watching TV. Lately my mother has become a bit hard of hearing. So, in my absence, the boys have joyfully let the TV volume soar out of control.

Over the noise, my mother calls from the kitchen, "How did it go, dear?" But I'm distracted by the answering machine whose blinking light displays two messages; everywhere I go blinking lights seem to tell me what to do. Hooray, the first message is Brenda Keenan's husky voice saying that she'd like to give me the job. I will be working at three Head Start centers, which are all in the Bronx: Mondays in Marble Hill, Tuesdays near Yankee Stadium, and Fridays in Castle Hill. But the part about my having to go back to the main office gets drowned out beneath little Simon's mounting protest.

"Haskell, I don't like this show. Turn it back! Mommy, Haskell is—"

"Shut up, Simon!"

"No, you shut up!"

"Mommy, he's fresh!" gloats Haskell as I try to make out the second voice that's purring underneath the TV with its frantic commercials, all of which seem to end with a man screaming: "some assembly required, batteries not included!"

"Could everybody please just keep it down?" I bellow, managing to stab the repeat button on the answering machine. "I think I've just been offered a new job!"

But as Brenda's message replays, I can barely listen. I know I will have to take the job; we have no other income. Can I imagine myself singing songs and playing musical games with young children from some of the city's roughest neighborhoods? What on earth can I offer them?

First Monday in Marble Hill

"Why do I need this?" I ask the orderly, whose hypodermic needle is poised above my arm to administer a tetanus shot.

"Because sometimes when you work with children, they're gonna bite you."

The Head Start offices are willing to wait for my finger prints. But I cannot be brought into the centers without the tetanus shot. So now I've found myself in the office of the physician who accepts our temporary insurance, realizing this job may bite me. I'm going to a foreign country and I need inoculations. I finish my paperwork just as their budget is confirmed. We enrichment consultants will be paid, and I am to begin work at Marble Hill the following Monday.

But with my family, the fun never stops. Monday morning Simon wakes up with his right eye plastered shut. He has to be kept home from school with a goopy case of pinkeye. With Mark to run him to the pediatrician, I have no excuse for not launching myself onto the Bronx-bound subway. I am frozen with dread, but after managing all the logistics at home there is a calming magic to floating over the river on the elevated Number 1 Train above Dyckman Street, traveling 'through the looking glass' to the north bank of the Harlem River—which I have seen before only from the protection of my father's car.

Looking down as we approach the river, I see a rugged procession of sprawling factories, their soot-blackened smokestacks rising out of the low buildings like birthday candles stuck on a sheet cake. Gray intervals of parking lots and warehouses are followed by a patchwork of tenement blocks, until suddenly a network of crisscrossing steel girders accosts my view and my train is on a bridge crossing the shimmering plain of the Harlem River, glassily mirroring the sky.

But soon enough my view is limited to the tar paper moonscapes that cover the businesses of what must be upper Broadway in Marble Hill. The stations we pull into are all fine old ladies up here, wonderful fleurs-de-lys medallions of cast iron and gargoyles spying down into curtained tenement windows like those in an Edward Hopper painting.

I try to peek into these windows, intrigued by the glimpses of passing rooms and figures. We are close to my stop, as indicated in the little yellow directory that arrived with my paperwork from Brenda Keenan. As the train pulls out of 215th Street I am on my feet and shrugging into my guitar case like a life jacket, waiting with a pounding heart for the doors to open at 225th Street. And then my pounding heart and I are abruptly under the sky where I have to walk some hundred yards on the long, narrow platform to find the exit to the street. Through the cool, piney mist, which tickles my face as I look south, I can make out the sandy bank of the river with bulldozers poised in their work, silent dinosaurs in the distance stooping to drink.

On this side of the tracks I find there is no station-house and I have to push myself through a rusty gate that swings in a circle to eject me to the top of a high, lonely, corroded iron stairway down to the street. Salt air from the river has been feasting on the iron for decades, and although there is not a soul beside me climbing down, many passing shoes have worn the steel treads on every step to smooth treachery. As I make my way down the three long flights I hold tightly to the banisters, lest a damp metal step should slip out from beneath my feet to send my guitar and me ricocheting like a pinball.

I reach the bottom, but wonder what this staircase will be like in December, covered with snow and ice. If anybody falls down, how long will they lie here before being discovered? Aside from the whistling traffic, the street is silent and the gray sky dark as a Brillo pad. Nobody will come to inspect this dilapidated stairway. If I should slip, fall, and die, they'll find a skeleton strapped into a guitar case.

Above 225th Street Broadway is grim. The sidewalk in front of the long, meandering housing project that occupies the entire east side of the street is encased in scaffolding, the windows choked behind black netting, like a caterpillar's tent. In my little yellow directory, I see that the address I need to find is an even number. Somewhere within this corridor of gloom my guitar and I will be expected to chime out the likes of "Twinkle, Twinkle Little Star," "If You're Happy and You Know It." How am I going to sing "You Are My Sunshine" in these doldrums? This will be like singing "Happy Birthday" from the crypt.

After two long blocks I arrive at a crossroad where Broadway makes a sharp, serpentine turn and curls off to the right, dragging the apparatus of the elevated subway along with it. I follow my housing project and all the darkness of the scaffolding to the left. Parting direction from the train tracks adds another level of uneasiness, but just around the corner I find a narrow cement path that leads from the sidewalk to a plain steel door. There is no sign announcing that this is Head Start or the Archdiocese of New York. But I can see by the address on a door that this is where my journey ends. A frank buzzer releases the lock and I am admitted to the corridor of a dull little school. The ceilings are low and fluorescently lit, much like the subway car that brought me here. The floors are blocks of lightly scarred linoleum and the walls contain bulletin boards with cutouts of apples and autumn leaves stapled on construction paper.

Miss Antonette

Three women stand over a coffee station holding small Styrofoam cups. My arrival interrupts their morning chatter. In the ensuing silence each lets her eyes travel from my ankle boots to the top of my shorn head. I try to smile.

"Good morning. I'm looking for Marble Hill Head Start?"

A short Asian woman, wearing a tan, ribbed turtleneck, brown stretch pants, and loafers, extends her hand. "How do you do," she intones, in a girlish singsong, "and welcome to our center. I see from your instrument that you must be our new music consultant. I am Miss Antonette, your site supervisor. And this is Miss Sandra, and this is Miss Kadrena." Miss Sandra is black and Miss Kadrena is Hispanic. They both tower over Miss Antonette.

"I'm Leah."

Miss Antonette glances at her watch.

"Please come with me, Leah. We have two classrooms here for you. Room One will be your first."

I follow Miss Antonette into the closer of the two classrooms. I notice a large sink in the corner, along with bins of colorful supplies like magic markers, crepe paper, and puffballs. In the center of the room little desks are pushed into clusters of four. Since the room is a big L-shape, we must round the corner ahead of us before coming upon two teachers sitting in chairs, and the circle of children sitting cross-legged on a big, round floor rug. Their big, round eyes are trained on me, their mouths dropped open in fright, as if they are watching the Hindenburg explode.

"Here we go," I think as Miss Antonette steps in front of me.

"Good morning, boys and girls," she announces in her high, syrupy voice.

"Guh-mawny Miss Antonette," the group responds flatly.

"And how are you today, my boys and girls?" Miss Antonette continues, slapping her palms to her thighs and bending forward with a smile.

"Fine. Thank you for asking and how are you?" they chorus back.

The teachers have these kids well trained. They respond to these formalities like a squadron of cadets.

"I am fine thank you, boys and girls!"

Miss Antonette turns to face me then and places a hand on my shoulder. "This is your new music teacher. She will be coming to sing with you on Mondays now. Her name is Miss Leah." There is silence. A ring of frightened eyes stares at me. I smile but my mouth feels spastic.

"So let me hear you say good morning to Miss Leah!"

One of the teachers makes this request. There is no response, but when the teacher stands up threateningly and claps her hands, the whole room seems to jump, myself included, and the children obediently mumble: "Guh–mawny, Mi ...," their voices fade as they get to the mystery of my name.

I rush to their assistance: "Miss Leah!" I say brightly. "My name is Miss Leah." They continue to stare, and I realize they don't know what's expected of them. So I try again. "My name is Miss Leah," I repeat. "But don't worry if you can't remember my name, boys and girls, because like Miss Antonette says, I'll be coming every Monday from now on to sing and play with you."

I look over at Miss Antonette and find that she's shifted her weight to one foot and is watching me with her head cocked to one side, so I hurriedly continue. "But you're the lucky ones this morning. Wanna know why? 'Cause you only have one name to learn!"

Then I point to myself. "But look! I have...," and I begin an exaggerated pantomime of making a head count, letting my knees begin to shake and making the corner of my lips quiver. As their number climbs over ten, I pretend to wipe away a bead of sweat, and thank goodness, they're beginning to smile. Two of them have become so bold as to giggle, and I'm becoming safer for them by the minute.

This is what I want more than anything. I want them to think that Music is going to be fun, something they'll come to look forward to on Monday mornings. As I begin darting around, talking about all the things that we're going to do together, a voice in my head keeps repeating, in the strong Queens accent that I first heard it: "Remembah, don't be too nice or they'll take you for all you's worth. Trust my word on this one: Don't smile 'til Christmas!"

Don't Smile 'til Christmas: Remembering the Korean School

The voice was Anne Nugent's. I met this teacher in a private Lutheran school in Queens where, many years ago, I taught the recorder to Korean students. After only a few months they'd all learned to play the recorder and to read the treble clef at least as well as I could. We had accomplished so much that I vowed I would always remember Anne's advice, except in that school I had certain advantages that I could not take for granted in other situations like the one I found myself in today. In the Queens school, I stood at the blackboard, in front of rows of immaculately dressed six- and seven-year-olds. I had the unsmiling Anne Nugent there to support me. In addition, the school observed a rigid behavior code, enforced by the very fierce Asian headmistress that everybody called "Moma-san."

In her late sixties, Moma-san was no "little old lady!" Lesson One, for me, was that you couldn't let yourself be fooled by the pink, fuzzy bedroom slippers in which Moma-san shuffled around the corridors of her school. They may as well have been combat boots goose-stepping through the halls and classrooms when she took to patrolling her domain. When a class became noisy, when the students grew restless and giggly, she would appear in the back of the classroom like the fin of a shark efficiently detecting blood in the water. Even the most fidgety boys would fall silent.

And I knew why. One winter afternoon a chubby little fellow missed his cue. This unfortunate child was lingering in his dreams when the classroom door creaked open behind him and all the other children clammed up. In fact, he was still singing and laughing to himself when an irate Moma-san descended upon him. She swooped him up roughly, all the while delivering a litany of unintelligible threats, her strong Asian accent made worse by her rage. Dragging him to the front of the room for all to see, she swiftly boxed the poor child's ears before sending him back to his desk, red-faced and stunned. Was it effective? Absolutely. Was it ethical? I knew it wasn't. In fact, it wasn't even legal—not even in a private school.

But I also knew that I liked teaching a classroom of quiet, orderly, respectful children. I'm one of those hypocrites who ends up letting other people do their dirty work. I needed Anne to scowl and not-smile. I needed Moma-san lurking in the hallways to keep the peace. But I found that for all of its obvious benefits, I just couldn't "not smile 'til Christmas" at the school in Queens.

Don't Smile 'til Chanukah: Remembering the Jewish School

Nor could I "not smile 'til Christmas" at my next teaching job, but for very different reasons. This time I would have to "not smile until Chanukah," because I found myself sitting on the floor in the middle of a circle of three- and four-year-old Jewish preschoolers at an orthodox synagogue near my home on the Lower East Side. As at the Lutheran school, my job had been made easy by a strict code of conduct upheld in this case by the pretty, young blonde—or at least blonde-wigged—*Rebetsen* (Rabbi's wife). This serene, surprisingly young woman presided over the preschool with all of its other young, serious women teachers in their long skirts, clunky shoes, and tightly buttoned blouses or shapeless turtlenecks.

The student/teacher ratio was in my favor. There were always three, sometimes as many as four, teachers to a room so that any children who fought, cried, threw up, or just wandered away were briskly handled, leaving me free to sing, play my guitar, and clown around with the others. I could "smile" without having to be a cop or the EMS guy. The retinue of serious young women was doing the dirty work of not smiling 'til Chanukah.

During the two years that I made my pre-Shabbat Friday afternoon visits I watched as month by month the staff of young teachers rotated out from under me. Every one of the girls who taught there would, in time, leave the school to get married. They'd return after a week or two of wedding festivities, scratching away at their "sheitels," the wig an Orthodox Jewish wife wears over her ritually cut hair. Once she's married, an Orthodox Jewish woman's hair is considered seductive to other men and therefore hidden in public.

In a few weeks their bellies expanded under those long, tent-like skirts. As their bellies grew and grew, it became harder and harder for the girls to bend over the children and sit toddlers in their laps. Suddenly they would leave to have their own babies, and I would be introduced to the new young women who were being cycled in. And the whole process would begin again.

Smile—You're Here

Years later, I can't use Anne Nugent's advice in this classroom in the Bronx. I have too many little eyes staring up at me, and too much sudden pressure. Here the ring of children at my feet are every color of the rainbow and every shade of the spectrum. Some have hair the color of sunshine and others stare at me with eye whites that shock, from faces as black as the darkest Nigerian nights.

Miss Antonette introduces the classroom teachers. Miss Nicole, who's Hispanic, looks younger than I am. She is rosy and plump with a short, blond ponytail. Miss Evangeline is an older black woman who remains seated when we meet.

"Show Miss Leah your good behavior, boys and girls," Miss Antonette advises as she takes leave. Now I clearly hold the stage.

"We are going to sing about the weather!" I lick my finger and hold it up, as if to test the wind. These children do not live on farmlands in Oklahoma. They have not read *The Grapes of Wrath*, and have no idea why I do this odd thing. They stare at me with undisguised wonder.

"We are going to sing about our bodies," I continue. And here I look down at myself and reel back in a double take, as if in utter surprise at what I've found.

"We are going to sing about our families," I go on. "Some of you perhaps have mommies...?"

I'm giving them a deep, exaggerated shrug when I get my first nibble on the line I've cast. Quietly, a lone voice whimpers that yes, he has a mommy.

"Are there any daddies out there?" I try. Another voice chimes in, "I got a Daddy," and still another voice says, "Oh. . . . Me! I got a daddy! One, one daddy!"

It occurred to me that not all of them had a mommy and daddy at home, and some might live with grandparents or other family. Nevertheless, the question began a dialogue.

I push forward with, "And maybe some of you have a pet animal that lives in your house with you . . .," and the floodgates are opened!

"We got a cat at our house!"

"Oh, oh, Miss, Miss Teacher, Music Teacher! We, we, we got a puppy at my house..."

"Oh, Miss Teacher, we got a fish!"

And someone else: "We got a fish, too, but it die!"

"Oh, Miss! My...my brother, my big brother...He got a dog now."

"My brother have a dog too!" cries another.

"And just who could it be at all of your houses who walks all these dogs, hmmmmm?"

I raise one accusing eyebrow.

"Oh me! Miss Teacher! We...we got a new puppy at my house and...and...he ...he done it on the rug, Miss...Miss...What's your name?"

"Are you telling me that your brother did it on the rug?"

There's laughter, thank heavens, there's laughter!

"We're going to sing about the days of the week and the holidays of the year," I attempt to plow ahead, through the algae of everybody talking at once. But at least now I have their attention. Four-year-olds are egomaniacs by design. Every four-year-old has a story. They're all talking at once because they're excited about what we're doing, and they all want to put in their two cents, their voices rising and scalloping each other to be heard. But at last I've got them happily starring in their own show, which is just where I need them—front and center stage!

"We are going to sing about what we eat . . ." Here I lean in abruptly, letting myself loom over them and scold with my index finger. "And what you should NOT be eating!" And yes, they're eating it up and laughing.

"Hey, Miss...You!...Miss Teacher!"

Some of them swat nervously at the air as they laugh and call out to me. "Hey, Miss—You funny!"

"Her name is Miss Leah!" Miss Evangeline bellows from her chair, with sudden impatience. Her eyes are clamped shut as if she's yelling from her sleep.

"Meees Leah, Meees Leah!" Just that quickly, a staggered chorus of my own name surrounds me like frogs croaking in a swamp.

Through the corner of my eye I see that Miss Antonette silently enter the room and my anxiety spikes to the ceiling. How long has she been watching me? What did she see? I turn to her and smile, but she remains maddeningly expressionless. She watches me with her arms folded as if I were a television set. As she stands, she shifts her weight from one boxy hip to the other and tilts her round face from side to side, wrinkling her little nose as if she was sniffing an onion. Do I stink? Does the Miss Leah Show stink?

Now my mercury is plunging as rapidly as it shot to the sky. I'm still on my feet and jabbering to the kids, but I'm suddenly afraid that I'm going to burst into tears. I believe that I'm failing my test.

Her face is such a downer that it almost makes me feel furious. Oh, give me a break, I could explode at her. *You think what I'm doing is easy? You try being silly and jolly with a group of new children at 9:30 on a Monday morning.* People who don't perform have no idea how much a little encouragement can mean at the right moment, and how hard discouragement can sit.

But there's no time for tears. No time for rants or outbreaks of any kind. No time to think at all, because I somehow have to bring to order this mêlée of everybody shouting about their pets before Miss Antonette's entirely inhuman face stamps me with a failing grade. After all, I haven't even broken out the guitar yet.

"She has no control over the children," my inner ear is already chanting in her high, childish voice. But I've dangled at wit's end many times, and now the usual zany energy comes to my rescue. If I'm going to be scrutinized like a television, then let's turn up the volume!

"Alright, alright. I get the picture," I tell them in my best sheep-herding yell. "I know. You have cats and dogs and birds and fish!"

And then to the loud little boy who's still babbling about his monkey, "I know, you got the whole Bronx Zoo at your house! Okay, that's great. That's fine but listen up. Hey out there, slow down. Shhhhh!!"

Finally Miss Nicole flies out of her chair and claps her hands. There is an abrupt silence and I jump on top of it for all I'm worth.

"Okay, let's keep it simple then. Who here likes to watch TV?"

A few little hands shoot into the air like Roman candles. There is a quick second and then a roar issues up from the floor as every hand strains toward me, pumping up and down as if the little life it's attached to depends upon it.

"Oh, me...MEEE! We watch...Oh Mees! Mees! Teacher...We watch Dora, Spiderman, Scooby Doo...."

"Wait, wait!" I'm crying. "Okay, hold the phone!"

I lean back to grab my gig bag from where I propped it when I came in, and deftly unzip the guitar case. My guitar is painted a minty aqua-green. I lower the strap over my shoulders while a shudder of ecstasy rises up from the floor. My heart is pounding. While I rush to tune my guitar I must remember to breathe.

Hurry, everything fast, fast, fast before I loose this moment of their rapture, this one chance to redeem myself in the expressionless eyes of Miss Antonette.

The quiet children watch me with open mouths. What will she do with that big green guitar thing? The teachers watch me. Even Miss Evangeline has opened her eyes and is blinking at me. And Miss Antonette watches. She has shifted her weight yet again for the beginning of the music and has pointed one of her loafers in the air. Overwhelmed, I try to meet all the eager eyes and hurry to tune my guitar.

The chord I finally strike sounds tainted and sour as goat yogurt. And yet it will have to do because, as every performer knows all too well, "You never get a second chance to make a first impression," and this is especially true with children. And so I pipe out, "Okay, now who knows of a little yellow fellow? What's his name again . . .? Something like Sponge Bob Square Guy?"

Almost in unison they all yell back at me, "Sponge Bob Square Pants!" And it's just the chorus of support I was looking for. I hit a sour D chord now. A fat, sour D7 rumbling in second position and let it resound beneath me as I hold the match to the gasoline: "Oh! Who lives in a pineapple under the sea?"

Why hadn't I thought of TV characters sooner? As I've been given no curriculum or guidelines, this is nothing short of the mother lode! Now we've struck common ground. The children sitting at my feet are delivering their beloved jingle to perfection, as though we'd been rehearsing together for months. They're even right on pitch, but better than anything, they are smiling and rocking away on their little rug. "Ready! Sponge Bob Square Pants, SPONGE BOB SQUARE PANTS!!" We all shout the finale together and I scrape out a lusty "Ho Ho Ho" behind them just as the pirate does in the TV theme song.

"Again, again!" shout the children. Miss Nicole giggles and applauds and even the sleepy Miss Evangeline smiles. I look around, hoping to finally catch some twinkle of approval from Miss Antonette, but she has disappeared at the very moment of my glory. At the side of the classroom where she and her pointed loafer were standing, there is only empty space.

The Land and the Sea

Not two hours later I collapse in the extra chair in Miss Antonette's office. I have just completed my very first two forty-five-minute music classes; I wrapped things up in Room One and then went on to Room Two. I met the two new teachers there, all the children in that room, and I am now painfully aware that very soon I will have to do it all over again: two classes again in the afternoon.

The teachers in Room Two are Miss Lucia and Miss Blanca. Miss Lucia is a black woman with gentle eyes. I would guess her to be my contemporary in her early forties, even though her children are ten years older than my boys. Although I am the newcomer, she has me feeling protective. Unlike the two titans next door, she possesses a sweetness in the classroom and speaks with a fragile, hoarse voice that is often overpowered by the children.

The second teacher, Miss Blanca, appears to be much younger. Like Miss Nicole in Room One, she is a light-skinned Hispanic blonde, only Miss Blanca is a waif, girlish and trim. She is considerably more reserved than Miss Lucia or perhaps just doesn't have as much to say in English. She smiles when we are introduced, but most of the time her mysterious eyes slide behind an almost Elvis-like sneer. You never know where you're going to encounter the very essence of cool.

"Have you ever tried Philippine food, Miss Leah?" Miss Antonette's question interrupts my trance, but I am limp from my exertions in the classrooms and can hardly focus my mind enough to answer her. Honestly, I don't think I've tried it, I respond. "Well, if you'd care to, you can join us in the staffroom. Today there is a hot lunch. You are more than welcome to eat with us."

Her smile brings relief—I seem to have passed muster; the Miss Leah Show is a wrap!—but also conflict. After sustaining the spotlight all morning, learning the names of four teachers and all the new children, I am overwhelmed. The idea of having to perform socially over lunch without making a bad impression on the staff and supervisor adds to what feels like yet more effort. I don't wish to seem rude, but I need a moment to catch my breath.

I don't know where in these new mean streets I will head, but I know I must shake off the rigors of the morning and pound the earth with my feet. I need to steam like a manhole. I must be alone.

"I may go out for a sandwich, if I can," I explain.

Amid the 99-cent stores, newsstands, and pizza parlors on Upper Broadway, I find the stone façade of the Land & Sea restaurant. Inside, I come face to face with a bubbling fish tank. Mirrored walls dimly reflect brown and maroon floral curtains and carpeting in the dining room beyond. If it looks like a funeral parlor, then I'm ready for death, or at least a grilled cheese.

I assume that the waiter who shows me to a booth by the window is cringing at my near-baldness. He is an older man with a gray mustache beneath his substantial nose and frightened blue eyes. He wears a forest green tailored shirt with a black apron, and hands me the oversized, vinyl-bound menu as if I were a leper.

When I was a teenager my father used to complain that my unkempt, frizzy hair was a "secret ticket to the underworld," as drug peddlers approached us during father/daughter walks through Central Park. I couldn't get it right. Now it's gone, and my missing hair is still raising red flags for innocent people. Perhaps my anxious waiter is guessing that I'm sick and that what I'm sporting is a chemo cut. What else could be the source of his terrible discomfort?

With eyes cast down, he tallies my order and flees to the kitchen. His squeamishness hurts my feelings and is making me jones for my home turf. I've never so much appreciated my Lower East Side stomping ground, where you can shave your head and tattoo rainbows over your scalp, for all anybody cares. Waiting beside my guitar case, I seem to be reprising my old role where, swathed in rags, I played mandolin for a skit in the Renaissance Fair when it came to Bryant Park. As the King's procession approached with fanfare, my tawdry ensemble and I were supposed to disperse as sword-wielding henchmen drove us from the stage bellowing, "Begone gypsies!" Nothing has changed. Here I am, sitting at this coffee shop in the Bronx, ever the untouchable troubadour.

As the waiter returns with my soup, I doubt I'll improve matters in accounting for my buzz cut by mentioning the lice. An itchy case of head lice is not good conversation for a first date. Instead, I spoon my soup and eat bread while he hovers from a safe distance, poised with his cleaning rag to wipe me away. I drink coffee and enjoy the easy-listening station that quietly plies me with gently familiar musical swill on this new planet.

We in Bluegrass have a saying: "We don't want to make you glad twice—Glad to see us come, and glad to see us go." When I'm ready to leave I spare the old man any further interaction with this bald extraterrestrial from the lower galaxy. I fold my money, including a generous tip for his suffering, beneath my saucer. Then it's out to the sidewalk where Broadway will wind me back to the housing project. Back to the Head Start Center where I can expect to be greeted with more of the same reserve and suspicion that I met at the Land & Sea Restaurant. Even the children I face in the afternoon will be a new group and full of wide-eyed apprehension. Of course, once I can trick them into having a good time they'll want to ingest me like a tank of piranhas, but that's not what I'm looking for. It would just be nice to be headed to where people would be simply glad to see me. Glad only once—glad to see me come.

First Tuesday in Highbridge

In all my years as a New York straphanger I have never used the Number 4 Train for anything other than a magic carpet to whisk me up from the Village to Grand Central Station. Today my little yellow directory tells me that I will be riding the 4 all the way up to 161st Street, abutting Yankee Stadium. As I head toward the IRT subway station at Astor Place, guitar in hand, I remember that Mark had returned from a baseball game with the boys, commenting that the neighborhood around Yankee Stadium was awfully grim. Perhaps this is why, though not yet awake in bed, he mumbled, "be careful" as I bent over him, kissed his cheek, and whispered, "I'm out of here."

But summer baseball traffic is long gone on the Tuesday morning when I make my first trip to the center in Highbridge. The subway station where I dismount is like a dirty castle. Many covered stairways with slivers of fortress windows peek over the intersection below. The muddy tiles beneath my feet are slick with decaying garbage, and when I step outside the sky is a glaring, yet murky white, like the coat of a dirty city dog.

Finally the subway stairs have deposited me on a small concrete island around which car traffic streams in both directions. Here is where I will catch my bus to the Our Lady of Miracles School, which hosts the Highbridge Head Start Center. The sidewalks on either side of this busy section of East 161st Street rise for several blocks, finally crowned on the left by the enormous Bronx Borough Courthouse, a square monolith of granite and bronze which broods disapprovingly over the delis, newsstands, diners, doughnut shops, and sports bars.

On the right side, a historic theatrical façade sweeps up the slope. It could have been an old movie house, or in it's first incarnation, a vaudeville stage. But at this time in history, it is Burger King, "Home to the Whopper." And downstream my eyes are filled with the white sprawl of Yankee Stadium with its highest bleachers arched above its walls like the back of a cobra poised to strike. My nose draws in a nauseating mix of sweet doughnuts and bacon, tainted with sour diesel fumes from the rushing cars, trucks, and buses.

On the sidewalk, the faces that huff past me mostly belong to young African Americans. Many of them have their heads clamped into headphones, while others wear durags—and quite a few are wearing both. A lot of the footwear I see, flamboyant high-top sneakers in phosphorescent colors, look fit for inter-galactic travel—while the old tenements that rise above the storefronts with their fire escapes and heavily lidded windows have seen it all come and go. Eroded grooves in their red-and-tan brick facades seem to hold the passing of time like the diagnostic rings of a tree.

The cracked sidewalk under my toes is polka-dotted with dark wads of chewing gum bulldozed flat by armies of trampling feet. When I look up my eye is caught by the very old-fashioned awning which droops demurely like a soot-covered petticoat above the ancient bakery whose inoperative neon sign tells me it is called Gordon's, and somehow, in spite of all the new electronics and car traffic, I am reminded of the descriptions of the teaming marketplace of Dickens's London.

The stop for my Number 13 Bus is dangerous. People standing in line seem precariously balanced on a submarine-shaped wedge of pavement that divides 161st Street. A tall brick planter of bare shrubs consumes most of the island. Everybody has to stand single file along the rim of the pavement to keep from stepping into traffic, which speeds past only inches from our toes and shoulders. The people on the line I join seem accustomed to perching on a lip of sidewalk cheek-by-jowl with speeding vehicles. But I'm not!

The only thought I can keep in my head as my nose catches the breeze of every car rushing past is that I am very glad not to have the boys wiggling beside me at this moment. Don't these people realize that if one of us were to faint or even as much as lose our footing and stagger, something tragic could happen?

Am I the only one worrying that if there's a psycho in our midst who was to push somebody, that person, or perhaps even all of us, could be roadkill just as fast as you can order a Whopper with cheese across the street?

But time is clicking away, and so, inside my shoes, I dig my talons into the pavement like the bird on a wire that I am today, and wait. Poised like this on the wall of death, I am reminded of my long, slippery descent yesterday at Marble Hill, slaloming down the long subway stairways at 225th Street that were more like a playground slide.

The cars rushing past us emerge from a tunnel that runs from the belly of the hill that holds the looming courthouse building. From the tunnel's black mouth, multicolored cars are spat toward us like gum balls. Just as suddenly the great reflective planes of a bus's windshield bursts from the darkness like some kind of oversized, prehistoric fly.

This great insect clamps on its breaks and eddies up to the curb, but it turns out not to be the Number 13 I'm looking for. Instead, a numeral 6 blinks in the corner of its windshield. I mention Nelson Avenue and Our Lady of Miracles School to the people around me, and a man who is not boarding the Number 6 Bus bobs his head in recognition. Through a thick Spanish accent, he talks about my having to go to someplace whose name I just can't make out. I nod politely, but what I hear him say sounds like getting to Our Lady of Miracles will require going up to something called "Plankety Plank."

Finally the Number 6 bus closes its doors and after a preliminary snort roars away heading downhill toward Yankee Stadium and the elevated subway bridge to disappear inside yet another tunnel. When I look back, the tunnel from which the bus had emerged is still implacably spitting out cars. In fact, two more buses roar toward us but neither one is a 13. Tuesday has already been a long day.

At last a bus sidles up, blinking the digits "13" in the corner of its windshield. Its doors open with a mechanical gasp, its steps lower to meet the curb with an earsplitting whistle. I have become separated from the man who talked about "Plankety Plank." As I join one more slow line of anxious commuters extruding ourselves into yet another sardine can, I am thinking that I need to elect a new guide to find Nelson Avenue and lead me to Our Lady of Miracles. As I creep up the bus steps, I ask the woman in front of me—and the man behind me—when the bus driver himself takes me by surprise by rising to his feet. He takes hold of my arm and almost pushes me into one of the seats behind his own, gruffly promising, "I take care of you!"

Umpff! Women lower themselves on either side of my seat, and I am forced to balance my guitar case and canvas bag on my knees, pinned as I am between two sets of thighs as broad and unyielding as cinder blocks. Nobody returns my nervous smile as I make adjustments. What if I make a mistake and sail off in the wrong direction? There's nothing to do but wait. At last the doors hiss together around my doubts and the last few dark overcoats rushing in. Like it or not, I am a prisoner on the bus, pinned against myself, leaving the safety of the green lines of the subway map with every thrust of the engine. Where will this bus, roaring downhill beyond Yankee Stadium toward yet another tunnel, take me?

But it is almost beautiful when we emerge moments later from the dark interval of cracked and grafittied concrete inside. A historic line of warm, earth-toned brick apartment buildings fills the windshield as the bus swings to the left. I see shades of chocolate, cinnamon, and honey and on its easternmost corner, a light pink building with a Jerome Avenue address written in italics across its blue canopy. The next block we roar past holds the surprise of a sprawling granite mansion that looks like the wayward little brother of the Museum of Natural History. It could be home to royalty. It could hold ballrooms. What an elegant neighborhood this must once have been.

Higher and higher we climb with the motor whining as the bus leans and labors against gravity. Tenements on either side of the street are actually carved into the hill, the second floor of one building almost aligned with the first floor of its neighbor on higher ground, as in Paris' Montmartre. For several blocks brick tenements continue to zigzag up the hill, climbing with the bus windows. Some that we pass flash only the solemn face of a stoop and front door, while others have small businesses at sidewalk level. We pass the windows of corner bodegas with signs that advertise "Food stamps and WIC checks accepted here." We grind past a travel agent with a neon sign of Spanish promises: "*Reservaciones, Pasaportes, Seguros*" ("Reservations, Passports, Insurance"). We pass a butcher's shop with the silhouette of a chicken on its dirty, yellow awning; a handmade sign for a social club with paintings of maracàs and conga drums; a community center; a Laundromat; an appliance repair shop; as well as a plentiful string of Pentecostal churches and unisex hair salons.

Eventually Victorian houses begin to appear, elbowing their wide porches between the tenements and the chain-link fences, all topped with barbed-wire tiaras that enclose vacant lots strewn with garbage. Some of these houses are freestanding, while others are conjoined to an identical neighbor. But almost all of them are covered with satellite dishes for cable television that are bolted onto second-story windowsills, or to the bars of child safety guards like a rash of facial moles. At street level where there must have been porch swings in better times, piles of black garbage bags now sit watching us pass, instead of people sitting on their front lawns. Plaster icons of Mary despair over broken flowerpots, litter, and fallen leaves.

Some windows are broken and taped while some panes have been replaced with plywood boards. In every direction, paint is chipping, unhinged shutters hang, and exterior aluminum siding is dented. Even the sky seems to be peeling like an old bathroom wall.

"Ah, sir? Have we come to Nelson Avenue?" I keep asking even though I can see that it annoys the driver.

"Lady," he sighs with the doors he is opening and closing. "I tell you when, I tell you when we be there. Soon."

He will be glad to be rid of me, I think as we pass a shabby parking lot. A hand-painted sign written on the wall beside it reads, "Fix Flat." A small shoe repair shop has also painted its own sign with primitively rendered shoes and boots surrounding the words. Half the letters are missing from the neon sign above the Chinese takeout restaurant whose interior is enclosed by bulletproof Plexiglas.

We rumble past the red plastic slides and wooden jungle gym of a playground sitting behind a chain-link fence. My heart leaps because although I am so far from home I can feel Simon with me. Even though this is such a grim and dangerous neighborhood, my five-year old son would notice the hanging tires and bright red slides. He would want to get off the bus and stop and play there.

We pass a church storefront and the awning for Sistah Love's unisex hair salon, before the restless local topography strains the engine again. The bus is almost pointed vertically up when my driver pulls to a stop beside a brick compound that occupies the entire hilly block it is built on.

"Go that way," he tells me.

Then he points to another slope, which runs perpendicular to the street we've been traveling. "Go that way. Is on the block. You see it."

I gather my things and struggle down the acutely tilted bus steps. I nod to him from the sidewalk. "Couldn't have done it without you, sir. Thank you so much!"

"Okay," he says before closing the doors to drive his lumbering bus away.

Our Lady of Miracles One and Two (The School on the Hill)

As I make my way up the slope, an old stone school appears which shares the block with a second, modern school building: these are Our Lady of Miracles One and Two. A church steeple and a rectory preside above the spread from still higher ground. On the old school I find the Head Start logo of alphabet blocks taped onto the buzzer beside the massive front doors. I wait before the scrutiny of the granite gargoyles to gain admission.

Just inside, a dark flight of steep stairs rises toward a rectangle of florescent light at its first platform. "Knees up, Farmer Brown!" One of my own children's songs plays in my head as I mount the stairs. The rectangle of light becomes the threshold of a small administrative office.

In the office are two brunette women. One sits at a desk against the far wall. The other, standing by the humming copy machine, smiles as I approach. We say our good mornings, and Miss Daniela shakes my hand. She is Hispanic, pretty, and stylishly dressed in a floral blouse and black slacks. I would guess she's in her late thirties. The woman behind her desk is also attractive and somewhat older, with a full compliment of makeup to match the red knit sweater that hugs her silhouette. "And this is Miss Inez."

As we are introduced, Miss Inez seems to recoil. Her tight smile and quickly averted eyes bring me suddenly back to the Land & Sea Restaurant from yesterday at Marble Hill, back to scaring the poor old waiter out of his apron with my baldness. I am grateful that Miss Daniela is not frightened, even as I remove my hat. She explains that the first classroom I am to visit is actually back in the modern building. In fact, I will be zigzagging between Our Lady of Miracles One and Two all day. When I return from my first class in Our Lady of Miracles One, my next two classrooms will be waiting for me upstairs, she explains, and points into the darkness of the hallway here in Our Lady of Miracles Two.

And then she tells me that I look worried. "It's a lot at first but you'll get used to us, Miss Leah."

"I'm alright. I guess I'm still taking in...all my new surroundings," I say.

Miss Daniela removes her pages from the copy machine. "As you can see ours is a poor district. A lot of our families receive public assistance. Many of them depend on the breakfast and hot lunch we provide, and of course, the childcare. Is this a new experience for you, Miss Leah, coming to a neighborhood like Highbridge?"

"Well, I come from the Lower East Side, which is not exactly Paradise." I think about what makes it different. "In my neighborhood people with diverse incomes live side-by-side. I don't know. Somehow the poverty around here seems especially intense...maybe more isolated."

She nods. "Let's put it this way. When the other social worker, Miss Gladys, and I used to make our home visits, I can tell you we didn't even want to wear open-toed sandals in some of the apartments because of the rats and the roaches." She breaks into Spanish for Miss Inez who says, "Ay-ay-ay," then covers her mouth.

Miss Daniela consults her watch. "You can get started, if you want. Just go back the way you came. You'll find our other school building, Our Lady of Miracles One, Miss Leah. Don't worry. You won't have no trouble getting in," she insists, smiling.

At the top of the stairs in Our Lady of Miracles One a statue of Jesus holds an infant in his arms and I try to take comfort as I draw near the statue. It is nice to see a kind face. Continuing to the right, I find that the halls of Our Lady of Miracles One are lined with artwork. Children have painted on construction paper, and teachers have captioned their remarks in bold magic markers beneath. Most of the papers just hold blotches of paint, but the remarks vary. Some describe firefighters. One says, "I've made a flower. I hope it will grow." One calls three spots a supermarket. "My Mommy buys milk and juice." Another one says, "I made my Daddy because he likes me." During my years at Head Start I will see many captioned drawings and paintings. Teachers are trained to elicit comments from the children about what they've represented. This practice helps parents become more aware of their children's artwork and what it might mean.

On the opposite wall older Our Lady of Miracles students have mounted their poems about the four seasons. Not surprisingly, most are odes to warmer weather. "Spring is encouraging. The flowers are flourishing," begins one. Another one describes "a spring day as soft as a pillow."

I can tell that the voices chorusing from behind the final classroom door are indeed my Head Starters because I recognize their monotonal salutations: "... Fine, thank you for asking. And how are you?" the group repeats as tunelessly as their counterparts at Marble Hill. Only today I have no Miss Antonette to introduce me to the class. Bashfully, I turn the doorknob and admit myself.

Inside, a group of children sit cross-legged on the floor with two female teachers presiding, swathed in their stiff Head Start smocks worn over shirts and blue jeans. At this center these canvas bib aprons are royal blue, as opposed to the red ones worn by the teachers yesterday at Marble Hill. The old-fashioned classroom with its blocks and bookshelves is standard issue.

The two teachers are friendly and rise to greet me as I walk in. I wave to the children who look back at me with frightened eyes. The first teacher to shake my hand is Miss Linda. She is tall and big-boned for an Asian woman, and has thick black hair reaching down to her shoulders. The second teacher, also large, is a nut-brown Hispanic woman named Miss Caridad. When I mispronounce it she laughs and repeats her name for me explaining that it means "charity" in Spanish.

Having faced yesterday's avalanche of exotic names, I plan to open the show today with something other than my litany of "Hello" songs. It is irksome to feel so overwhelmed by the many little faces in my classroom after a youth of memory-retention machismo. I was once able to gobble song lyrics whole, sometimes after only a single hearing. And I counted on being able to catalogue tall stacks of names: dorms of college students, and more recently, the boy's nursery school classmates and the names of all their parents.

With the unsettling discovery that there is now an abyss where my memory used to be, I decide to stick with the ABC's and "Twinkle, Twinkle, Little Star" —the old standards. I sit in front of the children with my guitar and begin to strum. It's going well, and I drive on with "The Wheels of the Bus," "The Eensy, Beensy Spider," and my special favorite, "If You're Happy and You Know It."

My own joyful memories of this song stem from the first four summers of my life. My father was a staff social worker at an Educational Alliance family camp in Putnam County. During July and August we accompanied him upstate, where my older sister and I were "staff kids" on a beautiful, woodsy campus where it seemed the whole day was devoted to singing. Before breakfast in the communal dining room, our voices rang out with the *Ha-Motzi*, a Hebrew prayer thanking God for bread. "We are marching to Pretoria," we cheered as we proceeded from the art pavilion to the lake in little groups of campers. There was folk dancing on an asphalt flat known as "The White Top." And every evening as the sun sank below the lake we lowered the flag with a solemn round of "Taps."

In the car rides that began and ended the heaven of these early summers, my family sang "rounds," taught by my mother. These little tunes are entered at staggered intervals—when the first person reaches Part 2, the second person sings Part 1, and so on—creating lush harmonies when they are sung by two or three voices. This is why singing in groups is in my blood.

Come Follow

Traditional English Round

"Wow, not bad for city kids!" I gush after we sing "Old MacDonald Had a Farm." We've covered the whole barnyard, and I found that they know when to *moo* and *oink* and *quack*, even though many of them have probably seen these animals only on TV. I am genuinely impressed with their abilities and before I leave, I tell them so.

I won't have to worry about getting my exercise on Tuesdays, I think as I walk around the corner. Even for a former long-distance runner like myself, the stairways at both Our Lady of Miracless are particularly steep. Back in the darkness of the old building, I huff past the narrow office and see that Miss Daniela is no longer there. Only Miss Inez is on the phone at her desk, and so I continue up the next flight and open the door to my second classroom.

Inside the room I blink as sunlight streams from the windows, contrasting with the deep shadows of the hallway. The classroom is expansive, with high ceilings, and the plaster walls have the attractive detail of wainscoting and molding. In one corner there is a water table full of soapsuds on which float colored measuring cups and other tub toys. In other areas I recognize the baby dolls and pretend kitchenettes for dramatic play. There are the usual cluster of tables and chairs, but the teachers are sitting beside the low shelves that hold books and building blocks in the far corner. Only as I move toward them do I see that the children are waiting for me in a circle at their feet.

In this room I meet Miss Felipa and Miss Gracia, both are pretty and robust young Hispanic women with lustrous black hair and large, equally dark, eyes. As in my first class, the children are mostly black with a sprinkling of lighter-skinned, mixed ethnicities. In cheerful bursts of heavily-accented English, the teachers coax their charges out of their initial shyness to sing and participate. Within the half hour I need these teachers on their feet, as my bodyguards. Invigorated from songs, joking and the flattery of my rapt attention, the kids must be forcefully told to stop shouting out of turn and putting their hands on my guitar.

"No, no, Poppy," the teachers say. "We listen, we don't touch!"

One devilish little imp clouds over with tears when she has to be dislodged from my calves for a second time. From the safe distance of Miss Gracia's lap she sits, alternately wailing and pouting through the second half of our time together: stormy weather from a little girl named Sky.

As I rise to leave, many pressing hands reach out for my shoelaces and the cuffs of my pants. "Don't go, Teacher; don't go, Miss," they call to me, as Miss Felipa, laughing and shaking her head, shows me out of the classroom. It is nice to feel so wanted in this new place.

With the closed wooden door at my back I find myself in a grandly proportioned, peach-colored hallway. Older students in gray and maroon plaid uniforms hurry past me with curious stares. I watch them disappear around a corner and note the sign for a Girl's Room on the opposite wall. As in Miss Gracia's and Miss Felipa's classroom, the hallway ceilings are cavernous. From a window at the other end, a stained glass panel illuminates the face of a saint. I will need her blessings. Already today I have scouted out new subway and bus lines, figured out the riddle of the two Our Lady of Miracless, and conducted two classes. I have made the acquaintance of two administrators—one friendly and one not, and four teachers. Also, importantly, I looked into the eyes of about fifty new children. Was that enough? Couldn't that be enough?

As I move down the hall and contemplate my third and final door of the morning, I realize that I am exhausted.

In Room Three my knock is answered by a Rubenesque giantess. Like Miss Gracia and Miss Felipa, she is a beautiful, mocha-skinned Hispanic woman with her eyebrows tweezed into arches, and full, painted lips. I think of Henri Matisse and his odalisques, his *Luxe, Calme et Volupté*, and the restful, tropical life. If I am going to survive this marathon every Tuesday I will need this woman's ease, and I appreciate her immediately. She turns around to take my hand and smile; this is Miss Magdalena.

Miss Pilar, the second teacher in this room, is also likable. A tomboyish and feisty young Asian woman, she, like the other teachers, speaks with a strong Spanish accent. She wears wire-framed glasses and her long black hair in two taut braids that fly behind her as she jumps up and down tending to the children. When a boy reaches to press his palm to the strings of my guitar, Miss Pilar grabs the child by the arm and yanks him to his feet.

"Why you did that! How come you did that?" she barks directly into his astonished face. But a moment later she throws her head back with spirited giggles, and the prominent teeth she flashes are as broad and white as piano keys. Miss Pilar, Miss Linda from my fist class, and Miss Antonette from yesterday: all three have the same round face, Asian eyes, and caramel-colored skin. I am guessing that Miss Pilar and Miss Linda are also from the Philippines.

Is It Lunch Yet?

After this third class, I stagger back downstairs to the office headquarters where I am surprised to find Brenda Keenan sitting at the little desk. She smiles and her small, friendly eyes disappear into her cheeks. She is having a conversation on the phone and gestures that I should make myself comfortable.

On the desk in front of her sit three open containers of Chinese food, from which she eats continuously. I pull up a chair and sit behind her, listening as she describes some upcoming staff event into the phone. "Aw, it's the same thing every year," she says, muffling her words beneath mouthfuls of *egg foo yung*, squeezing her napkin and licking her fingers. "The men will want to gamble and the women will want to go shopping." When she chortles, even from behind, I can see her neck and jowls quivering above the collar of her blouse, and I think of my Simon. If he were with me he would say, "her fat is laughing too."

"How did your first classes go, Miss Leah?" carols Miss Daniela from the back of the room.

"Very well, thank you," I call back to her, nodding. "Your teachers do such a great job in the classroom. Everybody was really helpful."

Miss Daniela turns toward me with hands on her hips and lowers her head coyly. "Did our children behave for you, Miss Leah?" she draws out her words with an indulgent smile.

"Oh, they did pretty well for meeting a brand-new person; THIS brand-new person." I laugh. "They were fine. There wasn't a lot of acting out, not too many tears."

Miss Daniela shakes her head. "Aye, *dios mio*," she sighs turning back to her copy machine. "What can I say, Miss Leah? They are a lively bunch, but we do love them very much."

She purrs Spanish to Miss Inez and then clucks softly to herself, continuing to shake her head and repeating, "Aye, we do love our children here."

When Brenda gets off the phone, she asks, "So how ya doing, kid? How'd it go yesterday at Marble Hill? How's everything going for you here at Miracles?" With as much alacrity as I can muster I field her second round of inquiries. My stomach is beginning to growl and behind my temples I feel the pressure of a gathering migraine. Can none of them see the light on my dashboard flashingthat warns of an empty tank? Is there no end to the hoops I must jump through and the balls I will be made to balance on my nose?

As happened yesterday, I fear that I am nearing the end of my capacity to perform for my superiors. All I want to talk to anyone about is my lunch hour. After the rigors of my morning, I feel like I am pulsing my gills before these women, like an expiring fish in the face of even friendly and concerned questions.

I have a question for them: Do open containers of Chinese takeout mean that it's lunchtime? No one tells me if this is my lunch hour and whether I'm free to leave the building. How grateful I would be for the clarity of a punch clock or a screaming factory whistle, but here in the little office "the five o'clock whistle never blew."

I realize that if I am to eat I must pose some questions of my own and begin with a segue remark.

"So Miss Brenda, will I be seeing you on Fridays at St. Anthony's?"

She goes for the bait and tells me that actually no two weeks were the same for her. Part of her job as the social services coordinator is to visit all the different centers. Before she finishes her thought the phone rings again to interrupt us. "Here, you want the paper?" she asks me, before taking the call. She tilts her head. "Come on, take one. I got all three. The *Times*, the *Post* . . . whatever you want, here!" She thrusts a copy of the *Daily News* into my hands and then picks up the receiver. "Good morning, Our Lady of Miracles. This is Brenda speaking."

Above us the clock on the wall reads a quarter to twelve but it is nothing more than a line in the sand that blows into my eyes. Brenda chats into the phone, eats her Chinese food, and my tense waiting in the chair behind her goes on and uncomfortably on. I am almost frying with restlessness to have to sit like this in limbo as invaluable minutes tick past. I am weary of having to await instruction in order to embark on my every move. I long to be a civilian again and reclaim the most essential of human rights—to blend back into a scowling, mumbling "anybody," free to prowl the neighborhood for the sanctuary of a diner counter or a coffee shop window to stare out of.

I decide to wait until 12:00—flat, high noon itself—before taking some action. I begin rifling through the newspaper, but I can't keep my mind on anything. I look for the funny pages and end up in the crime section where I read that many of the city's most brutal attacks have occurred right here in the South Bronx. All the more reason to stay put, and yet at seven minutes before noon, a ripple of frustration surges through me.

"Miss Brenda, am I on my lunch hour?" I finally ask. She's off the phone now, but doesn't seem to hear me. "Gee, would it be alright if I just take a short walk . . . try to scout out a little comfort food for myself?" I try again.

"Naw, you'd better stick around," yawns Brenda. I can feel the heat rise dangerously into my cheeks.

So now I'm to be put on a hunger fast before my afternoon classes begin?

At the very instance when I don't think I can stand another famished second Brenda turns around and smiles. "Go 'head, Leah. Go stretch your legs. Go find your comfort food, but don't get too comfortable, okay? Remember that we're pretty much on the wrong side of the tracks up here." And then she repeats what my husband said to me this morning, already so many hours ago that it feels like a different day altogether; she tells me to "be careful."

Outside the school I leap like a hound in the woods. I practically bound from the pavement. I could skip, I could cry. Alone at last with a breeze on my nearly bald head, even spinning with hunger as I am, I feel restored. Men sit smoking on stoops, or mill about by the open doors of corner bodegas. If I happen to pass closely by them and catch their eyes they nod and say only, "Okay, Mommy. Okay."

I walk and walk, devouring blocks and passing landmarks that I remember from my bus ride, small stores, slums with gated windows, and the dismal street-level entrance occupying an entire block for a goose-shit-colored housing project. My restless feet carry me far away from Nelson Avenue to the very lip of the plateau where the street drops abruptly. There I pause to marvel at the bluff, the distant cityscape below my feet, twinkling with highways and railroad tracks and the regal aqueduct beyond that arches to span the river. I have come to the edge of the world and must face that there is no way I am going to find the sugar decanter and ketchup bottle I was so hoping for. There is going to be no Land & Sea restaurant today; no chicken soup with rice; no honey for Poo bear; no place to sit down in these heights.

Threading my way back toward Our Lady of Miracles, I wander into a supermarket. But I can't trust the deli counter where flies land on logs of headcheese and pale bologna. With every block I walk, I learn that even fast food as we know it, MacDonald's and Burger King, doesn't exist in this neighborhood. At a bodega closer to the school I am grateful to find a stack of pre-wrapped squares of carrot cake that my sons sometimes want. I eat one, cherishing my final strides of solitude. In another minute I stand balling the sticky wrapper into my pocket as I wait to get buzzed back inside.

Miss Bilkis

In the office upstairs, Brenda Keenan is gone and the new inhabitant of her desk is a shock to the senses: a woman so short and broad that she looks like a square with gargantuan breasts, wearing slacks and a cardigan. Graciously Miss Daniela introduces Miss Bilkis, my site supervisor here.

"And Miss Bilkis, this is our new music consultant, Miss Leah."

The compact ogress named Miss Bilkis loftily offers me her hand but not her face. Instead I get the stiff ginger ale-colored plume of the back of her head as she turns to the clock on the wall behind us. Her hand is cold and her voice is low and muffled. By way of a greeting she says only, "Eh, the children are waiting for you." When she gets up to leave I find that she's even shorter than she looked sitting, not much taller than a third-grader herself.

For every day I work at Our Lady of Miracles, Marble Hill, and Castle Hill, I will be responsible for completing a consultant's form and an exit report. Once Miss Bilkis has scuttled away, Miss Daniela brings me my paperwork and shows me the routine of how to make copies and where to file them. For most people this would be a cinch, but with my dyslexia, numbers and dates and correct spelling in the exit report are a challenge. When I have finished I sit awkwardly at the front desk while Miss Daniela and Miss Inez speak to each other in Spanish.

They've brewed a pot of coffee, and of course it is Miss Daniela who offers me a cup. I drain it like an hourglass and by the time I leave to embark on my three afternoon classes I am too over-stimulated to even remember to be afraid.

Returning to the classroom at Our Lady of Miracles One the same teachers from the morning reappear with an entirely different crop of children—the afternoon class—at their toes. I smile and settle the guitar on my lap. Two rows of new dark and piercing eyes regard me, and I must jump into the cold water and make it warm all over again. Somehow I am able to recall Miss Linda's name, but Miss Caridad has to refresh my memory more than once. Thankfully, she is as charitable as her name.

Back at the old building and upstairs in Miss Gracia's and Miss Felipa's room, a boy named Quidar rocks back and forth when I'm introduced and breaks into a stunning smile, bright teeth and eye-whites beaming to contrast with his dark complexion. "Aw, anybody can do that!" declares another boy when the guitar comes out. But halfway through the class he sidles up to me with an opportunistic twinkle in his eye, asking, "You could get me one of those?"

In the first row a saucy little charmer, a fair-haired Hispanic girl named Lily, scoots closer and closer with every song until she is practically sitting on my shoes. The teachers order her backwards, but I don't especially mind her game. I am relieved not to face once again the tears and antics of the temperamental child named Sky from the morning class.

Inside Miss Magdalena's door the blur of my last class of children is punctuated by what seem to be at least three boys named Stephen and a standout voluptuous little giggler named Mariah. A tiny fellow named Manuel begins to whimper as I try to lead "The Itsy Bitsy Spider." Miss Pilar explains that this is his favorite song, but that the class usually sings it in Spanish. Suddenly a throaty contralto rises at my back with a tuneful "*La pequeñita araña subió, subió, subió, / Vino la lluvia y se la llevó.*" Miss Magdalena is translating for Manuel and for me!

I rush to find her key and accompany her on guitar. In a few bars *La pequeñita araña* is safely back up the spout. Out came the sun to dry up all Manuel's tears and Miss Magdalena and I smile because this song is our first collaboration.

She says that she'll write down the words in Spanish for me by next week. Toward the end of the class, teachers distribute the children's snacks, half pints of milk and wrapped Quaker Oats granola bars. "Do you have children at home, Miss Leah?" asks Miss Magdalena. I tell her about Haskell and Simon, and she hands me two granola bars. "These are for your boys."

The Itsy Bitsy Spider

Traditional

The it- sy bit- sy spi- der climbed up the wat- er spout.

Down came the rain and washed the spi- der out. Out came the sun and

dried up all the rain, and the it- sy bit- sy spi- der climbed up the spout a- gain.

Homeward Bound

"You're done." Miss Daniela smiles, back in the office. "If you've finished your paperwork then you're done and you can go." The day has been so long that I almost can't believe what I hear. In a trance I say good-bye to her and to Miss Inez, who is still on the phone, and barely acknowledges me.

Before pushing myself through the front door downstairs, I notice a door to my left with a small window. Through the darkness I make out the silhouette of a huskily built man on the other side—a white man with a porridge-bowl haircut. He turns his head toward me but I hurriedly push myself through the front door and out to the street. I am at my saturation point and simply cannot meet yet another person. Yet I wonder, who could he be, rummaging in the shadows of Our Lady of Miracles, and why is he wearing a frilly kitchen apron?

Retracing my steps, I find the bus stop without difficulty. Across the street from where I was deposited that morning, under the red sign for the *farmacia*, there is a glass enclosure. Among the bus travelers, I recognize children wearing the gray and maroon plaid uniforms of Our Lady of Miracles.

Once we're on board, bus Number 13, angles downward, breaking our fall in pumps and gasps as we descend the same long, steep hill that my bus climbed to arrive this morning. As I tuck away my Metro card, my hand settles on two unfamiliar objects in my jacket pocket. They turn out to be the granola bars from my final class. At this center, I can see that Ms. Magdalena's room is going to be my dessert.

On level ground at the bottom of the hill, instead of cutting through the tunnel, my departing bus swings a wide arc through residential blocks. The old apartment buildings that ripple past flash intricate Deco brickwork and Tudor features as ornate as any strip on Madison Avenue. Finally we double back to pass barren expanses of brown grass as we approach the dainty white oval of Yankee stadium. We are back under the 161st Street station, but I can't stop running impressions of Highbridge through my head. How everything—from the acute steepness of the incline it is built on, to the astonishingly blunt proportions of my supervisor—seems rendered in larger-than-life extremes. The heaps of garbage, the disheveled people, the massive goose-shit-colored slab of a housing project, all seem like enhanced effects for a horror movie or disturbing warps from an acid trip. As we pull to a stop beneath the elevated subway tracks, people stand to leave. I join their slow line, haunted to think that above us, the whole dilapidated kingdom remains perched on its mesa, awaiting my return next week and simmering like a cauldron.

Miss Catalina

"Listen, don't call me Miss Brenda. I hate that shit."

On my second Friday morning at the Head Start center at Castle Hill—St. Anthony's School— right in the middle of singing "Old MacDonald," I am summoned to the telephone in the main office.

"I hope one of my sons isn't sick."

I try making conversation with the secretary who escorts me from the classroom, but she only walks ahead of me, and shrugs. Behind the reception desk she shows me to an empty cubicle with a telephone. Then with a lacquered nail she depresses a button on the phone pad, hands me the receiver and sashays back to her habitat.

"That you, Leah?" My gruff-voiced caller is Brenda Keenan from her office across the street.

"Yes, it's me. Good morning, Miss Brenda—" and that's when I hear it:

"Listen, don't call me Miss Brenda. I hate that shit."

Such a long way from home I shiver for the grace of a moment to be naughty and natural and out from under the thumb of my stodgy supervisor here. Miss Catalina Vedan has a graying pageboy haircut. Behind her glasses her eyes are tense, and she speaks in a squealing singsong that can't disguise the fact that she hasn't decided whether or not she likes me.

The center at Castle Hill offers a full day at school, unlike Marble Hill and Our Lady of Miracles, where the children attend in two shifts. Here, after lunch is served, Teachers turn off the lights in classrooms as the children lie down for a Board of Education-mandated forty-five-minute nap. Because of this break, five of my six music sessions are crammed back-to-back before lunch with only one final class to be given at the end of the day. And here I'd been concerned about getting through my Tuesdays—such innocence!

Anticipating these long Friday mornings makes it hard for me to sleep on Thursday nights. Often I leave the apartment in the morning stressed and exhausted, but if I doze on the subway the recorded announcements zap me awake as my train approaches St. Anthony's. From my coma I hear the mechanical voice herald "Morrison-Soundview," and "Parkchester."

By the time the doors slide open at the Castle Hill station, I struggle to my feet and then walk the half-mile to Metropolitan Avenue in dread. The day before me feels like having to throw five children's birthday parties in a row, with a sixth tossed in just as I begin to recover. As I duck out of each class, shutting their cries of "Miss Leah, Miss Leah, Miss Leah!" behind me, I must manufacture the enthusiasm needed for opening the next door, to do it all again—and again and yet again.

By my fifth class I draw less on my musicianship and humanity, and more on what is left of my stamina as a former, high school athlete. When I was summoned to the phone in the middle of singing "Old MacDonald" to my third class, Brenda was calling to make sure that I was settling into my routine. I was able to assure her brightly that everything was fine because she had just pumped the blood back into my long hours with one gust of her bullshit-banishing informality.

But I can't get too comfortable. I hurry back to complete this class, and then two more classes like it before it can be my turn to sit down.

Ghosts in the Garden

Every October inventive neighbors overtake the wooden stage in the middle of our community garden to construct a "haunted house" with dark corners and crawl spaces for children to explore. In the nights before Halloween, neighborhood kids have a chance to test-drive their costumes and scare each other in the "cobwebs" of the primitive labyrinth while we parents sit looking on and chatting. My sons and Ananda's daughter are among the masqueraders.

"So what are you doing in your classroom for Halloween?"

Beside me in the dark of our East Village community garden, Ananda drops to the ground and folds herself into a ball declaring, "I got a good one for you!"

By day Ananda is the head teacher at a Village preschool. By night she bicycles up to the West Side where she's completing a degree in education from Bank Street College. We are both in the business of three- and four-year-olds, though she works with the privileged children of educated parents, while at Head Start I tend to the children of struggling immigrants. I am grateful to make a new friend with so much experience that I can tap.

With her head tucked into her belly, and with a deep, muffled voice, she slowly recites: "Pumpkin, pumpkin, round and fat. Turn into a jack-o'-lantern just like that!" Then she raises her arms to clap them over her head in perfect time with her final word.

Look, it isn't Shakespeare. It isn't A. A. Milne or even Mother Goose. But as she rises to her feet, brushing loose leaves and gravel from her knees, I feel grateful enough to embrace her. Only a fellow preschool teacher can understand the value of this short, silly routine and no Halloween candy could have been sweeter. It's simple, engaging, and the movements are well within the children's ability to master. It could be taught from the floor in a large group and it ends with the triumphant smack of everybody clapping their hands at once.

"Such simple brilliance," I declare. "I mean, the poetry, the choreography!"

"And with our set you know, you can never underestimate the power of end rhyme," she gushes back. Only another preschool-teaching dork can stand with me in the late October chill as we wait for our children, extolling the many fine attributes of "Pumpkin, pumpkin" like appraisers of some rare antique.

"Is Simon supposed to be an astronaut?" asks Ananda. Not to be outdone by Haskell's bum getup, complete with penciled five o'clock shadow, Simon has been transformed into a vacuum cleaner. We rigged a hose with an attachment to feed out of the hole we had cut in one of Mark's old T-shirts. When the big night comes, at Simon's insistence, we plan to let him do his trick-or-treating with an opened vacuum bag—a fresh one, of course.

"That's cute," Ananda says when I explain his intentions. "Can we borrow him to clean my house?"

I'm energized as I head home with the boys a little later. I don't feel quite so worried about the coming week because this time, thanks to our local haunted house, I have a pumpkin up my sleeve.

On Monday morning Ananda's pumpkin is making such good pie that Miss Blanca and Miss Lucia are practically leading it for themselves by the afternoon. As I thought they might, the children really love curling themselves into balls and turning their classroom floor into a pumpkin patch. To continue the theme we fit bats and black cats onto Old MacDonald's farm and I creep the "Itsy Bitsy spider" into a minor key.

Where the kids seem confident enough, I have its creepy cousin "the great big hairy spider" climb up the waterspout instead, but I keep this variation out of my final classroom at Our Lady of Miracles where I think it wise to spare the thin-skinned little Manuel any upsetting corruptions to his personal favorite. For the first time, I catch myself actually looking forward to bringing something so popular to the classrooms on Friday.

Trick or Treat

When I arrive at St. Anthony's, it's *my* turn to be surprised. Instead of beginning my usual routine in the classrooms on the second floor, I am told to take my guitar and hurry to one of the administrative buildings across the street from the school. There, in a crepe-paper-strung multipurpose room, I find my six classes with their teachers all dressed in costumes and ready to perform in a Halloween assembly for members of the administrative staff of Head Start, who sit in rows of folding chairs.

The teachers have rehearsed their kids all week. But having no prior knowledge of the event, I have no idea what songs the children are to present or how my guitar and I may best be added to the mix. As I arrive the dimming lights leave me no time to check in with the teachers. Even if I recognize a classroom song once it begins, the children tend to shout or drone tunelessly so that it is impossible to herd them into a key by the end of the piece. I decide that my best contribution is simply one of moral support. So I toss my guitar to the side and plant myself in the middle of the children, where I can hold chilly little hands in mine and embolden shy performers rather than muddy things up with an unhandsome searching for guitar chords.

Six times I accompany masqueraded performers, princesses and superheroes, who take their places under the lights. The real stars of this show are the children in their costumes. The undistinguishable, tuneless ditties, one after another, are only an excuse to earn applause from the indulgent audience.

And then it's done. In the hubbub of lights going on and everybody rising from their chairs, Miss Catalina steers me to shake hands with a couple of men in suits with titles like Associate Director or Branch Supervisor. I hear no trumpeted fanfares when a heavy, unkempt woman with ruddy cheeks pushes her hand into mine. She has a tuft of chick-yellow hair like the troll doll I remember having as a child. I'm told only that her name is Florence Galway.

There's an air of festive relief among the teachers as I head back into the glare of daylight to help shepherd their classes back across Metropolitan Avenue. I'm moved to see the kids so dazzled by the sight of their classmates and even some of their teachers 'in drag.' Back at the school I have to stoop to admire blue Spidermen, Kelly-green Incredible Hulks, and pink-and-white Strawberry

Shortcakes. There are also many Bob the Builders, Little Mermaids, and Dora the Exploras stretching out costumed arms for me to slip off their jackets. Behind glittered masks and face paint, their eyes are round with excitement and put me to shame. Just as all the same old commercial displays of ghosts and goblins are starting to get on my nerves, just as bags of miniature Snickers and Three Musketeers bars have lost their delight for me, here are the children with their young, unjaded hearts set aflutter. Hadn't I been teleported up here to bring music and culture to their classrooms? Three times a week I write on the top of my consultant's form that I am a music and movement specialist. Meanwhile, the look of wonder on the children's faces is in fact reminding me what Halloween is really about.

The center threw me a bit of a curveball by springing the assembly on me. Still, I believe that the kids are happy to see me. As I head to the staffroom for lunch I feel confident that I helped them through the whole ordeal of performing and put their best costumed foot forward. My job is to help make the Head Start center shine before its administrative officers. With no prior knowledge of the assembly, I don't know what more I could have done.

An Unexpected New Friend

Morning classes were difficult today. At Marble Hill the dowdy Miss Evangeline began to snore in the middle of the first class, and in Room Two—perhaps because Miss Lucia had lost her voice—the boys were loud and disrespectful in a way that they hadn't been before.

They tired me out, so, at the Land and the Sea restaurant—when the same nervous waiter appears— "yes, today I will have coffee before my sandwich, please."

My all-purpose shoulder bag is stuffed to the point of exploding. There are pens and pencils, crumpled invoices and receipts, old Happy Meal toys, straws, napkins, and water bottles, even a soggy pair of Haskell's gym shorts I've forgotten to remove. I would have to hunt under all this clammy domestic detritus to uncover my wallet.

I am a little embarrassed to be caught on my feet taking things out, one by one, when the waiter appears with a tray. I doubt that the mess I am making will further endear me to him. I mean to initiate only minimal contact, but the coffee set he presents with a cloth napkin, lace doilies, and my own prim little coffee pot is so much more than I had expected.

"Are all these lovely things for me?" I can't help asking as he carefully sets the table. "My goodness. You make me feel like a princess!"

And just like that the old man who wasn't able to look me in the eye five minutes ago sets down his tray and takes me into his arms. He hugs me tightly too, urgently, like a long-lost uncle.

Back at headquarters I find Miss Lucia sitting in the staffroom by herself. She whispers to me that she's trying to revive her strained vocal cords with a cup of herbal tea. Still in her carefully hushed voice, she tells me about a situation at her home. When her thirteen-year-old daughter washes the family dishes, she leaves a soapy residue behind that both Miss Lucia and her husband can actually taste. Miss Lucia is glad that her daughter helps out with chores, and is reluctant to criticize her. Still, she doesn't want to have to blow any more soap bubbles for desert, she chuckles.

Only a kind spirit like Miss Lucia grapples with this sort of dilemma. I wish she didn't have to go back into the classroom and further ravage what is left of her voice. While she drinks her tea, I congratulate her on raising a teenager with such good manners. She smiles when I tell her that the only time my boys ever clean a plate is with their finger.

"Here, these are my boys."

After the school photographer visited P.S. 63, I acquired a new set of wallet-sized pictures of Haskell and Simon, posed against the background of an American Flag. Miss Lucia admires the picture of Haskell looking like a young marine with his buzz cut still severely intact from our lice episode. But when I show her Simon she knits her brow and taps his photo with her finger. "He looks like Habib," she rasps. Habib is a quiet boy who comes to Room Two in the afternoons.

From down the hall the front door buzzes as the second shift of children begin to arrive with their parents. Miss Lucia leaves the staffroom to join Miss Blanca in serving lunch to their class while I head to Miss Sandra's filing cabinets to complete my paperwork while they eat. Once I collect my two forms, I plan to return to where I was sitting with Miss Lucia. But when I re-enter the staffroom I am accosted by the stench of eyeball-quivering bleach fumes. Mr. Justin, the janitor, is mopping the staffroom floor so I retreat to Miss Antonette's office to scratch out my forms in the chair across from her desk. As usual she is on the phone. In the background of her conversation a radio on her bookshelf wails to the climax of a song: "And I'm gonna keep on lovin you. Cause it's the only thing I wanna do."

I ask once she finishes her call. "Is that REO Speedwagon?"

"Yeah." She smiles shyly and stretches back in her chair. "The '80s, Miss Leah, that was my time!" I file this tidbit, noting that a compilation CD of '80s pop songs will make an excellent stocking stuffer for Miss Antonette from her music consultant. As everyone keeps reminding me, the holidays will be here before we know it.

With my guitar thrown over my shoulder like a pick and shovel, I make my way back to the classrooms wondering if it might be fun to teach Miss Antonette's golden oldie to the children. Its tragic refrain of "I don't wanna sleep, I just wanna keep on loving you!" is probably something any child can relate to. But once the door opens and I catch sight of Miss Nicole carping at her class over some misconduct that occurred during their lunch while Miss Evangeline slumps in her chair, I decide to play it safe.

> After unzipping my guitar from its case, I follow our ABC's with teaching everybody "Ragg Mop," a silly song with lots of singing out of the letters that spell short words. I am pleased that the afternoon kids are willing to learn something new. Soon I have everybody crying out "R-A-G-G M-O-P-P, RAGG MOP, RAGG MOP, RAGG MOP!" right where it belongs in the lyrics. (To see renditions of this wonderful 1950s hit, see Johnny Lee Wills and His Boys or The Ames Brothers perform it on YouTube).

I still wrestle with all the length and newness of children's names. For example, two little girls named Genesis are in the afternoon class of Room One. I never knew that Genesis was a girl's proper name. There are children called Angel, Heaven, and Perfection. By the afternoon a handful of Destinys arrive—all of them adorable. In Miss Lucia's and Miss Blanca's room, there is a tubby, double-chinned little madonna named Nioka. There is a Chardonnay to sip as well as a Princessa and a Delicia to stub my tongue on again and again. There is also a second plus-size girl like Nioka who comes to Room Two in the afternoon.

This girl, Undine, with skin the color of pumpkin pie, embeds her name in my challenged memory by being tough and lippy and spending most of our class minutes sneering at me from the "time out" chair in the back of the room. And, of course, there is Habib, the little boy whose sweet face is indeed as pale and round as my Simon's.

At the end of my last class, Miss Lucia tells me to show Simon's school photo to Miss Blanca. Around us the children press in, crying, "Lemee see. Lemme see it!" Suddenly everybody is determined to get a look at my son. Miss Blanca leads little Habib through his more aggressive classmates to where I stoop so that he can regard his look-alike. When he arrives at my side he takes Simon's picture in his hands and I loop an arm around him.

"Ah, yes." He nods as if spotting a relative. And then he melts me. Just as Miss Lucia had earlier in the staffroom, he taps the photograph with his finger "...And if I knew him we would be friends," he says.

Years ago a friend told me that in the eyes of his pit bulls he noticed either total love or total hatred, with nothing in between. His observation comes back to me that night as I ponder my long day. I lie in bed remembering that a short time ago, when I first walked into their classroom, the children at all three centers and some of the staff, for that matter, regarded me as the beast itself. But after a few songs and dances many of them were willing to drop their reservations. Suddenly rooms full of strangers became ardent fans, grabbing for my shoelaces and clamoring for more music. Total love or total hatred with nothing in between; perhaps we human beings are more like my friend's pit bulls than we care to believe.

Either way, I know that I will no longer be a stranger in a strange land when I next exit the train at 225th Street. Already people greet me by name at the Marble Hill center, even if that name must be Miss Leah. For starters, I have Miss Lucia to talk to. And surely Habib, the little boy in her afternoon class, will now remember me. After his disarmingly sweet remark it appears that even Simon's picture is making friends uptown. And grudgingly, slowly, I admit to myself that I am starting to get along with Miss Antonette. With her high, tiny voice and her hankering for '80s pop music, she is shaking out to be not a bad little confection, so far as administrative supervisors go. By the end of the day, didn't she give my guitar a playful swat as I headed out the door, calling to me: "I see the children enjoy what you bring for them today, Miss Leah. I see you always came to us prepared to work."

But that isn't all. I fall asleep smiling as I recall the surprise embrace from the waiter at the Land and the Sea. My new friend is from Greece and speaks English haltingly. Still, we've managed to establish that now we are buddies and I am to call him Nicky.

A is for Apples

One Tuesday I arrive in Highbridge to learn that I will not be making my usual rounds, but will instead join my students on an apple picking trip to an orchard in rural New Jersey. As happened at Castle Hill on Halloween, the administrators forgot about my music classes when they scheduled the outing. Consequently they don't know what to do about me showing up with an arm full of Hula hoops. I am told to stash them and my guitar in Ms. Bilkis' locked office. I leave my accoutrements leaning against the copy machine under a large framed photograph of Lady Diana hand in hand with a wimpled Mother Theresa stepping out of an orphanage doorway.

Two tremendous chartered commercial coaches will convey the inner city families of Highbridge, the staff of Head Start, and one displaced music consultant deep into the autumnal provinces of the other side of the Hudson. Sleek and tall with mysterious darkened windows, the coaches eclipse the Our Lady of Miracles complex behind them. As parents and children gather on the sidewalk the parked buses loom, dwarfing fragile trees and low buildings on the block as idling motors rumble.

Among the crowd I smile, recognizing faces from the morning and afternoon classrooms. But on this occasion the children don't call out to me. There is no spirited, nagging chorus of "Miss Leah, Miss Leah" as little ones hover by the knees of their parents, glazed, I imagined, from the over-stimulation of their altered routine, the sudden merging of teachers and parents.

It is also before eight o'clock. *"Isn't it a bit early in the morning for all of this?"* A character from a Harold Pinter play mawkishly entreats in my memory as I survey the parents shuffling self-consciously, sipping from their coffee cups and yawning. I wave when the sweet face of Nabid, a particularly lovely child who always thanks me at the end of my class, meets my eyes. I find him peeking from within the rainbow of billowing traditional saris worn by his relatives. I also recognize a pretty, light-skinned black girl named Essence from one of the morning classes. Dolled up in a trench coat, a dress, pumps, and hoop earrings, her mother stands beside her daughter holding her hand. The poor woman must have misunderstood the informal nature of the outing. Most astonishingly, her shiny scalp almost appears to have been turtle-waxed, like the hood of a Mustang. For no reason that I can guess, Essence's beautiful mother is balder than I.

At that moment Miss Lucy, an older black woman from the office, hurries out to speak to the families who have gathered in front of the buses. I've met this administrator before, seen her clowning around with Miss Magdalena, to whom she seems particularly close. Generally she wears glasses and restrains her graying ponytail severely close to her scalp.

But today she doesn't look good. Her gray hair is flying out of her bobby-pins, and there is a great sorrow I've never seen before etched into the bags and lines of her face. I hope that she is not unwell. And yet when she opens her mouth, her ragged voice carries the same authority it always has. She starts by clapping her hands.

"People!" She calls, her voice as hoarse as it is loud, and the crowd instantly becomes quiet with attention. "Okay, mommies, daddies...We're so glad to have your company today, but you do understand that we have a few rules that you need to observe here with your children. While you're with us, there's to be no smoking, no drinking." Some of the men smile guiltily or start to laugh. "I don't want to hear no cussing or no foul language. Y'all want a fight. You can do that on your own time. Not here," continues Miss Lucy. "We would like everybody to set a good example for your children. If any of you get out of order you may be asked to leave the bus at any time. And if you be way out in New Jersey you'n trust me, you ain't gonna like THAT! Emmm, Emmmm. You know what I'm sayin'?" And then she guffaws and the crowd follows her cue. They laugh at what she's told them and buzz again with conversation, but at least now they know the rules.

When we get to the orchard we are supposed to board a long mobile platform that is pulled by a tractor. I sit on the wooden boards along with the children and a bevy of older relatives. Grandmothers in brightly colored saris sit uncomfortably, bouncing up and down, as we are pulled, bumping, over a field and into the rows of trees.

But before we reach our destination the unthinkable happens: The sky opens to a teaming rain. We are helpless, drenched, trapped; brightly colored saris get soaked and cling to the grandmothers' thighs, wet children cling to the saris. Essence's mother wraps her trench coat around her daughter, and in spite of Miss Lucy's admonition, I hear forbidden words from the mouths of dads.

Are these administrators clueless? They forget my class, and they don't check the forecast when they plan a trip. The tractor turns around, wheels already spinning in the mud, and hauls us back to where the buses are parked and the motors idling. Since the rain shows no sign of relenting we are loaded back on the bus. Each child has been awarded a mini paper shopping bag of apples. There is even one being held out for me to take as we reboard the coaches. Lunch is handed out as the buses roll: some kind of pale pork meat sandwiches on white bread.

I find, however, that I can't eat. The bus is highly air-conditioned, and we are all drenched. I don't know how the others are managing but I have curled up in whatever dryness remains inside my wool sweater. Slightly motion sick and shivering in the seat behind the driver, I have retracted my cold knuckles deep into the sleeves, and dug my chin into the collar like a duck into her feathers.

Between my wet head and muddy shoes this thin, heat-retaining layer of wool alone keeps me from contracting any number of croupy, whooping conditions as the bus engine whines us back to Our Lady of Miracles. As a consultant with not a personal day off in her contract, I'm rather in awe that my ratty old maroon sweater has stood nobly between me and the setback of unpaid, missed work hours spent housebound with an upper respiratory infection. More immediately, it has spared me an hour and a half of sour, diesel-smelling, teeth-chattering chills. Wool! I've never been so grateful for the animal that produced it, and for the wheel that spun it. Now it means something entirely new when I sing "the sheep's in the meadow, the cow's in the corn" with the children. All the songs with sheep are suddenly imbued with new and passionate significance.

"Bah, bah, black sheep, have you any wool?"

"Yes sir, yes sir, one sweater full."

Boo!

Around Mount Eden Avenue, the larger neighborhood of Tremont was named by its first postmaster after the three hills it encompassed, which were probably known well by his carriage horse or his own tired feet: Mount Eden, Mount Hope, and Fairmount. But Castle Hill was named, by the Dutch explorer Adriaen Block, for the slight elevation that occurs at present-day Lacombe and Castle Hill Avenues. To his seventeenth-century eyes, the verdant, majestic mound he beheld there resembled a castle.

The Friday morning in early November when I arrive there with my guitar to trudge to St. Anthony's through an icy rain, it is more like "White Castle Hill." Rows of bargain emporiums, fast food joints, and shabby storefronts only reinforce the fact that Castle Hill, as well as my other two Bronx neighborhoods, has for decades been listed among the poorest congressional districts in the country.

At St. Anthony's Brenda Keenan wants to speak to me. The same secretary who summoned me last time is at my classroom door. Unfortunately I can't come to the phone as I did before. This time the secretary instructs me that I'm supposed to stay put, finish all my morning classes, and then report to Brenda's office in person. Before eating lunch, I head back across Metropolitan Avenue, not knowing what to expect any more than I had the week before when I was told to join the Halloween assembly. My days at Head Start are, indeed, full of surprises. The only thing I know for sure is that this time I won't have to call her Miss Brenda.

To find Brenda Keenan at the administrative building I trace my way back in time to the little office in which she had interviewed me so many weeks ago. The statue of Jesus still stands, palms out, offering his grace from the corner of the waiting room. His crown of thorns reminds me that, only a short time ago, I wondered if my head would ever stop itching from lice, and now blessedly it has. Miracles are possible, beginning with, for once, not having to insipidly call my superior "Miss" Brenda.

The door to Brenda's office is open and she waves for me to sit down in a chair beside her desk as she finishes a phone conversation. Something is clearly wrong. Her smile has no warmth—not a trace of her signature jolliness and nothing of the "cut the shit" informality that had breathed the life back into me not two weeks ago. Had it been just a hopeful dream, and am I waking up to find that she's turned back into Miss Brenda?

I take my seat beside her desk.

"So how are you?" she asks flatly, putting the receiver down.

I am just fine and so is she. My classes? Oh, everything is humming along. She nods, rubbing her nose, letting her small, mascaraed eyes blink around the room. Finally they come to rest on me.

"Yeah, but I gotta tell you, Leah, we've had a complaint about you from Florence Galway. You probably met her at our Halloween thing. Do you remember meeting her? Do you know who she is?"

Though I remember meeting her with her tuft of yellow hair, I do not know "who she is." But by now my heart is pounding with such vexation that I doubt I can remember my own name.

"Well, she's head of the entire archdiocese Head Start operations," Brenda explains. "That's right," she says, zeroing in on my frightened eyes and nodding cryptically. "I'm afraid this isn't good, Leah. You know, what can I say? She mentioned how disappointed she was that you didn't play your guitar last week." Brenda shrugs while shaking her head, and continues. "You know some of our top people were there—feds, grant writers, site supervisors—I mean, come on, kiddo. This is the big time. You really left me in an awkward spot. Aren't you aware that you were expected to accompany the children? I mean that kind of thing is supposed to be your department. That's what we hired you for!"

Did I know that I was expected to accompany the children?

Well, in a word, "no."

For a moment I just sit in a stupor. Does this mean that I'll be going home to tell Mark and the boys that I've lost my job, that I failed here, and that I won't be bringing home any more money? Doesn't Brenda realize that nobody had told me anything about this performance? Nobody!

"Brenda," I say at last. "When I arrived to work on Friday morning last week, I had no idea there was going to be a Halloween performance. Nobody gave me any kind of a heads-up. I was just told to go across the street, and boom—suddenly I found myself in front of a live audience, expected to play my guitar on the spot to songs I've never heard before. It was like something from one of those classic anxiety dreams where you don't know your lines in a play."

I check, but she isn't convinced. I sigh and continue rubbing my clammy palms on my knees and trying to still my racing heart. "Brenda, in order to accompany a song, I have to at least find out what key everybody is singing in. Without knowing that I would be all over the map hunting for chords, and that could have just made the whole thing look sloppy. I'm very sorry I didn't break out my guitar, but please, can you see that under the circumstances I didn't want to risk muddying up the children's performance? I thought I could be most helpful just making the kids feel comfortable on stage and supporting the teachers."

People with no experience playing music are often unaware of concerns such as cueing a group to sing in the same key in which they are being accompanied. To do a good job there has to be some planning—otherwise, big, hideous embarrassing train wrecks will occur, no matter how fine a musician or how good a music teacher anyone happens to be.

The fact is, and she damn well knows it, that I am just an afterthought. The center had completely forgotten about me, and so they had thrown me in cold last week and now here I am, on the spot, fighting for my life again. If the job description called for turning water into wine, then the man she wanted was Jesus and he was back down the hall in the waiting room.

Brenda taps the pencil eraser against her lips. Finally she shrugs, and I catch a semblance of the old twinkle in her eye.

"In the future it would be really helpful if the teachers could let me know in advance when we're having an assembly, and if we could use some of our time in the classroom to prepare for it."

How can she argue with that request?

"Then I promise you, my guitar and I will be all over it like an entire brass band."

At last she smiles. "Alright. Get out of here," she tells me with a wave of her hand. "Go eat your lunch."

Outside her office door I follow the narrow hallway back to the reception area, still dizzy from having argued my case. I have to wonder who might this Florence Galway be who'd felt compelled to put in such a bad word for me? Passing through the waiting room on my way to the street, I come eye to eye with the statue of Jesus and am struck anew by the exasperation in his perpetually heaven-turned glance.

On Pins and Hypodermic Needles

On Mondays I have my breakfast at the Land & the Sea restaurant. Upper Broadway at 225th Street is still a long way from home and after facing the inquisition at St. Anthony's concerning Florence Galway 's "disappointment," I am full of gratitude for the safe harbor of a cozy, upholstered booth against the window where hot coffee and a tight hug from Nicky begins my morning. And I happily discover that both the bran and carrot muffins on the menu are stocked with plump golden raisins, "berried treasure" to uncover after being torn from sleep and enduring the long commute.

Once I'm buzzed inside, I find the staffroom of the Marble Hill center to be a bustling souk of commerce. The Aflac insurance people are repacking their briefcases, having just completed their pitch to the office workers.

"Quack quack! Did anybody get the quack quack insurance?" Miss Sandra giggles to Miss Antonette, once they are gone. Last week, the Avon lady had come calling and we'd all gone jewelry shopping. Maybe next week there will be a Tupperware party at Head Start.

The staffroom has a vitality of its own where I am under no obligation to hold the stage, as I do in the classrooms. With each passing week, as even the oddity of my crew cut becomes an expected sight for the staff on Mondays, I find that I'm welcome to relax in front of my newspaper here, and nobody seems to be watching me. During the long break between the morning and afternoon classes, to my delight, I can catch my breath.

In Room Two by the end of the morning we sing our goodbyes to the accompaniment of gusts of wind that sent branches scratching at the window panes. By contrast, the interior staffroom is almost cozy as I settle into a folding chair and unwrap my tuna sandwich.

"It's a serious problem, Justin!" From the opposite end of the table, Miss Sandra bears down on the janitor, Mr. Justin, who is shaking his head behind the cover of his paperback.

"And what might your serious problem be?" chirps Miss Antonette, who has followed close behind me to pop a Hot Pocket into the microwave. We learn that Miss Sandra is moving her mother into a new home. The good news, she relays, is that after years on a waiting list for government-subsidized housing, her mother's number has finally been drawn. The bad news is that the brand new apartment is far too small. In the tiny kitchen Miss Sandra's mother, a big lady like her daughter, gets pinned between the countertop and the appliances as she tried to prepare a meal.

Miss Sandra's story brought to mind the conversation with Miss Lucia last week. I am actually looking forward to an update on her daughter's soapy dishes. But when I open the door of Room Two, I find that although she has recovered her voice, Miss Lucia is in no mood to chat.

"I just can't wait for the cold weather to set in. No sir, it can't arrive soon enough for me!" she mutters in her delicate rasp, feeding the arms of her children into their jacket sleeves and winding zippers up to their chins with Miss Blanca. I wonder if we are preparing the classes for a fire drill until the teachers explain what's going on.

After our blustery morning, the wind died down and turned the afternoon into one of the last temperate days of autumn. Outside, the sun streams out from behind clouds. Apparently Miss Antonette has taken a wild hair that the teachers and I should round up the children of Room Two for an outing in the small playground at the center of the housing project that encompasses our center. In a line with everybody holding the hand of a partner, I am to be the caboose. Still shaking her head and complaining to Miss Blanca, Miss Lucia leads the train of us along a narrow path of sidewalk that cuts through the patchy, brown grass between buildings.

When we come to the paved enclosure, grim with its deserted swing set and slide, Miss Blanca swivels to face the line with hooded eyes and a stony expression. "Nobody moves!" she commands, with a voice deeper than I've ever heard in her classroom.

"Company halt!" I add, trying to keep the restless class amused while ahead of us Miss Lucia snaps her hands into a pair of latex gloves and, clutching a paper bag, begins to stalk the periphery of the blacktop. Time and again I watch her bend to the asphalt collecting chards of broken glass or perhaps plucking condoms or cigarette butts from the dirt by the swings along with other nasty debris that has settled in the corners. Wobbling on her crepe soles, she steps up one or two rungs of the ladder leading to the slide in order to check the top of the platform. When Miss Lucia completes her inspection, Miss Blanca releases the class with a sweep of her arm, and laughs as the children stream into the little playground, chasing each other and shrieking with their sudden freedom.

Miss Blanca saunters easily behind the stampede, stopping to lean against the chain-link fence and yawn with her caramel hair blowing gently back against her open mouth. By contrast, Miss Lucia dutifully follows her children, helping them navigate the slide and separating brawlers. She remains tense and fretful until we are back in the classroom, closing the door decisively behind us.

"Bad idea, bad idea," I hear her fume as we peel down the same zippers it seems we had only just engaged. Sending the children with their arms full of jackets and sweaters to be returned to their cubbies, Miss Lucia draws Miss Blanca and me beside her. "Now why on earth would Antonette want us to do a thing like that?" she hisses. "And don't think in the past we haven't had to pick up syringes with our bare hands. Isn't that right, Miss Blanca?"

I agree with Miss Lucia that having to take her class to a playground that was frequented by vagrants and junkies at least as often as by children seemed a naive and hazardous whim on the part of our supervisor. I wasn't any happier than poor Miss Lucia was about the idea of encountering cigarette lighters, fish tubing, or hypodermic needles with a class of children in tow.

Later as I get to my paperwork in her office, I decide that I will try to plant some distressing image that might discourage Miss Antonette from indulging such notions in the future. But even after listening to my somewhat embellished version of our expedition, which included a barehanded Miss Lucia having to rid the area of crack pipes and razor blades, Miss Antonette closes her eyes before speaking.

"Yes, drug addiction is a terrible problem," she allows. "Although, you know, in my country it is not so much the heroin you have here as, how do you say it, Methone, methodine...?"

"Methamphetamine, or 'crystal meth,'" I correct her.

"Yes, that's right. It's that speed they can produce in their home laboratories. Most other imported drugs like heroin or cocaine are too expensive for a lot of young people to get their hands on. And of course there's plenty of marijuana back home.

"Even my little brother. In my family there are seven children. As the oldest, when I lived at home, I used to keep an eye on him. But now that I live in the States, my mother, you know, she spoils him, doesn't have any control over him."

Miss Antonette tells me that her little brother is beginning to hang out with the wrong people. She believes that he's starting to take drugs himself. Just last week he had called her to ask for money. He told her that it was for a new pair of expensive American running shoes, but she won't send him anything because she believes she knows exactly how he intends to spend the money. "I dunno how he's going to end up," she finally sighs, looking down at her fingernails and shaking her head.

"That makes me sad," I tell her. And then follows an uncomfortable silence. "Do you think it would do any good to tell your mother about these things you've been noticing?" I ask.

"I dunno what she could hear."

"Can you tell her what's making you worry? Can you talk about the kind of things that you were just telling me?"

But Miss Antonette only continues looking down at her nails. "I dunno," she repeats, in her high, tiny voice. "He's her baby boy, you know?" Having finished studying her nails, she folds her pudgy hands on the desktop. "All she knows how to do is to spoil him. She can't hear anything bad about him, you know?" she says, returning her sad eyes to mine.

She shrugs again but her wistful smile turns coy with a wrinkle of her nose. "I see you notice that I have no ring, Miss Leah, but I can assure you that my little brother is not the only man in my life." She caught me staring at her fingers although it's only a tick of bashfulness that brought my gaze to her folded hands.

Sensing, however, that a little girl talk is in order, I smile back.

"Do you have a boyfriend, Miss Antonette?"

"I have a sweetheart!" she tells me brightly.

Miss Antonette's beau lives in Texas. She hasn't seen him in a long time, each of them being so busy with their careers. But they speak on the phone whenever they have a chance. Until they can marry, Miss Antonette lives with her grandmother and a great aunt for whom she observes a ten o'clock curfew. I feel claustrophobic just hearing about what awaits her at home every night: two old ladies sitting in a living room in Queens, under a ticking clock. But Miss Antonette doesn't sound burdened when she says simply with a shrug, "They get uncomfortable if I'm not at home when they expect me to be."

I also learn that her boyfriend is a heart surgeon. "Can you imagine what our favorite song is now that you know that about him?" she asks.

When I can't guess she tells me, giggling, that it is Sheryl Crow's "The First Cut Is the Deepest."

Hands Up High, Hands Down Low!

At St. Anthony's my first two morning classes are located up a long schoolhouse flight of stairs. The children have learned to expect fun at the sight of my instrument and bag of props, so Miss Masaya and Miss Lisa, the teachers in Room One, have a hard time controlling the burst of energy as I duck into their classroom. Some kids simply run to greet me at the door and plaster themselves against my legs before they can be called to order. It's like the moment when the gates open and the bull charges into the rodeo, kicking and bucking. If I haven't been brought to my knees by the little mob, I'll hurry to the chair that has been placed facing the rug where they are supposed to be sitting with folded legs, "crisscross, applesauce," waiting for me "nicely." Now it's time to let the games begin!

"Wooo, okay, hold the phone! Everybody hold the presses!" I parry.

"Miss Leah, Miss Leah," the children cry.

Over the mayhem I attempt to grab the reins with a bright "Good morning, boys and girls!" I make sure to admire the barrettes and baubles in the hair of the little girls, while feigning alarm at the roars and dramatic faces made by the boys—every one of them little Max, jumping right from the pages of Maurice Sendak's *Where the Wild Things Are*.

> ### HANDS UP HIGH, HANDS DOWN LOW!
>
> "Alright everybody, hands up high!"
> I throw my hands into the air, inviting the children to do the same.
> "Hands down low!"
> I let my hands dangle, like an ape.
> "Behind your back!"
> I hide my hands behind my back.
> "Now, where did they go?"
> My hands still behind me, I shrug and shake my head.

"Behind you. They're behind your back, Miss Leah!" the children chorus.

We might repeat this three or four times, as more and more children begin to participate. Soon they will all be reaching their hands into the air, bringing them down to the floor, and then hiding them behind their backs with gleaming eyes. This exercise can be done with the children standing up or sitting down.

"Oh, my goodness, will you look at this!" I gasp, pointing to one of them. "This little girl must have left her hands at home. This little girl doesn't have any hands!"

I don't know how politically correct this is, but the children love being singled out, holding my astonished attention all to themselves, and getting to show me that they really do have a fine pair of grubby little hands to wave in my face after all.

"Here they are! I have hands. Here are my hands!" they cry.

Oh, you silly Miss Leah!

Entering the room with such pizzazz is fine, but in real time we are only two minutes into their session, and I still have a long way to go. I prefer to begin my classes with a warm-up or two like this one that unifies the room, using just our voices or our clapping hands before the guitar is brought in.

Appetizers

Young children don't generally sit and sing for forty minutes in the natural world. To keep my sessions from becoming dull, I've become a passionate collector of things to do with the kids before even going to the music. I've compiled lists of little "appetizers"—games and rhymes to engage their participation, like "Hands Up High and Hands Down Low." Here are some favorites, and how to do them:

BEEHIVE

Make a fist and say, "This is the hive. Where are the bees? Hidden inside where nobody sees. The bees are starting to come out of the hive . . ."

Release your fingers: "One, two, three, four, five!"

FINGER ROCKET SHIPS

Announce "Time to launch our Finger Rocket Ships!"

Place folded hands together with pointed index fingers touching, in a "rocket" shape.

Count backward from ten to one with the children. Then say, "Blast off!"

Raise your arms, maintaining the shape of the "finger rocket ship" and launch them as high into the stratosphere as everyone's arms can propel the pointed index fingers.

DIDDLE, DIDDLE, DUMPLING, MY SON JOHN

Recite simple Mother Goose rhymes like "Diddle, Diddle Dumpling"—which has proven particularly successful in my classes—or "Patty Cakes," which children always enjoy. Simple childhood classics can always be pulled into service.

TOMMY THUMBS

From Ananda I learned "Tommy Thumbs," a little finger game where the children get to call out a body part where the "Tommy Thumbs" can do their dancing.

"Tommy Thumbs up, Tommy Thumbs down,

Tommy Thumbs dancing all around the town

Dance 'em on your shoulder, Dance 'em on your head

Dance 'em on your... eyebrows, nose, bellybutton!

And tuck them into bed!"

(Tuck them "into bed" under your folded arms).

Having a good time with Tommy Thumbs"?

Try doing a verse replacing Tommy Thumbs with "pointer," "tall man," and the rest of the fingers.

CLEAN HANDS, DIRTY HANDS

Here is a longer "appetizer."

Children love pantomiming little stories together. There's a magic to something that's done by the whole room—teachers included. Lead this game with energy, funny faces, and a dynamic voice, and even the most mundane activity, like pretending to wash our hands, can morph into a beloved classroom routine.

This original routine to get the party started begins with me holding out my hands toward the children, proudly declaring, "Clean hands!

Once familiar with the game, the children hold out their hands to me immediately, shouting "Clean hands!" too.

Next I hold my hands before my eyes for a closer inspection. Rearing back in disgust I declare "Dirty hands!" and shamefully tuck them under my legs if I am sitting, or behind my back if I am on my feet.

The children either mimic what I do or they may just laugh.

In another moment I will let my rubbery frown flip back into a smile.

"Clean hands!" I chime out, proudly presenting my palms to the children again.

As with "Hands up High, Hands down Low," it always takes a few cycles of "Clean Hands, Dirty Hands" before everybody catches on and is able to join in the fun. When I sense we've passed our prime with this routine, I tell the group, "You know, maybe we'd better wash our hands now," and everybody nods eagerly.

"Let's turn on the water!" I instruct, pantomiming turning a faucet in the air. Together we vigorously rub our hands, chanting the little song I learned from my days at the Orthodox Jewish preschool. It was sung there as the children washed their hands in preparation for making the *bruchas* ("blessings") that were said before doing many daily routines, including just preparing to eat a snack—sung to the tune of "Here We Go Round the Mulberry Bush:"

This is the way we wash our hands, wash our hands, and wash our hands.
This is the way we wash our hands, so early in the morning.

Then we clap our hand together on each side of our body as we sing:

Once on the right and once on the left,
Once on the right and once on the left,
Once on the right and once on the left,
So early in the morning.

I created "Clean Hands, Dirty Hands" when I was two or three years old. I used to tease my mother when she sent me off to wash my hands before a meal. I'd return from the bathroom and hold out my paws for her approval, mournfully declaring, "Dirty hands." I used to enjoy the suspense of watching her frown because I knew that in the next moment I could delight her by contradicting myself, joyfully announcing, "Clean hands!" My poor mother! I seem to remember that I would repeat the words again and again.

Next I prompt the class: "And now we need a little soap!"

Here again I pantomime rubbing a bar of soap between my hands or pumping a bottle top, if soft soap is your thing. "Ooh, look at all the bubbly bubbles!" I exclaim. "Hey, I know! Let's blow a bubble—a big bubble, all together!"

Then I draw in a deep breath and begin exhaling a raspberry into my cupped hands.

"Wow, look at that! But I think we can blow a bigger one. What do you think? Shall we try?"

Once again I rear back and suck in a lungful, just as if I was blowing up a balloon.

And out goes another raspberry—this time even louder and ruder than before.

"Boy oh boy, that's a big one. But I think we can do one better than that. Come on, help me blow just one more bubble—let's blow a really giant one this time!"

Again I rear back and draw in as much air as I can. By the third time many of the children are sucking in air along with me. Now I cut loose with this final raspberry. I hold my arms out as if I were struggling to cradle a blimp. "Wow, Nilly, I think we'd better pop this mama bubble!"

I tell the gang, "Come on, everybody, together now," and I count, slowly, so the group can recite with me: "One, two, three!" Now I spread out my arms as if I'm anticipating a hug and clap my hands brightly together with a big smack!

"Whew, that was a big one!" I say, as I make eye contact all around with a smile. When you do this exercise, don't be surprised if you find yourself surrounded by a happy class of children, on their feet and ready for what's next.

Main Courses

It's important to get children up on their feet after they have been sitting for a while. After warming up and washing up, we're ready to tackle the main event. These easy activities are always a hit.

SIMON SAYS

We stand up to play Simon Says. I am the leader with very young children, and I tell them what Simon wants them to do. "Simon says, put your hands on your head." The children put their hands on their head. "Simon says, put your hands on your nose." They do so again. But when I say "Put your hands on your belly," everyone who does that is "out"—because Simon didn't say it.

(This is how Simon Says has been played for years. Nobody who's "out" needs to be eliminated. He or she can still participate in the game).

HEAD, SHOULDERS, KNEES, AND TOES

This song I can do a cappella or with the guitar.
You can find many versions of this popular song on YouTube.com.

Head, Shoulders, Knees, and Toes
Head, shoulders, knees, and toes, knees and toes
Head, shoulders, knees, and toes, knees and toes
and eyes and ears and mouth and nose,
Head, shoulders, knees and toes, knees and toes.

"Again, again! Do it again!" the kids cry.
We often do this three times in a row, going faster and faster, until we turn ourselves into a human blur. The official description of my consultancy is "Music and Movement," and I take the latter part of my title most seriously.

COBRA, CRABS, DOGS

There's plenty of fun to borrow from the animal kingdom to keep us in action.
I don't know a lot of yoga, but children love the downward-facing dog position, or
flipping onto their backs to walk like crabs. I ask them to lie on the floor arching
their backs like a cobra as I trill to them, snake-charmer style, on a recorder. This
activity is fully described in my book *Games That Sing* (Heritage Music Press, 2011).

Sometimes we let our faces take us to the zoo. "Come on everybody, open your
mouth! Yawn like a lion, show me tongues like a lizard, teeth like a bulldog!" We all
stick out our tongues and bring our bottom row of teeth over our lips. Together we
make funny faces.

Oliver

Hard as I try, and for all my bag of tricks, there is one little boy in my second
room whose attention I can never hold. I've been told that pale and fair-haired
Oliver is autistic. As I work with the rest of his classmates, presiding over the
crush of them kneeling in front of me on their area rug, or urging them to their
feet for a dance, Oliver floats around the outskirts of the classroom, anxiously
clutching to his chest a video cartridge of Thomas the Tank Engine as another
child might carry a teddy bear.

The head teacher in Oliver's classroom is Miss Natalia. Of the two teachers
in this room, invariably she is the one that springs from her chair to fetch Oliver
back from disappearing into a far corner, or to intervene when he throws a fit
of frustration, to which he's prone. She'll bark orders above his wailing and
yank him by his arm. And yet I notice that as she leads him back to the group,
he emerges pliant and noticeably soothed. What is it about this feisty, primitive
woman, Miss Natalia, that gives her the magic touch with Oliver? Is it simply
that he is as fascinated as I am by his teacher's flinty temper and gravelly voice?
I know of no way to find out.

Oliver is an enigma. For whatever reason it is clear that this autistic boy is
responsive to Miss Natalia's gruff ministrations, and that the two of them are

very much a pair. I know that Miss Natalia has no education or training that formally qualifies her to work with a special-needs student like Oliver. Yet she manages to keep him relaxed and comfortable as effectively as anyone with an advanced degree. The assistant teacher, Miss Mandy, a lanky, attractive young African-American woman, tends the rest of the children and pretty much ignores Oliver's incessant orbiting around the classroom. What more can she do?

I never feel as if I remotely inhabit the same classroom, never mind the same dimension, as little Oliver, clutching his video cartridge and muttering in the corners. Perhaps it takes someone as direct, instinctive, and cardinal as Miss Natalia to pierce the inscrutable membrane that confines him.

Crowd Control

By the time I walk down the stairs in a fog, having completed my first two classes, it will be 10:45. The sun has made considerable progress in its journey across the sky, and the staffroom clock tells me, happily, that I am entitled to my ten-minute bathroom break.

A crimped paper cup of cold water and a moment to close my eyes restores my energy. Still, three classrooms await me. It doesn't make it any easier that the very next classroom I face belongs to that vituperative little Napoleon, Miss Salomé. Admittedly in her class I do not have to worry, as I do in some other classes, that nobody will uphold crowd control as the group becomes stimulated by my music and games. Miss Salomé maintains excellent control of her children but poses a whole other set of obstacles to my leading the class. Often she snaps severely at a child who is beginning to fidget, completely oblivious to how much her finger wagging and rumbled threats interrupt the mood I try to create in the room.

As I pass through her door no children cry out and scurry to my knees as they had in my previous classes. Not one of them dares! While I do appreciate being able to safely cross the room, there is something about the sheer force of her personality that makes opening her door just as tiring as braving the madding crowd. With her ferocious energy and appetite for attention, Miss Salomé belongs in a preschool classroom just as much as any of her students. She belongs on her knees in a sandbox! In a way I envy her. Clearly she loves her work, and her arrested development gives her an edge over the rest of us—normal adults who appreciate lunch hours and battle professional burnout.

"Bubakar! Ibrahaima!" She belts out their names and claps her hands briskly.

We had just been launching our finger rockets. The countdown is interrupted, and everyone falters.

The two children who'd been singled out weren't nearly so disruptive as their zealous, disciplinarian teacher. Often she shouts out orders, overpowering our singing.

I know she means well. She wants to help me, but it's clear that she can't hear herself.

The other teacher, Miss Ascension, is so shy and accommodating that I can't turn to her for support. In this room, the crowd is controlled, but the head teacher is not.

It's Never Enough

With the passing weeks, and to go along with my cornucopia of openers, I begin presenting themes that can dictate the songs and activities I choose for a given session, just as the ghosts and pumpkins of Halloween had done for my classes not so long ago. My themes can be simple and broad, such as exploring shapes and colors, or they can be more specific, such as "the weather," "the circus," or "outer space and what we see in the night sky."

In my class about "cleaning up" for example, it is natural to begin with a round of "Clean Hands, Dirty Hands." This can be followed by Raffi's popular counting song about when to brush our teeth. A short discussion about what we clean up that's on our bodies as opposed to what we clean up that's in our homes provides a perfect segue for teaching a song of Woody Guthrie's where his verses sweep and bubble and polish until the whole room is "Pretty and Shiny-o." (For the full lyrics to this delightful song, visit: http://woodyguthrie.org).

Then for a wild finale I will hold my guitar by the neck and slide it lightly along the classroom floor like a vacuum cleaner. (I don't recommend this course of action to anyone holding a Stradivarius, but my ancient green Guild and I are willing to take our chances). "Look out dirt, look out dust bunnies! I'm coming to eat you up!!" I tell the children who scatter, squealing and giggling as I push my "vacuum cleaner" menacingly close to their shoes.

"Again, again, Miss Leah!' They cry when I finally sit down, putting the guitar to my knee to play a "good-bye song" at the end of our time together. I usually borrow the song from Barney the Purple Dinosaur, which goes, "I love you, you love me, we're a happy family..." to the tune of "This Old Man."

At the first cloying strains, some children are willing to sit and obediently mouth the words to this ubiquitous anthem that they recognize from watching television. Others stand to demand an encore.

"Oh, stay, Miss Leah! Play more, Miss Leah. Play more songs!"

Though utterly spent, I still blush at their show of ardor.

"But we've already had lots of fun and I have to visit your friends in the other class!" I remind them gently.

One Friday I make a case for packing it in: "We've sung. We've danced. We caught scarves in the butterfly net. What more can I give you? Isn't that enough?" I ask, edging to the door when a child named Ethan stands up to put in his two cents.

"No, Miss Leah," he answers, as earnestly as Oliver Twist asking for a second portion of gruel. "It's never enough."

Whether they happen to be the love of your life or just a four-year-old in your third period class at St. Anthony's, you always treasure being told that someone can never have enough of you.

Not all of my young cheering squad speak out as memorably as Ethan. Mostly they just whine and pull on my clothing until I feel like the Beatles trying to outrun their crazed fans in A Hard Day's Night. Many of them can't even remember my name and still call me "Music Teacher," or simply "Music." But in fairness, I can't remember most of their names. Honestly, I can turn it around and call them "Teacher" when I think about how much I learned from them in those early sessions.

For example, before my work at Head Start, I believed that if I gave a class of young children a directive such as "spread yourselves out" or "everybody find a partner" or "let's join hands and make a circle," that they would be able to follow these simple instructions.

I thought I complied with similar commands as a little kid in nursery school. And yet, what I quickly learned as a teacher is that instructions like these are not at all self-evident for this age group. To preschoolers, instructions such as "spread out" or "make a circle" are vague abstractions, difficult to understand and translate into action.

When I announce, "Alright, everybody stand up and give yourself a little space. Spread yourselves around the room!" The group of children looks blankly at me with no more idea of what has been said than if I had spoken to them in Swahili. Children this age are painfully literal ("They're not shoes. They're boots!"). Especially when in groups, young children need to be spoon-fed precise instructions.

For instance, if you want your children to stand apart from each other so that they are not touching their neighbors, ask them to spin around "like a helicopter" with their arms extended. Demonstrate this action yourself so they understand. You may have to take each child by the shoulders and gently guide him or her to take a spot. This is also true for getting children to form a circle. I found that joining the hands of first two children, and then two others—until everybody's connected—while sing-songing the words "a circle is round, a circle is round," is the most effective way to set the scene for "Ring Around the Rosy," "Bluebird Through My Window," and other classics done in the round.

Additionally, I discovered that children do not know their right side from their left. Not surprising, since even adults get confused over stage left and stage right. A little routine I developed helps clarify right from left, and proved fun.

Right Side, Left Side

Leah Wells

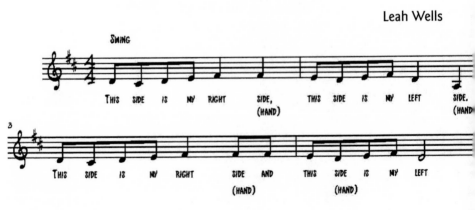

Raise your right and left hand as each is referenced in the song. You can also insert "right foot" and "right eye" (pointing to your right or left eye with a wink). Children will really laugh when you plug your right and left nostril—and you don't mind sounding ridiculous. Additionally, you may pluck a scarf or a beanbag you're holding, and pass it from one hand to the next with the song: "This scarf is my right scarf, and this scarf is my left scarf..." Even if you don't have enough scarves, beanbags, or puffballs for all the children to join you, they still enjoy watching you pass these colorful objects from hand to hand and it helps them to visualize their own right and left sides.

Do not be overly concerned if the children standing in front of you, mirroring what you do, may actually be holding up their right hands as you sing left, and visa versa. Rest assured that they derive benefit from having a good time as they learn that they have two sides to their body—one called "right" and one called "left." If need be, you might try standing with your back to them, so they can indeed model their right and left sides on yours.

The Red Truck

Right sides and left sides are very much on my mind over the weekend as I take my sons to meet a family friend at the Discovery store, an emporium for science toys and novelties in the middle of Grand Central Station. While the boys cruise the aisles for super balls, magnets, and gyroscopes, my attention is riveted by a small remote-controlled plastic red truck that keeps whizzing past me and bumping around the corners. The cab holds four seats occupied by a duck, a pig, a cow, and a chicken. Delighted children take turns manning the controls to send the thing zooming and zigzagging under our feet.

Soon my boys join the fun. As they take their turn at the joystick I listen to Haskell directing his brother: "Cut it to the left, Simon! Make it go to the left!" Long after my friend left the store, I stand watching the boys and the other children playing with the truck. The control can send it backward and forward as well as left to right. *Backward* and *forward* are also good concepts I am working on with the kids at school. I begin to wonder if my Head Starters uptown might like to practice moving in different directions by trying their hand at driving a truck.

Although I have almost nothing in the bank, I can't stop thinking of what a splash the remote control could make in my classrooms. What have I done to myself—setting the bar for fun in my classrooms so high that every weekend I feel under pressure to conjure new activities?

Creating a music class around the little red truck will take care of all fifteen of my sessions next week, so I decide to take the plunge. I ask the manager if I can possibly buy the floor model, which has already seen numerous collisions, at a discount. After a few minutes of wheedling and bargaining ("it's for helping disadvantaged preschoolers") I have myself a deal. I am able to put the thirty dollars on a credit card, being careful to save the receipt in order to deduct the expense from my taxes. At home I will add this receipt to my ever-growing list of the world's oddest work-related expenses: nose whistles, Kazoos, Jewish grogers and Chinese ribbon sticks, a litter of multiracial baby dolls, a gallon of bubble fluid with a wand the size of a frying pan—and now one remote-controlled, red plastic truck with a chicken at the wheel. To Haskell and Simon's astonishment we leave the store with the toy have been playing with under their mother's arm. We all agree that the Discovery store at Grand Central Station truly lived up to its name.

But my discoveries do not end there. At home I tell the boys that I am sure the kids at school wouldn't mind if we shared the truck with them. I leave Haskell and Simon in their room, still busily engrossed with the new toy as I make dinner. But repeated instances of objects clattering to the floor send me running from the kitchen to their room. Carrot and vegetable peeler in hand, I find that the boys have created a game for the truck with what little floor space they can clear in their crowded bedroom. Haskell and Simon have a ball by stacking high, precarious towers of books, toys, and stuffed animals—and then taking turns directing the little truck to plunge into their constructions like a wrecking ball.

There is so much glee and jumping up and down with excitement that the boys have forgotten the starting time of their favorite television show, which is unprecedented in our household. From where I stand in the doorway, chomping on a carrot, I see how deeply absorbing it is for the boys to construct their towers—balancing tilting objects, engineering foundations and spires—and then demolishing them again and again; they are having so much fun that even their hunger goes unnoticed.

Watching them, I remember that each classroom at Head Start is equipped with a full set of wooden building blocks. I can ask the children to spend some time building a little kingdom with their blocks. Then, when I unveil the truck, they can tell me which way it must be steered to knock down their creations.

So many children's songs are about building things. While the kids build with their blocks I can teach them any number of songs. In particular, a bluesy little number, "I Live in the City," from Malvina Reynolds' album comes to mind: "I live in the city, yes I do. Made by human hands." Numerous studies extol the benefits of letting children play with blocks. In my exit report I can describe this activity as a means of fostering cooperation and problem solving, while stacking and building develops children's fine motor coordination.

Of course the children at Marble Hill are dazzled by the red truck when it arrives at school with me on Monday morning. But there is simply not enough time for every child to have a turn demolishing the city of blocks. I avert the crisis by choosing a teacher to manage the controls while the children cry out directions as the truck lurches treacherously around the classroom floor.

"No...back, back, forward. Go forward!" This way everybody is in on the excitement. And maybe even "to the right!" or "to the left!" will begin to make sense.

By Friday I have honed running this activity to a science. First, I review the concept of left and right, playing "This Side is My Right Side" before the excitement of introducing the truck and the block building hijacks the children's concentration. Then wham-bam—it will be time to pull out all the stops! By 9:40 our truck-driving bash has already been such a joyful, noisy success in Room One that the uproar has drawn the attention of an anxious Miss Catalina.

"Is everything alright, Miss Leah?" she calls up a little too sweetly from the bottom of the stairs as I cross the small hallway between the doors of Room One and Room Two. "Is everything under control?"

"Yes, Miss Catalina. Everything's fine," I assure her, leaning over the bannister. "Music and movement can get very lively!"

I wait before letting myself into Room Two but she does not respond. More and more I feel her suspicion about what I am up to in her classrooms. Sometimes in the staffroom I catch her studying me. She puts on a show of clanging laughter when our gazes lock, but her tight smile can't cover her disfavor—in the same way that the lemony cleanser fails to disguise the bitter odor of the public bathroom just behind the heavy wooden door.

Being called to task for not accompanying Halloween songs that I had no knowledge of is still fresh in my memory at St. Anthony's. I shudder to imagine what other charges I may face from my developing critic, Miss Catalina. But at this moment it is I who must manufacture a smile because it is time for the pig, the chicken, the little red truck, and me to make our appearance in Room Two, the land of Miss Mandy, Miss Natalia, and her Oliver with his Thomas the Tank Engine cartridge still clutched tightly to his chest.

Beginning our session with a friendly round of "Clean Hands, Dirty Hands," I try to decide which of my two ladies here—the easygoing Miss Mandy or the volcanic Miss Natalia—will make the better demolition foreman to carry the show. This decision is surprisingly crucial. Over the course of the week I have seen how a fun teacher who understands the power and suspense that she wields along with her joystick can really enhance the quality of the whole experience, while having a boring or a clueless driver can rob even the culminating event of clattering, exploding blocks of its rightful punch.

Even with all the appeal and excitement of the red truck, anything undertaken in real time with children is unpredictable, and I am becoming nervous. If my activity loses its center, if my little architects quarrel over their blueprints, if the room degenerates into the Tower of Babel—then I know all too well what lies in store for the music consultant. The racket of tears and wailing and the commotion of falling blocks will indict me, and I will find myself facing Miss Catalina for a second time that morning.

Meanwhile the little campers of Room Two are gathered at my feet. Greetings and salutations have been said, our "Clean Hands, Dirty Hands" concluded. Still I can't decide who should be crowned Queen of our Wrecking Ball. I begin discussing left and right, backward and forward, but the children are growing restless and seems to intuit that I am holding out on them.

Still not sure which teacher to choose, I bring out the goods, demonstrating the little truck to the wonder of the children and getting them started on their block-building assignment. As I feared, something unexpected occurs. Oliver begins to have a tantrum. My voice already competes with Ms. Natalia growling her threats. I fear that my wonderful activity is going to bomb out for the first time all week. Leave it to St. Anthony's, the center of Florence Galway and Miss Catalina, to be my downfall at the end of such a good run at Marble Hill and Our Lady of Miracles!

Above the fray, a brisk knocking at the classroom door strikes terror in me. I feel certain that it can only be she of the shrill titter and tight smile, and I begin to wilt. Even the thought of her doubting voice has managed to rob me of all confidence. Has she climbed the stairs to investigate the hubbub and to find further fault with me? The next thing I know she will be forbidding me to implement original activities or to incorporate outside materials in my classes, like the red truck. I brace myself to meet my inquisitor— yet when Miss Natalia steps aside, I see in the doorway the most popular of all the janitors, Mr. Felix, a youthful Dominican man in his late twenties. He arrives to fix a clogged drain in the classroom sink, and I want to throw my arms around him and his plunger. How wonderful for him to appear at just that moment; the fix-it man here to repair the sink as well as my own quandary.

Impulsively, I hand him the controls for the truck and the little boy in him comes out to play. You have to love Mr. Felix! He looks as excited as Haskell and Simon did to be handed the joy stick. All the children watch him with delight. By the time a wide-eyed Mr. Felix has the truck poised in reverse, hovering as he shifts into drive, I strap my guitar back on. After the clatter of toppling towers and loud cheering has subsided, nobody notices that I have adapted the old Biblical hymn to suit recent events as I sing: "Felix fit the battle of Castle Hill and the blocks came tumbling down!"

"Well, just look at everybody having a good time."

I did not realize that, standing behind me, the real Miss Catalina has let herself into the classroom. Her words indicate approval, but as I wheel around to acknowledge her, my blood runs cold.

"Look at how all of my children are having a good time," she repeats.

Recited mirthlessly while turning to leave, even her praise stings like an accusation.

The Felix and Priscilla Puppet Show

In the staffroom I learn to make friends. Offerings of Tic-Tacs and sticks of gum earn me smiles from teachers who speak very little English. Also, my *People* magazine habit proves a good icebreaker. There are moments when I can't remember anybody's name, but together we can gush over pictures of George Clooney or Brad Pitt, handsome faces and names that everyone recognizes. We can laugh at the latest antics of Paris Hilton—and do we think that Britney Spears will find herself another husband? It seems that her first marriage has been annulled within a matter of hours.

So long as Miss Salomé isn't hovering, I can relax at the staff table in relative peace, if not in quiet. I'm always glad if Miss Priscilla, the fun-loving Puerto Rican head teacher in Room Six, happens to slide into the seat beside me. She seems to be no older than I am, although the children she speaks of as her own seem to be grown up and out of the house with their own families. Up here in the Bronx, a woman over thirty holding a baby is a grandmother.

Today Miss Priscilla points to the two large aluminum trays on a side table, which were left by the cooks. One holds mashed potatoes dotted with limp florets of broccoli. The other contains salmon filets covered by scaly flaps of their own gray skin so that they resemble a pile of severed tongues. For the first time in my secular Jewish life I find myself having to eat fish on Friday, at least if I want to be thrifty. Of my three centers, Saint Anthony's is the only staffroom that is spacious enough so that we teachers can be offered the same dishes that are served in the classrooms. I am grateful not to have to reach into my pockets to pay for a hot meal.

As I settle in with my plastic cutlery and my loaded paper plate, Miss Priscilla makes a face. "Every Friday I tell the kitchen that, you know, it's just such a waste." She leans in, pointing to the food. "Our kids won't eat it," she whispers wrinkling her nose. "It's too fishy for them."

"It's too fishy for me too," seconds Mr. Felix, who has joined us at the table and helps himself to the seat across from Miss Priscilla. He withdraws an apple from a brown paper bag and shines it between both his palms before taking a thunderous bite.

This Friday my *New York Post* is a hot commodity.

"Can I see your paper?" Mr. Felix asks between mouthfuls of apple. Glad to return the favor he'd done for me that morning, I slide it down to his end of the table like a hockey puck.

By 12:15 the staffroom is bustling at full tilt. Teachers sit down to eat and Miss Priscilla rises to offer her chair.

"Are you sure?" asks the newcomer, Miss Alison, the assistant teacher in

Miss Priscilla's classroom. Metal braces encumber this young Filipino woman's pretty smile.

"No, please! I can't eat no more of that." Miss Priscilla waves her hands. "Go ahead, honey. Take the chair for yourself. I'm good."

The table buzzes with conversation about everybody's plans for the weekend. Miss Julissa, who is from a military family, will be going to the airport to meet some returning soldiers. Somebody else is going to a wedding. What should she bring as a gift? Across the table Mr. Felix spreads out the movie pages, the apple he chomps almost reduced to its core. Behind him tiptoes a diabolical Miss Priscilla.

"Oooh, what we gonna see, Poppy?"

She gives his shoulders a playful squeeze and lowers her head to glance at the listings. In front of her Mr. Felix opens his mouth to respond, but produces a powerful belch before he can find his words. At his back Miss Priscilla recoils, waving a hand in front of her nose.

"Oh, please! You gotta be kidding!" she cries. Palms down, she gestures emphatically. "Tha's it. I'm not taking you to the movies, nuh, uh! Not taking you nowheres, *chiquito*. Once, baby, once, but not no more!"

And behind him she sashays a defiant meringue. From his chair Mr. Felix swivels to watch her, furrowing his brow like a bloodhound. "You never take me anywhere!" he finally croaks, his voice hoarse with incredulity. I realize that I am coming to love this odd couple, Felix and Priscilla!

All day long I do pratfalls in the classrooms and make faces and pretend to laugh at all the children's silliness. Now, here in the staffroom, how refreshing it is to have a puppet show that I find genuinely entertaining, that I find hilarious! And oh, how relaxing to be out of the hot seat of having to manufacture small talk across the many language barriers when my brain is as limp as the broccoli and mashed potatoes that swim on my plate.

Indeed, I can enjoy "The Felix and Priscilla Puppet Show" in utter passivity, as if watching them on a television set. Neither of them seems to notice or mind that I am almost splitting my sides by the time they get up to leave.

A Bug is a Bug

After a week of racking up miles on the classroom floors of my three Head Start centers, the truck is finally retired to the boy's toy chest. Seeing its four little animal drivers capsized in the already forgotten truck sets me to rummaging through the rest of the contents of the old wicker basket with a professional eye. What else do we have lying around in the house that can become a star in the Bronx classrooms?

Tangled with the partially dismembered action figures beneath the truck, eight fabric legs belong to a hand puppet of a gangly, brown spider. It was sent to us by Mark's sister, Gwen. How can I ever forget the circumstances under which that spider arrived? It had been the summer that Mark was hospitalized, sweat-drenched and babbling delusionally with a soaring fever. Two days and the-results-of-the-biopsy later, I was visiting him at his hospital bed in Beth Israel where he lay recovering from what was believed to be the bite of a brown recluse spider that had swollen his normally slender left foot into a pink watermelon. I'd fretted that he would be injured permanently. But within a week, he was home, his foot restored to its fine bones and high arches. Mark was able to walk to the post office to retrieve the gag package from his sister. The spider puppet from Gwen that we unveiled from the bubble wrap made us laugh now that Mark was over his fever; he had regained the use of his left foot and the boys had their father back.

But what was it about childhood and spiders that went together? Just as the weepy little Manuel did at Our Lady of Miracles, I also carry a lifelong torch for the sweet simplicity of the itsy bitsy spider, and when I was little would tug at my mother's apron for her to sing it again and again. I'd also enjoyed the Scottish parable of Elspeth, the spider who inspired tenacity in Robert, the Bruce, who watched her spin her web multiple times, sparing no effort until she was satisfied with the result. And of course I loved *Charlotte's Web* and had read the story to the boys.

Spiders, I've been told, are the beloved mascots of storytellers as they too are regarded as the spinners of silken yarns. The doctors at Beth Israel assured us that encounters with brown recluse spiders are highly unusual in our region. After the July of Mark's spider bite, all mythological respect was cast aside and

I became an avid squasher of all eight-legged critters whenever they emerged.

The children at Head Start love spiders and are always begging me for the theme song from Spiderman so they can dance and pretend to capture me. They joyfully point their upturned wrists at me to "shoot their web" and have no knowledge of Mark's trip to the hospital and the terrible scare it gave me. I sink my hand within the spider puppet and watch it come alive as my fingers undulate its spindly legs. I wonder if the spider should come with me to school where it can dance for the children. Perhaps if I can get it onto the hands of some of the teachers, say the robust and giggly Miss Nicole at Marble Hill, or my goddess Miss Magdalena at Our Lady of Miracles, I can then build my classes around little Miss Muffet sitting on her tuffet and getting frightened away by the spider beside her. And then—duh, of course—the obvious thing would be to dramatize the Itsy Bitsy spider, especially once my hands are liberated to play the guitar.

By Sunday night the spider puppet sleeps at the ready in my canvas bag along with the Chinese ribbon sticks we are going to unfurl for "spinning webs." I will get everybody wiggling spiders out of their fingers, and I'll round out the critter theme with "The Ants Go Marching One by One." We'll sing the old folky chestnut "There Ain't No Bugs on Me," and finally, "I'm Bringing Home a Baby Bumblebee." Yeah, yeah, yeah, of course everybody knows that spiders are in the arachnid family and not insects, but why let a little science spoil the fun when, to a kid, a bug is a bug?

LITTLE MISS MUFFET

Little Miss Muffet
Sat on a tuffet,
Eating her curds and whey;
Along came a spider
Who sat down besid her
And frightened Miss Muffet away.

To dramatize this Mother Goose rhyme, invite children who are interested in performing for their class to take turns being Little Miss Muffet. As the class and I recite the simple verse they take the stage, sit down in a chair and daintily pantomime eating "curds and whey" while the class enjoys the dramatic irony of watching one of their teachers creep up with the spider puppet. As the wiggling legs of the spider tap Miss Muffet our leading lady (or fellow) gets to pretend to be startled, gasp, and dash away from the scary puppet. The children enjoy mastering this simple sequence as performers, as well as giggling from the audience.

Tigers and Monkeys and Cranes, Oh My!

One evening Haskell comes home announcing that he wants us to buy him a berimbau. Matter of factly, he estimates that this will run us about four hundred dollars. The item in question is a Brazilian stringed instrument that he's seen demonstrated by the popular *capoeira* guy at his afterschool program. But even more than a berimbau, Haskell wants to study a martial art at a real dojo. He is thirsting for the full experience of a practice space with mirrors and mats. He wants a *gi* (the official white jacket and pants), competitions, and belt promotions, and of course, anything that Haskell wants, Simon is sure to be desperate for as well.

As if by magic we find a flyer tucked into our front door for just such a thing. It is called *Pukulan* and bills itself as a form of Indonesian kung-fu that utilizes techniques gleaned from the movements of jungle animals, in particular the movements of monkeys, tigers, cranes, and snakes. *Pukulan* was developed when the Dutch invaded Indonesia, and therefore it is excellent for teaching to children because this fighting system was originally based on little people defending themselves against bigger people.

Of course as a mother, I fret that learning how to punch and parry will make the boys more apt to get cocky and pick fights. On the other hand, isn't it wise to prepare them to meet whatever dangers a city kid might encounter in school playgrounds or on the streets? I don't want to be naive. I want my sons to be strong and nimble and able to radiate the confidence of knowing how to fight if they have to. The pamphlet promises a holistic philosophy that reinforces the responsible application of the martial skills taught at the center. The contact information listed is for a Sam and Karen Duffy. When I call to schedule a visit, we learn that they are not brother and sister as I'd thought, but a married couple.

On the second floor of a small building on West 14th Street, the boys and I watch as a children's class circles the floor and then, with a clap from the teacher, expertly pivots to run backward and then quickly forward again. Next come rounds of wall-to-wall sprinting. Then a series of calisthenics, counting their sit-ups and push-ups out loud in Indonesian. They receive a demonstration of various strikes and then divide into pairs on the mats for sparring. By the time the participants in their white *gis* are lined up for the ritual of "bowing out," my sons are hooked and clamoring for me to sign them up.

Behind the scenes, Sam and Karen are relaxed and informal, yet highly organized. I noticed that when the children in class become chatty, Karen cuts them off abruptly with a no-nonsense, "That's it! No more anecdotes. Times a wastin'!" How I wish I could lob this same decree at the little ones that swarm around my knees at school. I envy her being able to work with older kids who can process verbal instruction and who know when to be quiet. I can't count how many times children start talking to me in the middle of a song, as if I could split myself in two and continue playing to the group while answering their questions. Sometimes, hissed commands and hand-clapping from forceful personalities like Miss Natalia or Miss Salomé at St. Anthony's can bring the room to order. Sometimes nothing works at all.

I am glad that Haskell and Simon will be training in an environment where no misbehavior is tolerated. It is plain to see that Sam and Karen hold the complete respect of their students. I am also encouraged to notice that the equipment, mats, and punching bags, are all well-maintained and the shiny wooden floors are spotless. As the *Pukulan* kids disappear into dressing rooms to change into their street clothes, I get down to business with the Duffys. Up close Sam is tall and galumphing, with soft blue eyes and shaggy brown hair. He tells me that he was a couch potato before falling in love with martial arts.

Karen is higher energy. Shorter and solidly built, she has a crisp, bell-like voice and is pretty, with her blonde hair offset by her black instructor's *gi*. There are two other instructors to meet before Karen leads us to a small office where we can get registered. She explains that for an initial monthly fee the boys are entitled to take as many as three classes a week, and that all children's classes are offered on schoolday afternoons. I recognize some of the kids—like Ananda's daughter, Rainbow, as they emerge from the dressing rooms. Karen confirms that a lot of their students bus over from schools on the Lower East Side. She assures me that there is plenty of "carpooling" among the parents, which is great.

My boys can travel to the program with other families, even when I'm up in the Bronx. I can pick them up after the class ends.

Also, my mother has pledged her willingness to help us financially and even with transportation, when needed. "Well then, it's a wrap!" I tell Karen, smiling as we rise to our feet. The boys cheer, jumping up and down, and Karen playfully ruffles Haskell's recently sprouted inch of dark hair, sealing our promise to return with an enthusiastic "Awesome!"

I decide that I like the place and feel comfortable leaving my kids in the care of the Duffys and their team of cheerful young assistants. After all, how far astray can we go, enrolling at a dojo that calls itself "One With Heart"?

IF YOU'RE HAPPY AND YOU KNOW IT DELUXE

Pukulan even inspires an exercise for my preschoolers. Having seen the children so happy to work as partners on their mats, I think of how they might work in pairs of two with "If you're Happy and you Know It."

I'll call on my teachers to arrange the children into pairs. Then they can sing the song and perform with a partner instead of responding individually. For this purpose I will also adapt the activities we sing to suit this new form. For example: "If you're happy and you know it, Pat-ty Cake!" I can demonstrate clapping my palms together with a teacher, and the children can imitate us with their partners.

"If you're happy and you know it, let's hold hands." Again, with a teacher, I can demonstrate holding her hand and swinging it lightly.

Next: "If you're happy and you know it, hold both hands!" Now I'll have the children holding both their partner's hands and swinging them.

And after that, still with joined hands, "If you're happy and you know it, go round and round!"

I'll ask the children to walk in a circle with their partner as we sing. Then we give our partner a hug or a handshake. After all this fun I can play the song in minor chords, pretend to cry and ask that the children wave goodbye to their partner. Now we have a new hit variation to the old favorite, with a little lesson in partnership.

The Ballad of Miss Fernanda

By Monday I wish that I had some of Sam's and Karen's blocks and dodges for myself. That morning an anxious Miss Antonette meets me at the door of the Marble Hill center. As she takes my arm, her eyes give a paranoid dart from side to side before she guides me past the threshold. "We are informing everyone in our Head Start community that we have a lunatic who has been targeting our people as we come and go from the building," she whispers. Apparently, some troubled person living in the project has been hurling objects from his window which are aimed at the little path leading to the center door. Last week Delicia's mother was almost hit by a can of beans. There is no predicting when he may strike again.

"Don't forget to tell her that he's also been peeing out the window," calls Miss Nicole as she blusters by in her apron, wheeling a trolley of breakfast dishes toward the kitchen. The day is cloudy, and I silently inventory that I have taken my umbrella.

"Who would do such a thing?" I ask. "Are the police involved? Can't he be stopped?'

"Well, of course," Miss Antonette assures me. "We're doing everything we possibly can. Only believe it or not, as of yet we have no culprit. The police are still in the process of going door-to-door." Her voice trails away and I can see that her eyes have found my canvas bag, where the hairy brown legs of my spider puppet must only be adding to the surrealism of the morning. "You see, our parents are not looking up as they come and go," she explains. "And once things start dropping around them, of course everybody is too busy protecting their children to see where they come from." She shakes her round face from side to side. "I simply can't imagine why this is happening. We can only be thankful that he hasn't killed anybody."

She releases my arm with a small pat. "We want to be sure that nothing bad happens to you, Miss Leah," she says almost tenderly. "I know that you like to take a walk at your lunch hour, but until they locate our attacker I'm going to have to ask you not to leave the building." Not be able to go outside if I want to? I feel my lungs tighten.

"What it they haven't nailed the guy by the time I'm supposed to go home?

Are we going to be camping out here?" I ask.

Miss Antonette closes and rubs her eyes. "If they still don't have our guy by this afternoon," she sighs, "then what can I tell you? Just please walk as quickly as you can as you leave us. Oh, and you may want to cover your head with some kind of a book or something."

"And be sure to keep your mouth shut," Miss Nicole adds while storming past us to return to her classroom.

All morning the spider climbs and crawls for the giggling children of Rooms One and Two. As I've planned, we enact Little Miss Muffet who sits on her tuffet only to have the joy of running away screaming at the appearance of the spider puppet menacingly wagging its legs. In both rooms we cast and recast the vignette until all my little divas have had a go at the starring role. By the end of each class a particularly heartfelt rendition of "*The Itsy Bitsy Spider*" caps off the morning's theme parties. Fortunately today, I have thrown together a lunch. Perhaps inspired by Little Miss Muffet, I just happened to be packing curds and whey in the form of a blueberry yogurt and a juice box I've pinched from my sons' stash of lunch supplies.

After closing the door on the rowdy catcalls of Room Two, I go to deposit my guitar with Miss Antonette. She is talking on the phone as I enter, immediately shaking her head "no" to indicate that our lunatic was not apprehended that morning while the spider danced in her classrooms. Resigned, I head to the staffroom carrying the daily newspaper and my yogurt. But instead of seeing Miss Kadrena, Miss Sandra, or any of the dishwashers there, I find a middle-aged Filipino woman so petite that she is almost obscured by the stack of folders that sit on the table in front of her. Directly across from her sits the janitor, Mr. Justin, the only other person in the room. He sinks especially low in his seat, covering his face with one of his paperbacks. I am about to find out why.

"Oh, hello," I say quietly, so as not to disturb the small woman, who suddenly wheels around and leaps to her feet to introduce herself. In a high voice she tells me that her name is Miss Fernanda, squeezing my hand with the force of a man three times her size.

"Are you a teacher?" she asks. "Are you a regular teacher or ...Oh yes, you are a muu-sssick teaher, ha ha ha!"

Within seconds she becomes as demanding as the two classrooms of children I left behind. She even surpasses her Friday counterpart, the zealous little fire hose, Miss Salomé from St. Anthony's. I am no longer planning to eat there, but I can't escape, since she has not surrendered my hand. I try to slide away, but she bears down on my arm incrementally, like a tightening blood pressure cuff, while she continues her flood of questions.

"Oh, so you teach muuuu-sick to the children here! Oh, that is great. So what is your name, Muuuu-sick Teacher. Oh, that is so great Miss, Miss, Uh oh. Oh dear! Ah ha ha ha, I am so silly I have to ask you again for your name again?! Oh my goodness! I'm afraid I have already forgotten what you said. Oh, ah ha ha ha ha ha. Can you tell me what it is again, your name?"

I come to the staffroom to avoid the awkwardness of watching Miss Antonette take phone calls, but back to her office I race as soon as I can make my excuses.

"What's happened, Miss Leah? What's that look on your face? Has one of our people gotten hurt?" Antonette asks.

"Oh no, no, no. Everybody's fine," I assure her.

"Then what's the matter?" she persists.

I hesitate, and then on an impulse I close the door and whisper over her desk, "It's that tiny lady, Miss Fernanda. She...I guess she's a very sweet person but man, she won't stop talking and asking questions. I tried to leave the staffroom but she actually grabbed my arm and wouldn't let me go!"

Miss Antonette claps a hand to her mouth and doubles over with giggles. "I see you've met our assessment lady," she says, once she's recovered. "You're not alone Miss Leah," she hiccups and gives me a wink. "I know. Believe me, we all know. That lady's a bit of a nut. She comes to us once every three months or so to evaluate the children so our grants get renewed. Miss Leah, do you need to sit down?"

I am fending off a light-headedness and am grateful to take her suggestion. From the chair Miss Antonette offers I shake my head in a daze. "I mean I couldn't just say a simple hello," I marvel hoarsely. "You know what? In the five minutes I was with her, I think she's managed to give me a migraine."

Miss Antonette nods toward the door. "Oh please, you don't have to tell me about her and her questions. And do you know what else?" She leans across her desk and continues in a loud whisper. "Every time Miss Sandra and Miss Kadrena see her coming, they run!" She makes a slashing gesture. "Which isn't very nice because then I get stuck with her."

"One of the perks of being head supervisor," I tease her and she grins.

"But you know, Miss Leah, I think that it's because of her nerves that she is...that way."

"Her nerves?"

"It's because, well, you know, she lives in New Jersey and one day . . . it was a few years ago already, she was going home and she got mugged."

"No," I say.

"Yes, Miss Leah. They mugged her. Some guys did. They threw her down. They broke her shoulder."

"Oh no!"

"But wait, Miss Leah. Listen to this." Miss Antonette draws a breath. "Apparently one of them held a gun to her head and the other guy was shouting 'shoot her, just shoot her!' And she told us she thought she was going to die right then and there with her face pushed down in the mud."

"Oh, how horrible," I gasp.

"She was out for a good long time after that," Miss Antonette says slowly. "A very long time."

"How did she finally get away?" I ask.

"You know, I'm not exactly sure." Miss Antonette touches her lip with a pencil. "I think somebody was coming and her assailants decided to flee. I just don't know, Miss Leah. I really don't know. I don't even think Miss Fernanda herself really knows how she survived." She shrugs. "Maybe that's why she asks so many questions."

Later that afternoon Miss Antonette pokes her head into Room Two with an emphatic thumbs-up for the teachers and me. Just moments before, she tells us, the police escorted an older man who lives alone and has a psychiatric history from one of the lower floors of the adjoining building.

"Thank God it's over!" cries Miss Lucia, clasping her hands in prayer. "You know, Blanca, imagine if he had been throwing that debris from a higher floor?" As I walk out and close the classroom door I hear her say, "Suppose one of our children had been struck on the head?"

"Well, the coast is finally clear, Miss Leah," carols Miss Antonette. "No more lunatic, no more flying pots and pans." She glances at her watch. "Plus, your Miss Fernanda has been gone for a full hour. And Miss Leah, you'll be glad to hear this—she won't be back for a couple of months. When she comes next, it will be a Tuesday. You're safe!" Her signature giggle is fully restored.

I make my way down the little cement path at my leisure. The worries and overcast skies that began the morning are gone—there is no need to open my umbrella.

In English and Spanish

I'm trying to learn more Spanish. Often in the staffrooms I miss the liveliest conversations. Many children speak it at home, and might be drawn to participate if the songs were in Spanish—like Manuel's *La pequeñita araña*. The next day, in the classroom of Miss Linda and Miss Caridad at Our Lady of Miracles One, I hold up my hands for the children sitting before me in two rows on the floor.

"Come on! Who can show me two little ducks?" I hold my thumbs apart from the rest of my fingers and then snap them together.

"Quack, quack!" My hands pantomime two quacking duckbills. The children mirror this back to me, holding their hands in front of their faces.

"Good! Now can we make them fly? It's easy. Just do what I do!"

I demonstrate flapping my wings and the group at my feet instantly churns with flying elbows. This "appetizer" of duck was introduced to me by a Spanish-speaking mom with a young daughter whom I met at the annual Harvest Festival in our community garden. In a barter for allowing me to show up at her office so I could capture her rendition of "Patito" on my old cassette recorder, I agreed to play music for her daughter's upcoming sixth birthday party. Although heading to a kiddie party with my guitar is the last thing I want to do on my weekend, the party turned out to be a no-holds-barred fiesta with *tres leches* birthday cake and a pink *piñata*—and I was able to learn even more traditional Spanish games and dances for children. But of all the takeaways in my goody bag, I was especially excited about having learned "Patito the Duck," a short dramatic routine requiring nothing more than a pair of hands. It was simple enough for me to lead in both English and Spanish, and the children at Head Start, despite their varied backgrounds, request of me to perform it again and again: *Otra Vez!*

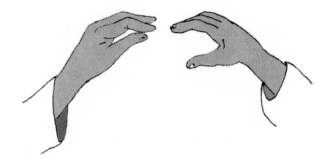

PATITO THE DUCK

Patito, Patito,
Qué comes? Qué comes?
Arroz! Arroz!
Da me! Da me!
NO! NO!

Patito, Patito,
What are you eating? What are you eating?
Rice! Rice!
Give me some! Give me some!
NO! NO!

Turn your hands into two quacking duck bills by separating your thumb from the rest of your cupped fingers and then bringing them together; *quack, quack!*

Recite the small script with your class of ducklings echoing you after each utterance and moving their hands as you do.

When you get to the part where Patito demands "Give me some" or *"Da me"* in Spanish and his companion answers, "No!" swivel one of your wrists so that your duckbill shakes its head "no" from side to side.

The naughty finale is non-verbal as Patito doesn't take "no" for an answer. Make one of your duckbills clamp shut over your other hand, maybe with a swallowing sound or gulp, as Patito devours his unabliging companion. Not a model for enduring friendship but a silly and often requested classroom routine.

As Patito arrives in the second morning class I teach, Miss Felipa smiles and tells me that in her Dominican family she grew up playing a little finger game called *El Panadero,* or "The Bread Man." She pulls her chair beside mine so she can teach it to me in front of the children. Soon my fingers can speak more Spanish than I do.

EL PANADERO

To play *El Panadero,* make a church out of your hands by holding them palm-to-palm, finger-to-finger. Begin by tapping your thumbs together.

"*Tume Tume,*" (the group can respond the second time) "*Tume Tume.*"

Next, tap your index fingers together.

"*Quién Es? Quién Es?*"

Tap your middle fingers.

"*El Panadero! El Panadero!*"

Tap your ring fingers.

"*Que quieres? Que quieres?*"

And finally tap your pinkies. "*El dinero de pan! El dinero de pan!*"

THE BREAD MAN *(in English)*

"Knock knock, Knock knock!"

"Who's there? Who's there?"

"It's the bread man! It's the bread man!"

"What do you want? What do you want?"

"The money for the bread! The money for the bread!"

After three classrooms of Patito, *El Panadero,* and the happy hands of the children, I run into Miss Magdalena huffing upstairs. With a strap across her shoulder she is lugging the blue insulated nylon container that holds the makings of her students' lunches. She smiles warmly, making me realize that I haven't seen Miss Lucy all morning.

"Where's your friend today?" I ask, trying to be sociable, as I bob past her on my way to the street.

She stops in the middle of the stairway and asks, "Do you have a moment, Miss Leah?" With a sigh she sets down the heavy rectangular bag at her feet and I double-back upstairs to her so that we can talk.

Miss Lucy's daughter has cancer. Terminal pancreatic cancer. Miss Magdalena tells me that it's already been a long, heartbreaking struggle and that just recently things have taken a turn for the worse. This is why Miss Lucy is not at work today. Now I understand why she looked so haggard when she addressed the families on the morning of the drenched apple-picking foray.

I tell Miss Magdalena that I'm deeply sorry and wonder if there's anything I can do. She asks me to include Miss Lucy and her daughter in my prayers.

"Do you pray, Miss Leah?" she asks.

I tell her that I pray constantly and we share a small laugh. As she bends to hoist her lunch bag, I want to tell her something that I hope will brighten her spirits before she returns to her classroom. And yet it backfires.

"I want to thank you for our song today." Half an hour ago in her classroom, Miss Magdalena and I discovered that we both harbored an enduring affection for a crossover Spanish hit from the late 1970s called "Eres Tú" that briefly made the Top 40. We sung it for the children. The harmony she nestled beneath my voice, and the shimmering tambourine she tapped to her hip made our duet outstanding.

When I finish gushing, Miss Magdalena folds her arms and smiles.

"You think I'm good?" she says. "You should have heard my father." She tells me that her handsome father was a professional singer with prestigious club dates, a band, and a manager. "Like a Spanish Frank Sinatra," she remembers. In her home there was music all the time as she was growing up.

"Your father must have been so proud of your talent," I say and she agrees. Yes, her father was very proud of the way his daughter sang. But as she got older (and her hands dart over her breasts and rest on her hips) he would never allow her to perform in public—never! And she slowly shakes her head.

"He said that if I will be singing for people I'm going to look like a prostitute!" she whispers fiercely, and her face darkens with the old wound. "Now I sing here!"

A moment later she shoulders the insulated bag and disappears at the top of the stairs without a backward glance.

Wonder Borough

New York, New York it's a hell of a town,
The Bronx is up, but the Battery's down...
—lyrics by B. Comden and A. Green

So often on my route to work in the Bronx I find myself hurrying past abandoned buildings and vandalized streetlights. I want to understand what forces created this sprawling, embattled ghost town of what was, at the turn of the century, hawked to the upwardly mobile as the Wonder Borough.

Everyone I consult about the Bronx immediately cites the devastation brought about by the construction of Robert Moses' Cross Bronx Expressway. They talk about the displacement of thousands of families and the destruction and isolation of what had been stable neighborhoods and vital ethnic communities. I learn that the intriguingly named Mount Eden Avenue commemorates Rachel Eden, an early nineteenth-century property owner. I wonder how typical it was for women to own property back then, and to have an avenue named for them.

In 1790 Lewis Morris, founder and namesake of the historic Bronx settlement of Morrisania and signer of the Declaration of Independence, proposed that his property be the site of the future capital of the United States. Almost 100 years later in the 1880s, realtor and neighborhood developer James Lee Wells (not related to me) zealously campaigned for the government of New York City to concentrate its resources, promoting the Bronx to the exclusion of the about-to-be-annexed districts of Brooklyn and Queens. "Just go north," he besieged politicians and city lawmakers. "The territory can easily accommodate a population ten or fifteen times as great."

At that time the Bronx was a hot new area for real estate development. Prospectors set their sights on the rolling country and breathtaking vistas of the lower Hudson Valley. They perceived residential gold for the taking in "them thar hills"—beginning in the Bronx. With the advent of improved transportation that accompanied the industrial revolution, urban developers were eager to exploit the potential for settlement and expansion that lay in developing the estates and manor houses to the north of Manhattan. They advertised in newspapers and broadsides, offering to those who could afford it a bucolic alternative to the teeming streets of the Lower East Side—where I happen to live now.

In anticipation of future prosperity, rural properties were auctioned off and divided into lots intended for development. These lots were sold and then re-sold, each time at a profit, as the railroad expanded its reach into the Bronx. Low-rise apartment buildings and tenements sprang up around the convenience of train stations and ferry landings. At five cents a ride, subways provided residents of these new buildings cheap, easy access to the lower Manhattan business district. Almost overnight new housing rose up accompanied by modern amenities: roads, hospitals, churches, fire departments, schools and social clubs, sewers and garbage removal—all serving a new society of commuters and supporting a local, robust economy.

But the same forces that had stimulated such sudden development just as quickly created the same hazardous, problematic conditions like those afflicting the squalid and densely populated ghettos of the Lower East Side. All at once the settlers of the Bronx's Mott Haven, Morrisania, and Hunts Point found themselves having to contend with the issues of an aging housing stock and with colonies of overcrowded tenements that were beginning to crumble.

Once again, economically successful families migrated north to better housing in the ever-beckoning suburbs of lower Westchester County. In the Bronx, departing second-generation German families, both Christian and Jewish, were replaced by an influx of renters looking for cheap housing. Many of the newcomers were first-generation immigrants seeking to realize the American dream: a place to work and raise their children, who would benefit from attending free elementary and public high schools.

In an attempt at civic improvement, housing projects like the one encompassing the Head Start center at Marble Hill were designed to address the overcrowding and unsanitary housing conditions. Despite the good intentions, the housing projects created a litany of deprivations and dangers all their own. These clusters of massive, depressingly identical units lacked the intimacy of the stoops and stairways of the tenements built on a more human scale. In these huge projects neighbors were less apt to bond with neighbors. Alienation and isolation increased. Renters did not feel safe using the elevators. In time even the most modern public housing projects sank into the same crime-ridden decrepitude as the tenements they replaced. It seemed that those living in the South Bronx couldn't catch a break.

Beginning around 1948 the Cross Bronx Expressway bulldozed a long bloody gash through miles of residential East Tremont, demolishing thousands of homes and shredding the diverse cultural fabric—like taking a scissors to a fragile heirloom quilt from the old country.

As a child growing up in Westchester County, I felt that the twisting high-way ramps and nexus of dark tunnels through which our family car entered the city made me want to roll up the window and lock the car door. The Bronx depicted in the 1970s and 1980s was a dangerous planet of vacant lots and graffitied walls. This image was reinforced by the movies of the time—like *Fort Apache the Bronx* and *Bonfire of the Vanities*—and broadcasts on the news. Current crime statistics for the South Bronx are twice as high as for my neighborhood. So many more people are murdered there. They even get killed underneath it, in the subway where I so often find myself.

In the Red

"Do you know anything about this?" Mark asks.

While I was at work, apparently, a bank representative called to inform him that every check we'd written and payments made against the money from my last pay period were all boomeranging back to them. There is no other explanation: The Archdiocese of New York has bounced my paycheck. The delinquent funds put us in arrears with our mortgage and maintenance so that we will have to pay late charges to both our managing agent and to Citibank. It's a night-mare: processing fees and overdraft notices piling up on top of our usual debt, as if we weren't in a deep enough hole to begin with.

That night neither of us can sleep. In the kitchen Mark sits chain-smoking while I toss and turn in bed. Usually Friday nights are the best time of the week, with Saturday and Sunday to look forward to. But a bounced paycheck is no way to begin the weekend. As an unprotected, fireable-at-will consultant, I already feel like a second-class employee. Before every holiday and "staff development day," I receive a memo from the main office reminding me to "Enjoy your day off" —as if I have any choice. Now in addition to no benefits, no insurance, and no sick days, there is also no money. And for the moment there is no action to take and nothing to be done. The Head Start offices will be closed all weekend so I will have to wait until Monday to find out what the hell is going on and to make it right.

Until this snafu gets resolved, we are reduced to using the one credit card we have between us that hasn't been maxed out and things quickly get entirely bizarre. Living on plastic, the four of us can sit down to an expensive dinner at a fancy restaurant, but we can't pay for the boys to get a candy bar on the way home. We can go to P. C. Richard's and buy a washing machine; we could buy a car—but, humiliatingly, we have no money for a newspaper.

The last time anything remotely like this happened dates back to my days of working at the Orthodox Jewish preschool. In Yiddish the word for a female teacher is *Morah*. Therefore, when I showed up to sing with the children my name was Morah Music. Everybody there called me Morah Music: the staff, the children, even the parents who picked up their children early on Shabbat afternoon. One day the rebbetzin, the rabbi's wife, mistakenly issued my check to Morah Music instead of Leah Wells.

"Morah Music is me! It means 'music teacher' in Yiddish. Look, here's my guitar." I'd had to make my case before the perplexed bank teller as well as her supervisor who suspected that I was attempting to scam some poor Morah Music out of her thirty-dollar wages.

Under the Bus

Alas, on Monday morning there are subway delays. When my train finally pulls up to 225th Street, breakfast time has passed and I rush not to be late for my first class.

To make matters worse, Miss Antonette is not in her office as I arrive, breathing hard from having to gallop all the way from the subway station. On this of all mornings, she is not at the center yet. The mystery of my bounced paycheck persists, but I must manufacture pep and good humor for visiting Room One.

How fortunate that today I have a brand-new activity that I have been hatching despite the weekend's turmoil. Oh sweet inspiration! While I found that all my students love "Head, Shoulders, Knees and Toes"—and they know where these parts of their bodies are found, just as they know pointer, pinky, and all of the fingers in between from singing "Where Is Thumbkin?" hundreds of times—I realized that secondary areas, such as wrists, ankles, and elbows, are still a mystery for most kids. Perusing old songbooks over the weekend, I found "Ezekiel connected them dry bones," a catchy musical anatomy lesson that was sung to the children of slaves, to teach the sequence of bones climbing from the toes to the skull between refrains of "and we all praise the Lord!" But as I'm singing to children of all faiths, I devise my own game: we will play dress-up as we sing the names of these body parts.

I have the whole routine pre-structured in my head and can leave difficult emotions about my paycheck hovering at a distance while I jump around implementing my scheme on auto-pilot. What I do involves leading a simple jingle I've concocted while the room sings along with me. Each repetition of our little song is accompanied by dressing up, adding item after item that I pull from an oversized, floppy shopping bag.

MOMMY IS GETTING DRESSED FOR A PARTY

In a large handbag collect costume jewelry such as a necklace, a bracelet, a chunky, twinkling finger ring, funky hair clips, dangling earrings, and sunglasses. Sit in front of the room with the bag and explain to the children that Mommy is getting ready to go to a party but she needs help to get all dressed up. Encourage the children to sing this little phrase with you: "Mommy is getting dressed for a party. Where does her necklace go?" Having sung this question, open the bag and dramatically remove the long, oversized string of beads or fake pearls and ask cluelessly, "Does it go here?" and try draping it over your knee. "Does it go here?" Try putting both arms through it like a shirt.

Most likely the children will be crying out that it belongs around your neck. When they've had enough, thank the children and oblige them with slipping the necklace where it belongs. Now it is time for everybody to sing the little song and for you to add the next item, such as "Mommy is getting dressed for a party, Where does her bracelet go? or "Mommy is getting dressed for a party, Where should she put her ring?"

Perhaps ask the children to show everyone where a bracelet goes, and where a necklace goes. Continue this routine until Mommy is all gussied up. Conclude this activity by saying good-bye to each item as it returns to the bag. Children enjoy the ritual of rewinding this activity and the chance to review what they have been seeing.

Another activity, "Nose Nose Nose," which features secondary body parts can be found on page 40 of my book *Games That Sing* (Heritage Music Press, 2011). In this engaging guessing game, children also identify their wrists, ankles, elbows, kneecaps and other parts of their bodies.

Mommy is Getting Dressed for a Party

Leah Wells

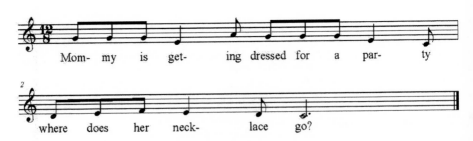

Mom- my is get- ing dressed for a par- ty

where does her neck- lace go?

This dress-up routine is a huge hit with the children. At the end of my second class, Miss Kadrena photographs me dripping in chiffon scarves and costume jewelry, for the Marble Hill newsletter. But even a successful morning can't prepare me for the almost sociopathic nonchalance that I encounter from Miss Antonette when at last I can tell her about my financial plight.

"We bounced a paycheck. It happens." She shrugs with a maddening disregard that leaves me scrambling to restate my concerns.

"But Miss Antonette," I try again. "Can you understand that we've already drawn against the money? We're in big trouble with the bank. We're up to our eyeballs in processing fees!"

Across her desk from me, Miss Antonette impassively twirls a strand of her bangs. The longer she sits there, clicking her chewing gum, the hotter my face becomes until I feel that my cheeks must be glowing like a neon sign.

"We've been living on credit cards all weekend!" I all but shriek.

And still she won't meet my eyes.

"I suggest that you speak to Brenda Keenan," she says mechanically at last, shrugging again. Her utter indifference paralyzes me. For a few minutes I watch her shuffling papers with her infuriating detachment until the telephone rings, startling both of us.

"Talk to Brenda," she repeats before taking the call. "I can do nothing for you."

On the first three attempts, Brenda is unreachable. I duck outside and call Mark from my cell phone to give him an update, which is to say that I haven't learned anything at all. He sounds upset and mumbles something.

"What? I didn't get that." I cover my other ear to blot out the traffic noise and squint against the wind.

"Nothing," he says. "It's just a lot to expect of us."

I sign off feeling helpless. I had no good news and now Mark is angry. Even if he knows it's not my fault, the situation makes him cold and cross. It may not be Miss Antonette's fault that the check bounced. Still, I thought she was supposed to look out for me. Was it really too much to expect a little show of concern and compassion?

Why did my favorite of the three supervisors have to go all body-snatched on me just when I needed her the most? Where did she go? Where was the friend I'd made who lamented to me about her little brother and who laughed with me about her boyfriend? Was she being coy? Or was she clueless? Was it cultural or was she just being a good bureaucrat, saving the face of her organization at the expense of the individual when something went wrong? If my situation genuinely meant so little to her, couldn't she at least have faked it? Here she was supposed to be my supervisor when a carpenter ant could have shown me more empathy. Wasn't it her job to be my advocate and see that my needs were met so that I could bring my full attention to the children? Even if she truly could "do nothing for me," had she no idea how much a simple human-to-human apology would mean at such a time?

As I speed out to lunch after my classes, I wonder: how am I ever going to face her again without exploding? Until now I regarded her as one of my first friends at Head Start. After this morning her stock with me has definitely plummeted. There will be no more social chitchat with her, no more girl talk, no more obligating myself to make nice in the staffroom. As far as I'm concerned, she's on probation!

As dawn breaks on Tuesday morning my life starts returning to normal. When I got off the subway Monday evening I received a message from Brenda Keenan in which she apologized profusely. My reissued check will not kick in for a few days, but thanks to a small cash loan from my mother, at least my wallet is full. We are no longer reduced to walking around in credit-card fantasyland.

"Oh, we're so sorry, kid." Over my voice mail Brenda assured me that it was some kind of agency-wide computer snafu that had invalidated many consultants' checks. "Yeah, yeah, I know. It's terrible. Just send me everything you got and we'll take care of all your fees," she promised, every bit as warm-blooded and reassuring as Miss Antonette had been remote.

When Miss Inez, in the little office, graces me with a fleeting smile I reflect that ironically she's become friendlier to me than Miss Antonette. Of course Miss Inez, as before, is still recognizably herself, with her skittish glances, and the same pursed lips and short answers in broken English. But last week, a particularly drafty day, she had surprised me with a gush of candor about the chilly room and lack of coffee supplies. "You see that, no cups!" she'd complained, rummaging in a drawer. "We gonna have to buy it ourselves. It's not right."

And just like that—in spite of the cold—the ice was broken. Miss Inez did not take me in her arms as Nicky had. Still, we'd had a laugh.

This morning I find the chair beside her desk occupied by a mother who balances a young child on the peaks of her ample lap. Miss Inez speaks to her in Spanish but I understand what is happening. Parents who wish to register a child at the Head Start center at Our Lady of Miracles are told to come to be interviewed between the hours of 9:00 and 11:00 AM or 1:00 and 3:00 PM. They must bring proof of income (budget letter, pay stub, or a notarized employment letter), the child's birth certificate and an immunization card from the doctor, as well as social security cards for the entire family. And, of course, the children themselves must be present in order to be assessed for admissions.

Miss Inez and Miss Lucy conduct these interviews at their desks and I've overheard parents or guardians asked questions such as: What language do you speak with your child at home? Does your child have a nickname? Is she toilet trained? Does he sleep through the night?

From the look of the families that show up to be interviewed, I wonder how many will be capable of producing all or any of the required documentation. Some of the mothers show up in the November cold wearing house slippers and dirty sweatpants. Many struggle with literacy and can hardly speak English. *Tax returns, notarized employment letter, social security cards for the entire family?* I'm not even sure where these documents are for my family.

Some mothers are obese. It pains me to see them huff and puff to climb our steep, dark stairway to the crowded office. Other children are clearly brought to the center by their grandparents.

As I walk by I look into the eyes of the girl on her mother's lap and wonder if, one day in my class, she will be laughing to "Clean Hands, Dirty Hands."

We Gather Together

The following Saturday is cold and rainy while golden sunshine has graced our bank account. My reissued check has finally cleared and at least for the moment we're out of the red. Since the boys want to practice their strikes from *Pukulan*, I am inclined to splurge on the bucket-sized punching bag they've been asking for. In the afternoon we hike through the drizzle up to Paragon, a sporting goods store near Union Square.

But what does one do with a punching bag in a small city apartment? At home I loop a string through an eyelet at the top of the punching bag so that it dangles like a churchbell and lead the boys outside our apartment door. All weekend long we play with the bag in the hallway: I stand high on a chair, halfway between Haskell and Simon, holding the top of the string while the boys bat the bag back and forth to each other like a tetherball. I don't know how I will use it in my classes but I do know that one way or another, this punching bag on its string is coming to Head Start with me next week.

Bright and early on Monday morning I have Miss Nicole line up her class so that every child gets a chance to punch the swinging bag and send it flying back and forth as my boys did at home. I ask them to punch it with a fist or slap it with an open hand. I build on past lessons and ask the children to use their right and then their left hand. Next I have them push it with two hands together so that they can use their body in still another way. I instruct the teachers to maintain the line of waiting children carefully so that nobody gets hit by the swinging bag.

At some point Miss Antonette investigates the happy commotion. She smiles and doesn't seem to mind that I stand on a chair, as I feared she might. She and I have been pleasant and civil to each other, but after last week I still keep my distance; I am minimal in my occupational banter, and intentionally cool. It probably helped to have a punching bag at my disposal all day.

In 1431, Joan of Arc was burned at the stake for hearing voices. Today, every other person on the street is plugged into some device, hearing voices and music, and suddenly I've joined their ranks. My friend Daniel Mackler has compiled a wonderful tape from his collection of vintage folk music and children's recordings. I buy a small, battery-powered cassette player that I can clip onto my belt loop, and now Malvina Reynolds, Pete Seeger, Burl Ives, Woody Guthrie, and still others accompany me to the land of gated windows and vacant lots—innocent songs about the fields and farms of a vanishing America that offset the present-day decay.

"On Top of Old Smokey," "Big Rock Candy Mountain," "Pop Goes the Weasel." Listening to Daniel's cassette on the subway makes me realize that there are certain nursery rhymes and children's classics that straddle time and social classes and seem to spring from the collective unconscious of all childhood.

Singing the ABCs is almost in our DNA, while "Twinkle, Twinkle Little Star" seems to be written across the sky—although I can't remember having learned it.

By Tuesday I begin planning Thanksgiving, wondering how the new punching bag may fit into the feast. I'm trying to weave some holiday imagery into our classroom songs, but I find that harvesting vegetables, good nutrition, and the meaning of Thanksgiving in general, is a hard sell in the Bronx. Naturally the children are more attuned to the candy and costumes of Halloween, and the Catholic school bulletin boards around us are more focused on Christmas and the saints of the Vatican than on the nerdy, buckle-donning pilgrims of the Mayflower.

From Daniel Mackler's tape I learn a lively version of "The Garden Song" as sung by the actor John Lithgow. I also bring in the story of *The Carrot Seed* by Ruth Krauss for dramatization. The challenge is blending the food of Thanksgiving with the punching bag. By my second class at Our Lady of Miracles, a lone plastic corncob left on the floor plants the seed for an unorthodox Thanksgiving activity.

Before I can try out this new possibility, a gruff voice interrupts me.

"Get offa the chair. I don't wanta have to write a report."

Miss Bilkis's muffled voice orders me down from the chair where I'm delighting the class with the punching bag. No matter how well things are going she never supports what I do here. After I step down, she waits at the back of the room with her fists held to her waistless sides to be certain she has stamped out any lasting embers of merriment before rolling out the door like a tank.

Now the children are confused and upset. The teachers see that I'm flummoxed. "Don't take it personal," they tell me. "It's just that she don't want to have to do no paperwork."

The chair I was standing on was barely a foot from the ground. I'm wearing sturdy shoes and feel confident. It's true that the unforeseen can happen, but the risk is minimal. It hadn't seemed to trouble Miss Antonette.

Happily, on Friday I learn that Miss Catalina will be out all day, attending a conference at St. Rita's. Nobody else at St. Anthony's seems to mind when I hop back on top of a low chair and line up the children for swinging left and right hooks at the moving target. I think of it now as a kind of piñata and plan to try out the idea inspired by the corncob.

In a variation on demolishing the block cities with the red truck, the children arrange piles of plastic fruits and vegetables from their play kitchens in a large shallow basket. As we pile up the play food—a green pepper, a drumstick, an onion—I try to get the children to identify what they have in their hands. We discuss the difference between fruits and vegetables, and food from animals and food from plants.

Finally, having completed the educational portion of my class, I am ready to give the kids a chance to clear this holiday table with a wrecking ball! They take turns at swinging the punching bag to knock the whole plastic cornucopia asunder. I will justify this activity in my exit report as "developing special awareness, turn-taking, and problem-solving." How about letting off steam?

The kids are restless today, and they love the excitement. They get very meticulous in assembling the pyramids of plastic food and enjoy watching the others take their turn to strike them down just as much as having their own turn. They have been so absorbed and well behaved that Miss Natalia and Miss Mandy are able to sit down to relish a moment off their feet.

After a second child has taken his turn, suddenly Oliver is behind me, handing me pieces of fruit and vegetables as they fall to the floor. The autistic boy remains at my side for the rest of the class, picking up every toy food item wherever it tumbles down with the attentive singularity of a Labrador retriever fetching a stick. I speak to him but he never responds. He will neither look me in the eye nor answer my questions. The next Friday when I come to visit his classroom, it will be as if we never shared this mysterious interval of harvesting plastic food together.

Without Miss Catalina, the staffroom is full of spirited chatter at lunch. Instead of the usual scaly salmon filets, the aluminum tray left by the cooks bubbles with lasagna. Ding-dong, the witch is dead! Even the food seems to be celebrating her absence. I snip the rubbery mozzarella topping to serve myself a square, wishing for a good Montepulciano to wash it down.

Around the table while I eat there is an air of tense excitement. It seems that a passenger has left $1,500 in the taxicab of Mr. Felix's cousin. Apparently the poor woman was distracted and hysterical because her husband had just had a heart attack. "I get that she was upset," says Miss Priscilla, "but what's she doing with $1,500 on her?"

"Maybe she had it to pay off the hit man," says Mr. Felix, taking a provocative bite of his apple.

"Up, thas it!" cries Miss Priscilla, grabbing the newspaper that was spread on the table in front of him and rolling it into a stick.

"What? What I do?" he protests.

Above these two flirts, the hands on the staffroom clock wind through my lunch hour. Reluctantly I rise from the table to toss my empty plate in the garbage bin and assemble my paperwork from the filing cabinets in the main office. I leave Mr. Felix covering his head while Miss Priscilla beats him repeatedly with his own newspaper, scolding, "You gonna act like a dog then I gotta treat you like one!"

After the weekend, my attempts to continue playing it cool with Miss Antonette are a dismal failure. Turning on the charm, she wants to know if my family will be doing anything special for the holiday. I answer her with a bland "not really," and absent myself to use the bathroom. But no sooner do I return when, humiliatingly, she gets to hear me bother Mr. Justin for the use of his master key to reopen the bathroom door because I left the key inside. So many times I was told that the staff key attached to its tricolor, braided pipe-cleaners must be returned to the hook outside the bathroom door where the next visitor can find it. To my chagrin, I'm no better than the children when it comes to following oral instructions.

There is worse bathroom trouble on the final Friday before Thanksgiving at Saint Anthony's. Opening the door to Miss Natalia's class, I am hit by a stink so powerful that it almost throws me backward. It's like a wall of raw sewage and I don't honestly know how anyone inside the room can stand it, I am gagging.

"What happened here?" I manage to ask Miss Mandy who has pulled her T-shirt over her nose like a surgical mask. She explains that Oliver has backed up the plumbing. He made a poop, she says, and then tried to flush an entire roll of toilet paper along with it. She says that poor Miss Natalia is in the bathroom furiously plunging, up to her elbows in feces and filthy water, that is spewing onto the bathroom floor.

I am dispatched to inform Mr. Felix of the emergency—before this foul, surging water can reach the children. Just as I turn to leave, I spot Oliver from the corner of my eye. He is clutching his Thomas the Tank engine cartridge and spinning around in the back of the room as he usually does, oblivious to all the havoc he occasioned.

Feliz Navidad

Through the windows of the bus on Tuesday, "Simon's playground" looks lonely. Over weeks of passing this little yard surrounded by barbed wire, I have never seen a single child at play there—not one.

From over the deli speakers at 161st Street, where I now buy my lunch, 106.7 Light FM—the radio station that follows me everywhere—Bing Crosby and Nat King Cole serenade me. Christmas is in itself a gift to my music sessions. Just breaking out "Jingle Bells" and "Santa Claus Is Coming to Town" puts everybody in a good mood. I don't have to rack my brain strategizing themes and activities to fill the time. I have Frosty the Snowman and Santa Claus and all his reindeer to help me. I am heartened to find that "Jingle Bell Rock" and "Rudolph the Red-Nosed Reindeer" still excite children just as much as they did a hundred years ago when I was learning them. In late December snow arrives, draping a bridal white veil over the steep sides of Highbridge, and leaving me to believe that miracles are possible.

I now take my lunch in the privacy of a nook backstage, in the vast, blue auditorium downstairs. Last week, seeking a hideaway with my sandwich, I'd come upon a lone folding chair in the wings. Heading there now I know I'll wade past stacks of textbooks and a large crucifix that leans against the wall. The blue darkness that stretches beyond me is as intoxicating as an ocean beach and I almost feel like running onto the stage as if into the surf. There are steps on either side, but I climb onto the stage from the center and head into the shadow of the wings to find my chair.

Behind mobile partitions in front of the auditorium an art class is in session for the older students at Our Lady of Miracles. The teacher, Mr. Brock—the man I had spotted in an apron on my first day—instructs them to add a frosting of glitter to the cardboard Christmas tree ornaments I heard them design and decorate last week. "Control the nozzle," he tells them now. "Think of your bottle of glue as a paint brush."

The children get boisterous and Mr. Brock reprimands them repeatedly.

"Francis...don't make me ask you again..."

As I relax and enjoy my sandwich I ponder the irony that I'm on stage, yet never so invisible.

Happy Birthday, Dear ... Who?

"The next stop will be Zerega Avenue."

Early Saturday evening I find myself on a Bronx-bound Number 6 Train headed to the stop above Castle Hill Avenue with my guitar and a bag of old clothes because I have accepted a special assignment. The assistant teacher in Miss Julissa's class, a robust young Hispanic woman whose confusing name is either Miss Cresi, Cresme, or Cresimi, asked me to entertain at her small daughter's fourth birthday party. Normally I would make excuses, but I have grown especially fond of this candid and playful woman who works with Miss Julissa. Also, she insists that she wants to pay me seventy-five dollars and waves away any negotiation on the matter. I had not realized until recently that the tiny, weepy, olive-skinned little girl from Miss Lisa's room upstairs is this nice woman's child.

The mother told me that it is hard for her somewhat fragile daughter to attend Head Start where she teaches, and to be separated from her all day in a different classroom. Apparently Miss Catalina would not allow them to be grouped together in the same class. Before I left on Friday I stood with both mother and daughter, scribbling their address and phone number on the back of an old consultant's form.

"Tell me again how to say your name. I want to get it right."

The teacher laughed, saying, "Oh, it's easy. Her name and my name are the same," leaving me just as baffled as I'd been to begin with. Before I sing "Happy Birthday," I hope to glean the spelling of it from the top of the birthday cake. Still, I knelt beside the anxious birthday girl and told her how excited I was to be coming to her house. "What shall we do at your party?" I asked, and the child whose name I would never be able to decipher threw herself into her mother's arms and shyly buried her face.

"Okay, Mommy." The teacher rocked her daughter and laughed indulgently. "She's overtired," she said, smoothing her hair.

"Does she have a favorite song?" I asked, rising to my feet.

"Not really," shrugged Miss Cresmi, or Cresi or Cresime. "You know, she likes all those princess movies. Maybe you could come as Cinderella."

Me and my big mouth! How was I supposed to come up with any kind of Disney duds by the next day? Fortunately I happened to mention my dilemma to an old friend later.

"Gee, the girls and I just got finished cleaning out their closets!" she exclaimed. "We're getting rid of tutus and leotards from their old dance classes and all kinds of other stuff. Maybe you can find some rags for Cinderella in there?" she offered.

Of course, once I got through rummaging in their bag of castaways, I looked more like a homeless Little Mermaid, but the billowy fabric and bright colors show an effort to be somebody from the world of make-believe. In return I wrote a card for my friend, thanking her and her two daughters for saving Cinderella.

I arrive at the two-family house in the Bronx, excited and curious to step into the private life of a Head Start student and teacher. It's a small apartment, cheerful and orderly. I say hello and quickly excuse myself to put on my costume in the bathroom—where Barbie doll torsos spring out of crocheted toilet-paper cozies. For her special day my teacher friend has twisted her daughter's long black hair into elaborate ringlets with a curling iron. Wearing a saintly white communion frock, the girl looks as stiff and frozen as the tops of the Barbie dolls do on their bathroom shelf.

To a group of cousins and local friends assembled in the living room, I begin with "If You're Happy and You Know It," and get the children on their feet for a freeze-tag song called "Play and Play!" I am glad to learn that these kids know Chiqui Morena (also spelled Checki Morena), a musical circle game from Puerto Rico. And then finally, I am off the hook as a Piñata is dangled for the blindfolded party guests to swat. No Miss Catalina or Miss Bilkis to stifle any of the joy and natural rowdiness of children. Clearly, this family wanted to see the birthday girl and her friends have fun.

Alas, the vast pink-and-white sheet cake has no flowers or lettering beneath its lighted candles. The many voices singing out around me engulf my fudging of the birthday girl's name.

After an interval of strenuous efforts to engage in small talk—I can't understand their questions and they can't understand my answers—by nine o'clock an exhausted Cinderella returns to her street clothes and subway car. Looking out the window from the elevated subway, I recognize familiar blocks of Castle Hill, swathed in darkness at this late hour. I shake my head, troubled that by the end of the ball, this Cinderella still has no idea of the mysterious name of my hostess and her birthday girl.

Play and Play

Public Domain

Play and play, play and play, play and play un- til the mus- ic stops.

Play and play, Play and play, play and play un- til the mus- ic stops.

repeat as desired

HOW TO BAKE A BIRTHDAY PARTY

Second only to their names, a birthday is every child's prized possession. Never mind the time of year, a child's birthday is his or her own personal Fourth of July, complete with fireworks! What can be better? They get a holiday of their own just for being born and they get presents and cake, and are showered with attention just for being themselves. At Head Start, when I enter a classroom and spot a child brimming with pride beneath a yellow construction-paper crown, I instantly know that today's music session will entail a birthday party — and with the experience from my own two boys, after all these years, I know how to start the action.

I found one of my all-time favorite birthday-party openers in the pages of Abigail Flesch Connors' wonderful activity book *101 Rhythm Instrument Activities for Young Children* (Gryphon House, 2004). To lead this delightful routine I lay aside my guitar and join the children on the floor, where clapping and hand play accompany the short verses of a song.

In the playgrounds and classrooms of my sons' schools I learned this pluckish regional variation.

Birthday Song

East Village Anon.

And please try out this next idea with any birthday children in your life. I would love to believe that I founded a new tradition with this original spin on everybody's grand old chestnut from the late nineteenth century—the Happy Birthday song.

MISS LEAH'S ALPHABET BIRTHDAY FUN

It's so simple but it works! To extend the excitement of singing "Happy Birthday" in the classroom, take the first letter of the birthday child's name and use it as the first letter for each word in "Happy Birthday." So, Simon's birthday would yield "Sappy Sirthday Soo, Soo!" And Ms, Ps, and Hs are all fun, as well as consonant blends when they present themselves. Francine finds her classmates giggling to Frappy Frithday, Froo, Froo. To get the whole room involved, the first thing to do is to ask the group what letter their birthday friend's name begins with. It might take a moment but there's always a few hotshots who figure out what I'm

---

looking for and eagerly shout out the answer for the rest: "T! It's a T, Miss Leah. Tyisha's name begin with a T!"

Admittedly, names that begin with a vowel don't quite pack the punch of the consonant names. Still, for all the many birthdays I serenaded at Head Start I never had a birthday boy or girl upset by the attention.

Everybody enjoys the silliness. Try it!

Over the years, I have entertained at many children's birthdays. I have called square dances and kick-started the Hora lines at weddings and bar mitzvahs. I've competed in string band competitions sponsored by the Moose Lodge of Galax, Virginia, and led the Hanukkah portion of the Christmas tree lighting at the Bronx Botanical Gardens. And yet before every new event I still break out in the same cold sweat.

Live music is, by its very nature, unpredictable; it hasn't happened yet. As entertainers and musicians we now compete not only with each other, but also with all the greats who ever lived and left footprints on the earth or at least audio tracks in the studio. An audience can run hot and cold, and my less-than-state-of-the-art sound equipment may act up. All the digital tuners and computer apps in the world can't keep me from breaking a string or blanking out on the words to somebody's favorite song. In our YouTube universe, why listen to me anyway when you could have Glenn Miller put you "in the mood" or Elvis himself to get you "all shook up"?

Even what I do for children isn't safe from this technological encroachment. In the classrooms and at private parties I have to squeeze myself in between all the bells and whistles from the children's favorite cartoons and movies. At one party, I arrived at a penthouse where the six-year-old birthday boy was screening an episode of SpongeBob for his friends on a flat screen TV the size of an Imax. Needless to say, they didn't want to turn it off to play Hot Potato with me. I show up to gigs and find the rooms roaring with CD players and DVDs. How can I compete? I feel embarrassed to ask the hosting parents to silence the iPods and boom boxes so I can take the stage—as they've hired me to do.

But nowadays, will children and their parents or their nannies and caregivers still fall for London Bridge? And is the Hokey Pokey really what it's all about? Can the old beloved songs and games that I grew up with and that have delighted children for generations still cut it? Will the music and my props and puppets be enough to amuse today's world-weary birthday kids? Will I be enough? What I have going for me is that unlike their holograms and devices, I am alive. My guitar and I are right in their face, capable of touch and interaction. But in these fast times will that still be enough to bake a birthday party?

Alas, even for children it's become a scratch-and-sniff culture and a strip club world of screaming commercials and flashing lights. Gunfire is everywhere. Smoke machines, synthesizers, car chases, nudity—with the bar for stimulation set so high these days, is it enough to be alive?

The Week Before Christmas

To my surprise the Marble Hill Center is almost a cozy place on a winter afternoon. Miss Sandra and Miss Kadrena sit in their offices typing or talking quietly on the telephone. From across the hall in the kitchen, plates clank as the cook loads the dishwasher. And in the staffroom, Mr. Justin sits alone at the big Formica table reading a paperback. A soft din of children's voices emanates from the classrooms. Everything feels drowsy and warmly insulated from the shadows of the scaffolding outside.

I go to say good-bye to Miss Antonette and wish her a happy holiday. Her door is cracked open, and I am about to knock when her phone rings. "Antonette Conendes," she tinkles her greeting into the receiver. "Ah, yes. Thank you for getting back to us. I am calling you from Marble Hill Head Start. We have a child with the address of your shelter who has been absent from our school for three days. We are wondering would you have any information about the family of this little boy, O'Neill Blevens? Yes, I see...Okay, we can try," she says with a discouraged laugh.

After she hangs up the phone, I tap softly on the cracked-open door.

"No news about O'Neill?" I ask. I remember the shy African American boy in Room Two. I had no idea he lived in a shelter.

She closes her eyes and squeezes the bridge of her nose with her fingers. "Ah Miss Leah. You can never tell me that we have a level playing field," she says with a sigh.

After we've said our Merry Christmases, one of the cooks runs out of the kitchen in her hairnet and gray uniform. I am gifted with a five-pound bag of frozen pork taco meat and a foot-long ingot of government-issued mozzarella cheese. The unexpected booty droops like an anvil in my canvas bag.

At home Mark whips up a "Head Start Chili" with the ingredients. After having been grated liberally over the chili, the tall block of mozzarella cheese still dominates our refrigerator shelf like the ponderous slab motif from *2001: A Space Odyssey*. The boys are a little young to remember this movie. But they intuitively understand why I feel compelled to sing the iconic opening bars of its theme whenever we open the refrigerator door to see the great block of cheese looming over the mustard, the orange juice, and the ketchup bottle.

On the final Tuesday of the Christmas season I fight my way to Our Lady of Miracles through a blizzard. Before class begins I duck into the girls' bathroom. The new motion-activated toilets that were recently installed never worked and still don't. I must use the same plunger that has been sitting in the bowl for two weeks. What good are high-tech mechanisms that are too complicated to repair? Give me an old-fashioned pull chain that actually flushes. Give me an outhouse! Give me a bucket! Fortunately I have discovered a little blue bathroom all to myself downstairs, near the stage where I sneak my lunch, with a good old-fashioned toilet. It lies behind a secret door in the farthest recess of the darkest wing backstage. What with my breakfast nook, a cozy radiator, and a private bathroom, my every need is taken care of, and I am almost going to miss this secret, musty little suite—my home and hearth away from home.

Today, having braved the elements like a fool to procure a cup of coffee, I arrive back behind the heavy stage curtain thoroughly soaked. In warm shadows, I roll up the drenched cuffs of my pants and take off my boots. I drape my wet socks over the ribs of the old sputtering radiator to dry and sit down to the hot coffee, and my egg salad on rye.

Behind partitions in front of the auditorium I can hear Mr. Brock addressing his art class. "Remember what I told you—never paint two wet colors side by side," he booms. "You're going to get mud."

At the end of my afternoon classes, I say bittersweet good-byes to the teachers. Miss Magdalena gives me a box of chocolate mints wrapped in Christmasy green foil. I offer them to everyone in the staffroom before ducking into a squeeze with Miss Lucy.

"I wish you and your daughter a blessed season," I whisper.

"Alright, baby." She pats my back.

Miss Bilkis is lurking somewhere in her mouse hole. I'm sure she would turn to look at the clock if I were to seek her out to wish her a happy holiday. Instead, I gather my belongings, looking around at the teachers for the last time this year, and zip into my jacket.

"So?" I turn finally to Miss Inez and we both giggle with embarrassed shyness. "Have a wonderful holiday with your family," I say. She bids me the same. "Be joyous, be safe," I continue, "and God willing, we'll all see each other in this dump next year. Maybe we'll even have coffee cups by then."

"*Aye Dio!*" Miss Inez covers her mouth and over her shoulder Miss Lucy guffaws and shakes her head. "Come here, Miss Leah!" Miss Inez continues laughing as she pecks me on the cheek and folds me lightly into a perfumed hug. "*Feliz Navidad*, all the best," she calls behind me as I start down the stairs.

CHRISTMAS VACATION

Vacation?

Ah, but it isn't.

On the second day after Head Start closed its doors for the holidays, Hospital Audiences Inc. has booked me to perform for special needs children. I find myself scaling the hinterlands of Queens in search of their elementary school. But the travel route mapped out by the school secretary just leads me in circles. I plead with locals and MTA employees for directions and almost break down in tears at the Euclid Avenue subway station. Two hectic phone calls to the principal's office, three retraced subway stops, and one very long bus ride later, I arrive at the low red brick school. Arriving impossibly late, perhaps I no longer have a gig.

I shake the hand of the school principal with ready apologies, only to learn that the starting time of 9:30 represented on my agency contract is two hours early, and every bit as incorrect as the travel directions they gave me. Because of this odd confluence of events, I receive a hero's welcome—with the embarrassed secretary who botched my route apologizing profusely. With the incorrect starting time canceling any "lateness" from my being sent in the wrong direction, I am perfectly on time to begin my back-to-back shows. And they say that two wrongs don't make a right!

At the head of a large classroom I tune my guitar and set out my materials: some hand puppets, a picture book, a snare drum with sticks and brushes, a weightless foam rubber ball the size of a cantaloupe. Behind me, a line of young children accompanied by their teachers enters through a back door. I've been told that each of my sessions will be composed of two classes put together. In no time I find myself sitting on a small wooden chair, facing sixteen children with at least half as many teachers—all women, who surround their students at the periphery of the classroom.

New troubles immediately become evident: Even the excellent teacher-student ratio at this school will work against me. As soon as the teachers settle themselves on desks and table tops, they begin to talk to each other—loudly, obliviously, as if nothing about to happen with their children and me concerns them in the slightest. I can't get their attention, not one of them meets my eye. The room I am supposed to perform in is as loud as any cocktail party; the din of conversation enough to bury my voice and guitar chords.

"Shhh!" I press my finger to my lips but get the attention of only one teacher who glances at me with annoyance and continues to talk. Lacking the courtesy of a quiet room and with no one to introduce me, I am truly grateful when a learning-disabled child on the floor finally takes matters into his own hands. Fixing on me with eager eyes behind his glasses, he cries out "Ready, set, go!" I can't think of a better opener, and I will use it many times in my work with children.

With the teachers maintaining their racket, singing "The Wheels of the Bus Go Round and Round" is like trying to drive through a snowstorm. Why don't I put my foot down and make a direct appeal for the cooperation of the staff? Because an over-worked, tired teacher may feel that it's her right to relax while a visiting artist performs. She may believe that she is off-duty and that she should be able to socialize with her colleagues. She doesn't realize that her talking in the room creates another layer of noise for the music consultant to have to fight against.

Also, this chatty teacher models for the children who look up to her that a visitor to the classroom can be ignored. Children are nobody's fools. If their teachers demonstrate that they can ignore me, then why shouldn't they? Occasionally a teacher whose allegiance I seek may feel pestered and become belligerent. They can report to the agency that I was unable to manage their classrooms and tarnish my reputation. They may do this whether I intrude upon their conversations or not...and this is when it is time to break out my secret weapon! This is why I carry a snare drum under my arm in addition to lugging my guitar and my bag of props. With the beer garden din created by the teachers swallowing up song after song and no end in sight to the problem, this is a job for "drum ball."

DRUM BALL

The wooden-framed snare drum is a one-hundred-year-old relic from a New York City high school marching band that Simon discovered at a sidewalk sale. Nobody had played the dusty drum for quite a while so I was surprised one day to hear a deep, steady thump emanating from Haskell and Simon's room. Peeking inside the door was like entering the chamber of a giant's heart. I found Haskell bouncing a light yellow foam ball off the head of Simon's old drum.

"Look Mommy, 'Drum Ball!' he announced.

When Haskell tilted the drum toward me, I could toss the ball against it like a backboard and, we could play a deeply resonant game of catch together. Of course, the music teacher in me took note.

To bring Drum Ball to the Head Start classrooms, I first demonstrate drumming on the snare with my hand, and then with a pair of sticks. Next come a set of steel brushes.

"Are these the kind of brushes we use to brush our hair?" I ask.

"No!"

"Are these the kind of brushes for brushing our teeth?" I touch the metal bristles to my lip. "Ouch! No again!"

After showing the kids how to tap and shuffle on the drum with the brushes, they have done enough watching and it's time to get them on their feet. "Everybody stand up and give a wiggle. I bet you've never seen anyone play the drum with a ball before!" And out from my bag would pop the yellow, blue, or the orange Nerf ball, at which they cheer. As Haskell did, I throw the ball in the air and let it land on the drum with a little boom. As the ball bounces on the drum—boom, boom, boom—I travel around the room with it. Then I gather the class into a circle around me.

With teachers in close attendance for containing the excitement, each child has a chance to launch the feather-weight foam ball toward the drum, hear the boom it creates, and perhaps catch it on the rebound. With Drum Ball there is no waste, even stray balls that roll to the ground or fly over everybody's head are as much fun for the group as landing a bull's eye that keeps the beat.

I use Drum Ball not only to delight the children here, but also to engage their AWOL teachers without having to utter a single reprimand. As the children take aim, I angle the drumhead up and give the ball an extra punch so that it sails in a high arc to land where the seated teachers are forced to catch it. Once the surprised women get into the fun, the whole room brightens. The children are excited as their teachers join the game, and I receive a round of applause at the end of the hour.

Saved by the ball! Between Simon's drum and Haskell's ingenuity, it almost feels as if my sons had traveled all the way out to Queens with me.

In the days that follow, Hospital Audience books me for another solo holiday show at The Center for Childhood Cerebral Palsy in Brooklyn. Then it's back to Manhattan to entertain children awaiting chemotherapy at a cancer treatment center. (Here I get stationed in the family waiting room beside an ethereal teenager who wears butterfly wings and leads a glittery art project. The challenge here is that the music I am to provide isn't always wanted. Often the older children are absorbed in hand-held video games and have no interest in joining me for early Beatles songs and Christmas carols). I receive a call asking if I would be willing to teach line-dancing to the residents of a maximum-security psychiatric hospital? My line-dance calling is rusty. However, when you're hungry enough and the boss asks if you can ride a horse, the answer is always "yes!" I also say "yes" to neighborhood parents who want their children to study guitar and mandolin with me.

Some vacation! The stress of cooking up idea after idea for my Head Start classrooms is replaced by designing shows for special populations, and meaningful music lessons for young 'millennials.' How much longer can I "fly by the seat of my pants," saving the day with Drum Ball or a red toy truck? I am not cut out to teach guitar playing by method. I never learned to play music that way. But improvisation is chancy. Indeed, if Haskell hadn't happened upon Drum Ball, or I hadn't found myself in the toy store that Saturday afternoon, neither of those favorite activities would have happened.

Still, chance graces me again as I'm struck by a Musak version of Pachelbel's Canon when I bring the boys to Dunkin Doughnuts one morning. The piece begins ponderously, with a single note for a measure before shimmering to its iconic climax. The kids I'm teaching, who are perhaps putting their fingers to the neck of a guitar for the first time, will be able to play this slow first section with a little coaching. Then, I will accompany them on my own guitar. *Voila*, my students will be able to make beautiful, satisfying, and even seasonal music in their very first lesson. Over the next week Pachelbel's Canon proves to be a winner for students of different ages. Beginners are proud to be part of creating music that they can instantly recognize and perform with reasonable ease. I extract yet more bite-size excerpts from other classical compositions for the new musicians to play in duets with me. From Pachelbel and Straus it'll be on to Beethoven, beginning with the "Ode to Joy" theme from his Fifth Symphony. By isolating well-trodden snippets of melody I imagine enough curricula to last through next July. With a dash of music appreciation and composer recognition thrown in—pun intended—"for good measure," I'll get no complaints from parents.

After school reopens and I'm working again at Head Start, these private lessons will be compressed into the weekends, when Mark takes the boys for a few hours of Daddy Duty while I knock on doors with my instrument, collapsible foot stool, and music stand in tow. Then I can dedicate not only vacations but also weekends to the pursuit of playing and teaching music. As Mark still has not found work, I am singing for all of our suppers.

Soon a new semester will begin for all of us—children, parents, teachers. With my new 'Pachelbel' method shaping the lessons with private students, I worry about returning to my Bronx preschoolers with as much pizazz. Should I continue to invent musical exercises on the spot for them, relying upon games learned from mothers in the community garden, and remembered from my childhood? What music did we sing and dance to when I was that age?

Mining my own childhood for what had been fun, I remember winding in and out of a circle of classmates, singing "Bluebird, bluebird through my window." Bluebird was great for a big room indoors, but outside where we were allowed to run it was a different story. In the open air our play got rougher with tag, dodge ball, and tug of war. And then there was Red Rover, Red Rover, a game where two lines of children holding hands face each other from a distance of several yards. "Red Rover, Red Rover let Leah come over!" The child who has been summoned with this taunt lights out from his line toward the chain of his classmates ahead of him with the intention of breaking their grip.

This activity is not used in the boys' classes at school. Perhaps assessed as too violent and dangerous by today's more safety-conscious standards, Red

Rover, like the long wooden sea-saws that once jarred our spines, has vanished from the playground, rendered extinct by insurance concerns. But back in the 1960s, in my public school yard, I remember the excitement of trying to hold on as charging classmates hurled themselves against our joined arms like battering rams.

The varying rules of censorship are hard for a traveling minstrel to keep up with. When I was a teenage camp counselor, I was forbidden to run relay races because competition was discouraged at that progressive camp. I also couldn't sing the story of Noah and the Ark because it mentioned God. Years later, at the Orthodox preschool I was forbidden to sing "Michael, Row Your Boat Ashore" because the song was thought to be "too Catholic." Even as a parent, I ponder exactly when the world changed and peanut butter sandwiches and wheat gluten, of all things, became toxic. When did competition become a dirty word? Even Musical Chairs, an exciting elimination game, seems to be retired from classrooms and from the birthday parties that my sons attend.

Call me a cretin, but in my day we didn't need "events planners" to have fun. We knew how to throw a party, an exciting, ego-bruising, unpolitically correct, hazardous, vanilla, chocolate and strawberry wingding! But was that spirit welcome at Head Start, where I wasn't allowed to stand on a tiny chair?

Maybe I should try to plan my classes along the lines of an established music curriculum. But where can such comprehensive curricula for the very young be found—where oh where can they be? (Of course, since 2003, a number of new preschool websites offer researched-based music curricula. We have listed some of these programs in the Appendix. When I began teaching, the pickings were slimmer).

My mother and I undertake research together at the computer. We find one or two programs that offer certification at a fee—integrating an early childhood background into music lessons. The fees are reasonable, but I still cannot afford them. Since Head Start doesn't pay for my extra classroom supplies, I doubt they'd pay for such certification. As it appears that I must continue to 'certify' myself, the site we find for discount school supplies most meets my needs and inspires me.

My mother helps me fill my cyber-shopping cart with bunches of rhythm sticks and stacks of "day-glow" colored scarves. At home a lifelike baby doll waits for me, next to a jack-in-the-box of a little clown, slide whistles, bells, kazoos and a wooden whistle that moans like an oncoming train. Soon I will need a circus tent or at least a new corner of the apartment to fit all my early childhood paraphernalia. With the slab of government cheese still dominating its shelf in the refrigerator, Head Start has already laid claim to my kitchen. Now it's coming for my bedroom.

The single most exciting gift from Mommy Santa is the "classroom size" — six foot in diameter–parachute. When the parcel of goodies arrives, I take the parachute into the hallway where the boys and their friends can play with it. The kids love pulling and pumping the fabric to make waves, and fanning themselves with the breeze it creates. As always, I watch their activities, on the lookout for what I might do in January when the parachute and I will touch down in the Bronx classrooms for the first time.

PART TWO

That's Show Biz!

Miss Catalina tightened the thumbscrews on my first day back: Extravaganza or bust! Over the weekend I apply myself to the question of how not to be 'deficient.'

I must come up with an idea for an Extravaganza show. Well, what is theatre? What makes something theatrical? What catches my eye and captures my attention? Is it for example, the Doberman Pincher on its short leash that growled and lunged at Simon, making us both cry? Is it the fragrant roast chicken that Mark lifted from the oven on Sunday night? And isn't it also the lone saxophone player serenading the dawn that I pass on my way to the subway that morning, my first Monday back at Marble Hill?

What makes good theatre? Certainly it has to include the Number One train thundering up to the platform at 59th Street with its gust of wind that sends papers flying and blows off our hats. How can I enlist these elements of surprise, suspense, and even danger in order to enhance my productions? As the train enters daylight, crossing into the Bronx, I look down from the elevated tracks to meditate on the pearly textures of the Harlem River roiling below. I recall how on the first leg of my commute, the soft melody of the sax player had so sweetened the empty blocks of my neighborhood. I realize that such beauty by itself is even more powerful than anything loud or sudden, contrived purely for shock value. I commit myself to coaxing a truly musical performance from the children for the Extravaganzas; a thing of beauty with dynamic contrast and charming bits of simple choreography to match.

Realistically, I'll be grateful if the kids behave during rehearsals, much less sing in tune for the performances. Loud noises and abrupt movements may be used to startle an audience from its slumber, but only beauty can enchant it.

But what will beauty enchant? What is the theme? By the time we reach 225th Street, I think of "Head Starters: Who We Are" as a theme with music that represents the children's different backgrounds. We can start with Native American chanting and rattling. We'll perform "Shay Shay Koolay" for the African countries, "Mi Cuerpo Hace Musica" for Latinos, "Swing Low, Sweet Chariot" for African Americans and Harry Belafonte's "The Banana Boat Song" for the Islands—with all nations building toward our grand and feel good finale of Woody Guthrie's classic "This Land is Your Land." Of course in my movie I have everybody—families, teachers, and administrators—clapping and swaying in the aisles, raising the roof with gospel enthusiasm. As we conclude with the emotional refrain of "This Land was Made for You and Me," those who are not already on their feet spring out of their chairs for a standing ovation. Who will you call *deee-ficient* when there isn't a dry eye in the house, Miss Catalina?

I arrive at Marble Hill stoked and ready to cast my shows only to find that, as Mark had predicted, nobody there is particularly thinking about the Extravaganzas anymore than I had before last Friday. "You are deficient!" So much for Miss Catalina making me dance over hot coals in her office. Relieved, I see no reason when I'm teaching the children, not to revisit my eclectic sets of folk and early labor songs from Daniel Mackler's tape, Mother Goose rhymes and bubble gum pop that we enjoyed in the months before Christmas.

I was also glad that on the strength of Mark's prediction, I had rebelliously tucked my new scarves and parachute into my supply bag along with my notes for the Extravaganzas.

I still have to cook up three different musical reviews with a cast of restless preschoolers on no budget...but for the moment I am safe, and have a parachute to break my fall.

I have not yet seen Miss Antonette, but the door to her office is open, the light is on, and the clock over her desk tells me that I have just enough time to pee before I'm due at my first class.

After only a couple of weeks of vacation everything is new again. Even small routines become brain benders, just as they were when I first arrived. I have to remember to bring in paper towels from the coffee station in the hallway since the dispenser in the bathroom is always empty. But most importantly I must remember to take the key with me when leaving the bathroom, lest the door lock behind me with the key inside—which, humiliatingly, already happened twice last semester.

The only upside about having so much to keep track of is that it reminds me of what life is constantly like for the children. Three- and four-year-olds struggle every day with the sequence of washing their hands, eating and drinking without creating a mess. And of course, the big kahuna—making it to the potty in time to do their business. It reminds me that songs about these things are important and have meaning for them. Maybe this is why they love my routine about clean hands and dirty hands.

During their long hours in school, preschoolers face many challenges, just as I must keep track of the procedures at my three centers. The children have to share, and wait their turn, which is still a challenge for plenty of adults. This morning, distracted, I again leave the key locked in the bathroom, and must trouble Mr. Justin to find his master set. This is not an auspicious beginning to the new semester. I could break down and sob from sheer embarrassment—just like any child in Room One or Room Two, after they are singled out and scolded.

Only the success of the parachute can banish my shame over forgetting the bathroom key. The children are mesmerized as I unfurl the parachute for them, spreading its rainbow of colors over the classroom floor, then inviting them to hold it, to pull on it and then to sit beneath it while the teachers and I fan them with the breeze we create by raising the fabric to billow over their heads and bringing it down to where it grazes the tops of their outstretched hands.

The kids are enthralled, making ripples and waves, as if on the surface of a kiddie pool. Even Miss Evangeline hoists herself from her chair, grabbing parachute handles with her class and helping with the fun. At the end of my first class, Miss Nicole giggles as I crush the colorful parachute back into its tiny stuff bag, an event to watch in and of itself. I am glad I was bold enough to bring the parachute to Head Start.

Number 15

Later that afternoon as I prepare to leave, an African American woman outside the center door notices my guitar and calls me out. "Did you see my son? His name is Kaleem. He's in Room Two with Miss Lucia and Miss Blanca." Parents assume that I know each child individually and are quick to put me on the spot. I hate admitting to them that I don't know who their kids are. In fact, sadly, the better behaved their children are, the less likely they are to stand out. Usually I remember only the real troublemakers.

"I'm sorry. They're all precious to me," I explain to her. "But I'm here only once a week and I visit so many schools that I don't always remember names. What does he look like?"

"Well, he's wearing a sport shirts," she laughs, "a green football jersey with a number 15." She tells me that at his old preschool, when her son misbehaved, the teacher locked him into a dark supply cupboard where the Pampers and wipes were stored. "I told the supervisor there that I'm gonna call A.C.S.," and she said, "'Look, you know, you gotta do what you gotta do.'"

"Really?" I say. "That was it? She wasn't horrified? She didn't apologize or say she'd do something immediately?"

The mother shakes her head sourly and gazes into space.

"So I pulled him out of there," she says. "Now I got him here; my God this year is easier for me!"

"I'm glad he's with us now," I say. "So what's happening with the other pre-school, the bad one?"

"Oh, you know...they're being investigated, but it takes a long time." She shrugs.

"Room Two, you said, right? I'll look for Kaleem," I promise her.

Highbridge High Drama

In my ongoing search for good theatre I find that Plankety Plank constitutes a genre of performance art all its own.

The next morning clear and present danger on the train interrupts my reading in the paper that a cop was killed in a shoot-out at a Bronx White Castle. From the other end of the car mounting voices kindle a fireball of hostility as young men in jackets shove each other and throw punches. From our seats we bystanders wince and cover our heads.

"If I gotta go back upstate I'm taking you with me, bro!" booms one of the hoods and then from the loudspeaker right on cue: "This is a Woodlawn-bound 4 train..."

"If it's Tuesday, this must be Highbridge," I whistle to myself, relieved to be exiting the train when at last the doors slide open at 161st Street. It is a hard landing to step down to the potholes and uncollected garbage, the barbed wire and bulletproof Plexiglas of the South Bronx. On the bus, I realize that the opulent department store windows and pretty Christmas lights downtown have made me grow soft. There is nothing up here to sugarcoat the slow hand of poverty. I will have to grow accustomed to the graffiti and degraded streets all over again.

Squeezed at the back of the bus, I notice that Simon's playground continues to look neglected as we roar past it. A snarl of weeds encroaches on one of the red slides and the wooden climbing structure with its hanging tires lists into the snow like a sinking ship. I have come upon the fall of Tara. I no longer think that Simon would want to play here. Now I think that he would be afraid of it.

After walking the last few blocks, I get buzzed into Our Lady of Miracles and mount the dark stairway to echoes of laughter. The small office as I arrive is unusually full and festive. In a semi circle, Miss Inez, Miss Lucy, and Miss Magdalena stand together by the coffee maker. In her old spot by the copy machine, her shining lips forming the same slow smile that first welcomed me here months ago, is Miss Daniela. "Well what a surprise!"

Genuinely glad to see everybody, I lean in for hugs and wishes of Happy New Year. Even with all the extra bodies, the office is drafty. We hunch our shoulders and blow on our hands but yes, there is hot coffee this morning and what a long way I've come to be able to laugh about it with these women, like old friends. In another minute the party disbands and Miss Magdalena saunters back upstairs to her class. Miss Lucy and Miss Inez return to their desks and Miss Daniela pulls up an extra chair to sit beside me. "So, are you back with us for good?" I ask.

She is here only for the day, to update some paper work. Soon she will receive a promotion, and next year she will become the site supervisor for the Monsignor Boyle Center when it opens in the fall. I congratulate her and she nods and wrinkles her nose. "Thank you," she says. "But Miss Leah there is something of a more serious nature that we need to discuss."

She pulls her chair even closer to where I can inhale the feminine cocktail of her hand lotion and chewing gum. "You may be seeing this on the news," she whispers—and of course, I already had. Without looking into my eyes, she tells me that the son of the slain police officer I had read about on the train attends the afternoon session in Miss Linda's and Miss Caridad's room. "Do you know which one is Pablo Hernandez?" she asks.

As with Kaleem's mother, I am asked to recall a child that doesn't stand out in my memory. Later that afternoon Miss Caridad discretely points out Pablo, a lamb with his curly brown hair and trusting dark eyes. He appears small, per-haps barely three years old. He sits cross-legged on his mat. Shyly eager for fun with our games and routines, he is sent giggling and squealing with the others to play with my parachute. But his gleeful oblivion presses on me. I want to take him in my arms and protect him, but I know better. Following Miss Daniela's instructions, I stick to business. I sing only about pies, puppies, and Spiderman for his class and remove all the daddies from my songs.

After class, in a corner of the lobby downstairs it is finally safe to break down. "Let it be known to all who enter here that Jesus Christ is the reason for this school. The unseen, yet ever present, teacher in its classrooms. The model for its faculty and the inspiration of its students."

Through my tears I can barely read the mounted plaque on the wall.

When I return to Our Lady of Miracles One, the joy that my parachute brings to the children of Miss Gracia's and Miss Felipa's room begins to restore my spirits. I move toward the finale with teachers and kids on their feet in a circle shaking the fabric so that the foam balls jump.

Unfortunately John Christopher is acting out, aggressively pushing class-mates on either side of him and lunging for the balls as they dance by. He knocks a child to the ground and the commotion draws Miss Bilkis, who moves in like a storm cloud. For a moment she just stares froggily behind her glasses at the laughing children and at the colorful undulations of the parachute.

We teachers know exactly what's coming. "This is an outside toy!" I could take the words right out of her mouth, and we all flash forbidden glances and roll our eyes.

"All right everybody, back to your mats," I sigh.

"The ride is over. Scat! Everybody go sit down." Miss Felipa claps her hands.

As I settle in front of the group with my guitar, I find it ironic that in this class it is safe to go back to songs about mommies and daddies, but here the colorful parachute is off limits. In this fly-free zone, Miss Bilkis has shot down my parachute as if it belonged to an enemy soldier. Now the only rainbow I can bring to the children of my final class is the *arco Inez* from the pretty lyrics of "*Des Colores*," the Spanish folk song that I sing with Miss Magdalena.

SMOOTH LANDINGS WITH A PARACHUTE

Sorry Miss Bilkis, but I beg to differ. A "classroom size" parachute actually makes a wonderful inside toy! "Want to see a rainbow?" I ask before shaking the multi-colored nylon of my parachute from its deceptively small stuff bag. If there are at least two other adults in the room, then you may begin by "taking the kids for a ride." Have them huddle together either on their bottoms or kneeling. Have the adults stand above the children spreading the parachute above them like a tent and together flap your arms up and then down so that the Parachute alternately rises and falls. This will create a billowing breeze.

The children want to put their hands over their heads and touch the parachute as it gently grazes their fingers before rising again. When the children have enough, invite them to stand up and grab a handle for themselves from the rim of the parachute. If there aren't enough handles, children can double up or others can simply grasp the edge of the fabric. By now everybody big and small should be standing in a ring around the parachute. The kids are restless, anxious to start cranking their handles. So why fight it?

Grab the energy and lead the group in a mass frenzy of shaking and pumping the handles so that the parachute vigorously ripples and snaps. Ask the children to stop and then tell them to pull backwards on their handles. The surface of the parachute will abruptly flatten and become as still as a millpond. When the children are ready for round two shout "Get all messed up!" and start madly waving and shaking again. After a few seconds cut off the ruckus by yelling "Stop!" Enjoy the contrast again and again. For an encore, throw a couple of colorful balloons or light foam balls about the same size onto the undulating fabric.

A lively song from the CD player is welcome, although once the foam balls or balloons are bobbing and snapping like popcorn, laughter from the children may be all the music that's needed.

As a grand finale, the children learn that now you're going to make the rainbow fly. With only you and your teachers holding the parachute, together bring your arms slowly up and down just as you did when you were making a breeze for the children. Give the teachers a count of "One, two" and on "three," have everybody let go of the handles at the same time. The parachute will fly out of your hands and sail over the classroom for a few seconds of glory before collapsing to the floor.

"Goodbye, Red. Goodbye, Yellow." Don't forget to say goodbye to each color as you fold away the rainbow.

On Friday I stubbornly smuggle the parachute into St. Anthony's. I want as many children as possible to enjoy it before Miss Catalina undoubtedly announces her sanctions. I play a game: betting against myself as to which of my six classrooms I will be visiting when I get the ax. I have put my money on door Number Three, which is Miss Salomé's room, but the grim reaper doesn't darken the threshold until I am a little further down the hall and deeper into the morning, in classroom Number Four.

"What is this I am seeing? Why are these children not preparing for their assembly?" Miss Catalina interrogates with folded arms.

But I have a reply. "Oh, these children have already done their practicing, Miss Catalina. The parachute is their reward for all the good work they've done at the beginning of class. Hey kids, let's show Miss Catalina how well we can follow directions. When I say 'three' let's show her how we make the balloons dance on the rainbow!"

It is the second Friday in January. The Extravaganzas are scheduled for the end of June—and still, she shutters my joyful activity with her sanctimonious, "But you're not giving the children what they need!"

Into the Fire

I'm an outright outlaw with my contraband "outside toys." Supporting this perception, Miss Antonette announces that I must be fingerprinted immediately, or she and I may both face some kind of penalty. When I began working at Head Start, fingerprinting had been postponed, in order to expedite my job application. Now, getting me into the system must be our top priority, she says, and waves away my concerns about the Extravaganza like a fly on her nose. "Oh, there's plenty of time," she scoffs, confirming my belief that Friday's ultimatum was only Miss Catalina's way of busting my chops.

She hands me a Xeroxed page bearing the Lower Manhattan address of a federal bureau. Tomorrow, rather than going to Our Lady of Miracles as usual, I am to report downtown and get fingerprinted.

"Will I miss a day's pay for this?" I ask. In a call to the main office we learn that I will be paid on the condition that after being processed, I subway directly up to Our Lady of Miracles and deliver as many classes as time will allow. Clearly a long day of strap-hanging lies ahead.

Snapping back from my private calculations I see that Miss Antonette is glancing at the clock and that it is ten minutes past my starting time. Apparently this morning the Fire Department is giving a presentation to the children. She waves me down the hall to begin the music session in Room One as soon as their program is finished.

Inside the classroom a fireman in full regalia of yellow coat, hat, and boots looms above the enraptured children. "Do your eyes go to sleep? Yes!" he lectures. "Does your mouth go to sleep? Yes, but your ears don't never go to sleep. Your ears can still wake you up. That's why you need to have a smoke detector at your house." To this Miss Nicole oddly adds, "You hear that boys and girls? You need to stay away from things that is hot." I keep to myself that at our home we had to disable our hyperactive smoke alarm, which instantly produces an ear-splitting pulse any time we so much as make toast.

At the end of the presentation, each child receives a coloring book in which Spot the Firehouse Dog reviews the golden rules of fire safety, and a mini pack of crayons.

Later, in our circle of joined hands, the scab I see on a child's skin is not a burn. The South American boy named Jesus beside me has marks that eerily resemble the stigmata on his palm. I flip his wrist and find bloody scrapes and cuts on the back of his hand as well.

"What happened here?" I ask .

"Poppy, who did you like this?' Miss Nicole comes up behind us. She kneels to take his small hand in hers.

Jesus looks into her eyes and in the thin panpipes of his voice he answers, "Mi madre, she...." He removes his hand to scratch at the air like a cat.

In her chair Miss Evangeline shifts her weight and issues a sigh like the airbreaks releasing on a train. "Write it up" she harrumphs, without seeming to open her eyes.

Into the System

Who could have known that having to get fingerprinted would occasion such a treat? On Tuesday morning I wake up naturally at 7 o'clock and get to linger in my kitchen with a cup of coffee—an enormous luxury. I let Mark sleep in and take the boys to school myself, for a change. On the way they chatter feverishly to me and insist that I take them right to their classrooms and that I say hello to both of their teachers. "Oh, Good Morning, Mrs. Wells. We don't get to see you very often!" You'd think the president was in town.

When I leave the school I stop at home to pick up my guitar before heading downtown to the massive court buildings and government agencies just north of City Hall. In the florescent-lit cubicle of a large, shabby office, an official pushes my fingers, one by one and rotates them against a glass plate. But something is wrong with the scans; my fingerprints don't register. Three times the computer shows a red "X" to reject the image of my fingers as unacceptable.

"You must do a lot of house cleaning with powerful chemicals. What are you, some kind of domestic?" asks the baffled clerk.

"I'm a mother," I tell him. "I wash floors and dishes and children's noses. Not long ago I was scrubbing diapers. Were these household activities really enough to obliterate my finger prints?" The clerk tells me that my fingerprints are so worn away that the computer may not be able to scan them.

"What happens then?" I ask.

"Oh, worst case scenario, some federal offices won't be able to retain you if they can't get you into the system," he says—which makes me want to sweep away the objects on his desk. Already for this job I've been stuck with needles and immunized against the venomous bite of a child. They have my social security number. They have my blood sweat and tears and still, as with Miss Catalina,

I'm found to be "deficient". In medieval times a man missing the first digit of his middle finger was ineligible to become a priest. It made no more sense to me that in Twenty-first Century New York City, fretting a steel string guitar and tending to children—the very things that most qualify me for Head Start—were about to defeat me. Of course I knew that all the elaborate screening was ultimately to protect the children from being placed with criminals. I got that, but if one's prints had been eroded from honest work, surely there must be some alternate means of obtaining a swatch of personage.

For example, couldn't a test tube of my type B positive blood be somehow paired with my ever "B positive" attitude as evidence of my spotless record? There was a comb in my purse. How about a distinctive follicle of my newly-sprouted ducktail or a q-tip of DNA swabbed from the lining of my cheek? In the words of the old standard "Why not take all of me?" The authorities were welcome to harvest their discharge of choice— stool, a healthy chunk of mucus, some nice urine perhaps...if only I could keep my job.

"Could we try one more time?" I beg. The clerk squints from my apparently bald fingertips back to his scanner, concluding at last: "I tell you what. We're gonna do you the old fashioned way." He produces an inkpad and presses each of my fingers onto its cool, porous tongue.

With the help of the dark ink the machine at last approves what broken spirals remain of my individuality, and I leave the office confident of remaining employable. On the subway ride uptown I plan to tell Miss Lucia this cautionary tale when I next see her. I want to make sure that she warns her daughter not to wash too many of her soapy dishes so that she doesn't erase herself by the time she's in her early forties, like me.

Back atop the cliffs of Highbridge, white, green and black garbage bags snagged on the crags of bare branches, ripple and snap in the icy wind like some banner of defeat. I learn that every so often Brenda Keenan conducts workshops that the families of the children are encouraged to attend. She holds them in the brief interval between the morning and afternoon sessions, and I come upon one at Our Lady of Miracles.

The little office is packed with the mothers of our children. Miss Inez and Miss Lucy are not around. New faces occupy all the seats while others crowd against the walls as Brenda holds court from the middle of the room.

The subject of today's workshop is child abuse. I come in at the point where

Brenda is saying that not getting a child to a doctor or dental appointment is neglect. Not bathing a child until he or she smells is neglect. Not getting a child to school on time, or at all, is neglect. Leaving a child in front of the T. V. too long—these are all forms of neglect, she reiterates.

There is no room for me in the crowded office, so I stoop in the dark hallway outside to organize my things. Before leaving for my first afternoon class, I hear a woman suggest that anybody who hits their child should cut a heart out of a piece of paper. "Any time you raise a hand to that kid you got to tear the heart," she instructs.

When Miss Catalina undermines my work or when Miss Bilkis obtusely dismisses my activities as "outside toys," I feel like they have lost touch with the founding mission of Head Start—which is to help disadvantaged children meet the challenges of entering public school and to enable them to thrive there. When teachers whisper that certain supervisors "can't be bothered with paperwork" to write a report about marks and bruises on our children, I worry that the program itself has deteriorated in the hands of complacent bureaucrats who are primarily interested in collecting their pay checks. I feel heartened when I hear Brenda talking to families about nutrition and neglect.

Brenda's outreach bears the torch lit by Dr. Robert Cooke, Sargent Shriver, and other founders who designed Head Start as a wholistic approach to supporting poor children. They conceived the program to reach beyond academic early intervention to minister to the needs of the entire child, to their physical health with vaccinations and medical screenings, to their emotional well-being, to their families, their culture and the community around them. Getting to eavesdrop as I do on Brenda's workshops on a range of subjects, from cutting board hygiene to the importance of fatherhood inspires me to find the humanity within the inhumane poverty and housing projects that trap these families, and to look beyond the fast food to find the soul food.

Into the Desert

By Friday morning I am trying to do exactly that. I embark from the train and for the first time in months I stride past the Dunkin Doughnut store at the foot of the station and begin scouting the long stretch of Castle Hill Avenue for a superior breakfast nook. Having stumbled on Brenda's staffroom workshop on preventing adult-onset diabetes, I find that even the candied pink décor of the chain store is enough to bring on a flush of insulin.

Foolishly, I consider skipping breakfast altogether. But my resolve vanishes as the steam-covered window of a coffee shop awakens the gnawing hunger I'm left with from my commute. I push open the glass door, hoping that my fierce opponent, the minute hand on the wall clock, will permit me time to eat a plate of eggs and home fries. Inside the store a child screams and an unkempt mother is woofing threats to it. Worse still, the whole place throbs with a rap station that practically shakes the plastic tables, which are bolted to the floor. No, this is not going to be my new breakfast spot. I pull my head from the door and keep walking.

I have heard of badlands such as this stretch of Castle Hill Avenue, offering little more than discount centers and national chains, referred to as 'food deserts.' With my growling stomach and the guitar heavy on my back, I am not proud that in the space of only a few doors my knees weaken and I surrender to the pre-fabricated oasis of a garish fast food chain. Inside it is warm, clean and quiet. My easy listening station purrs at a civilized volume and, unlike the coffee shop, the customers keep to themselves.

When I am seated at last beside the plastic tray that holds my equally plastic food, I open the *Post* but news of the war in Iraq makes a poor dining companion and I prefer the Horoscope: "Focus only on what you can improve in your immediate surroundings and trust the universe to take care of the bigger picture."

In my final class of the day, Miss Priscilla and Miss Alison have their hands full with the addition of a clingy new child. This pretty, light-skinned African-American girl, Tenacia, is aptly named. She is nothing if not tenacious. She disrupts all my activities, grabs things out of turn, interrupts songs, cries loudly. Even the other children complain, but Miss Alison only shrugs sweetly and says, "I know, but what can I do? You see how she is."

Privately, Miss Alison tells me that every morning when they serve the children breakfast, Tenacia will stand up and try to lock herself into the bathroom with her tray of food. "She's still so afraid someone gonna take it from her," she sighs.

A teacher in Room Three has traveled to her native Chile for a dental procedure.

For the second week in a row a likable Hispanic woman with a flying ponytail and good sense of humor has replaced her. Already we have caught eyes to wink over some of the choice antics of Miss Salomé and the children. Her name is Miss Regina. Her son is the same age as my Haskell and her husband is an orderly on a Psychiatric ward of Bellevue Hospital. He has told her that sometimes the patients will smear themselves in their own feces when they don't want to be handled by the staff. "And we think we have it bad." She shudders.

STOP, DROP, AND ROLL

Over the weekend, lingering reflections from the firemen last Monday kindle a flame of inspiration. During the presentation children took turns pretending they were on fire. A fireman instructed them to drop to the ground to roll out imaginary flames as the rest of the class incanted, "Stop, drop and roll! Stop, drop and roll!" Of course, Miss Leah will find music and movement potential in this lively simulation.

"Remember when the firemen visited us last week?" I ask when the children of Room One at Marble Hill push closely around my feet. "Well, today we're going to practice what we learned by playing a game called Stop, Drop and Roll."

At home I had prepared some orange and red construction paper flames for demonstration purposes. But Miss Nicole upgrades the concept to a four-alarm fire with her brilliant idea to tape these directly onto the children's clothing.

As each child takes a turn, two or three paper flames get tagged to their clothes with Scotch tape. "Ooh, you on fire, Mommy, watcha gonna do?" Miss Nicole prompts the next child on line. With the tagging of each shirt or pair of leggings, the tape on the paper flames acquires lint and becomes dull, making it easier for the line of children surfing onto the floor to emerge fire-free. A little upbeat music from Elmo on the CD player provides fire safety with a back beat. "Never forget this dance!" I tell them.

I plan to repeat this exercise with Miss Nicole's twist all week. But by ten minutes to seven on Tuesday morning neither fire alarm nor mechanical announcements can puncture the comatose-like slumber of the entire car of the

Number 4 Train. Across from where I nod, an unconscious team of canvas-clad construction workers share the subway car with me like a flophouse, as together we shudder through the darkness of long tunnels and screech into the glare of each successive station.

The men lean against each other like a row of dominoes and sleep with their tool bags and shovels resting against their boots. At some future time, as the northern-most lip of the real estate frontier creeps into the South Bronx, the elegant ghetto of Plankety Plank with its stately Art Deco buildings will be discovered by property tycoons. Eager developers will prize the decayed apartments for their historic features and for their plunging, expansive views of the lower Hudson Valley. When this happens, the guys across from me will be commissioned to carve out floor-to-ceiling picture windows and install skylights. They will crowbar ancient moldings and ceiling medallions, gloppy with generations of lead paint into dumpsters to be replaced by chic track lighting. Most likely as they usher out the decrepit to make way for the pioneering gentry, my undocumented companions will encounter fine lead paint dust and airborne asbestos with nothing to protect them but the bandannas they tie over their noses.

I am on my feet by the time our sleeping car meets daylight and slides beside the white walls of Yankee Stadium. And half an hour later, when I leave the bus "on top of old Smokey," Highbridge still snoozes without a shred of evidence of any gentrification to come.

I kick garbage out of the way as I push forward, cursing as I realize that while I have enough paper flames to consume the neighborhood, I have forgotten the all-important tape with which Miss Nicole elevated my routine to a party game. In the cramped, dimly lit aisles of a corner bodega, I try to scope out something that will do. Beside a stack of cardboard boxes holding stiff green plantains and, of all things, dollar packages of English tea biscuits, I ask the clerk in halting Spanish for Scotch tape. Although we stand less than a foot apart, the man behind the counter and I can't make out a word the other is saying and we have to keep pecking back and forth like guinea hens, asking, "¿Qué? Qué quieres decir?"

It could well be my Spanish, but more likely the problem is one of noise. Perdone, Nueva York, ¿has oído la última? Keeping the manic Latino radio announcer amped to a rattling volume has to be some kind of local practice. Here in Plankety Plank all commercial interiors rage with relentless, driven commentary, broken only by blasted intervals of highly percussive salsa bands.

Not only do I carry construction paper flames today, but also, in my determination not to be found "deficient," I bring baggies of dried black-eyed peas and Dixie cups—the makings of ceremonial rattles that will accompany Native American chants in the "Head Start: Who We Are" Extravaganza. But all I have brought will be rendered useless without some kind of adhesive tape. Inside my head, Miss Catalina chides me for forgetting this essential.

Fortunately, Mr. Brock, the art teacher, is willing to dig into his supply cabinet when I explain my dilemma.

"I didn't hear your guitar this morning. I thought maybe you weren't coming," he says, handing me a fresh roll of masking tape.

In the early morning, after my coffee and breakfast ritual enjoyed from deep within the wings at the back of the auditorium—time permitting—I had practiced my small classical repertoire on the guitar. I had no idea that anyone could hear me behind the heavy velvet stage curtain. I must have blushed, because Mr. Brock smiles and says, " I didn't mean to make you self-conscious. But I've come to look forward to my private concerts on Tuesdays." So I secretly listened to his art classes and he heard me practicing. I suppose we are even.

After completing my three morning classes I enter the office, filled with mothers in sweatpants and curlers attending a workshop on literacy conducted by Miss. Pilar. "Read from left to right," she proselytizes in her bold voice. "Tell them not to do like this," Miss Pilar says, dragging her index finger over the text from a page of Dr. Seuss's *Green Eggs and Ham*.

"After you done reading, let the children learn the importance that the book be returned to its proper place," she goes on. "We are teaching them to identify letters, numbers, colors, even how to hold properly the pencil. Let them draw. Ask them, 'What is this thing that you draw? What is this picture about?' Most important, we are teaching children the letters of their names. Show them M for McDonald's. Show them letters for the traffic signs, "R" for right, show "L" for left. Show them that a book has a title, author, illustrator. Let them get used to it. Then when they grows up they will be used to it and they will read with their own children."

When she ends the workshop Miss Pilar receives applause, and I feel the sleeping giant that is Highbridge stir ever so slightly.

Nathan

Just as I embrace the all-important business of preparing the Extravaganzas, the Castle Hill center receives another undiagnosed autistic boy. Assigned to Miss Lisa and Miss Masaya, Nathan is a white child; curly-haired and the most heavily muscled four-year-old child I've ever seen. Like Oliver, Nathan is left to roam around the classroom, where he chatters constantly to himself.

I am getting used to little meteors orbiting the classroom. One day, however, there is a collision in space. Nathan comes up behind me while I'm seated in front of the class, wearing my guitar. With what may have been a wooden maracà or a building block, he strikes the back of my head.

"Ow! I cry, hands flying from my strings.

I hear Nathan's monologue buzzing behind me, and suddenly the teachers are on their feet.

"Fill out a report!" they tell me. "Speak to Miss Catalina. Tell her what you see here. Tell her the way it is. We try to tell her but she don't listen to us!"

Miss Catalina sits across the desk from where I am filling out an incident report. Her chin rests on her fingers as she listens stiffly to my account. Despite her skeptical expression, I go to bat for the teachers and invoke her *cause celebre*. "How can we rehearse the children for the Extravaganzas if we have to worry about a random classroom attack?"

I remind Miss Catalina that Nathan is a large, husky child who becomes violent at times. The teachers are not qualified to deal with this kind of problem. After I've made my case, Miss Catalina says that yes, of course she has spoken to the family about getting a diagnosis for Nathan, but that they always refuse to do so. "They're in denial about his condition. Here, of course, we are aware that he doesn't communicate normally, but did you know that Nathan has computer skills that far exceed his age level? He can type and they tell me that when he types on the computer he writes in full sentences."

"Wow, that's extraordinary!" I say.

"So, in the meantime..." she shrugs a little too brightly, "What can we do? We keep him here with us. He has to be somewhere."

"But he could hurt somebody," I counter. "He could hurt one of the children or a teacher. He's already hurt someone," I say, rubbing the back of my head.

"I'll look into it," she says crisply. I wonder, who else besides Nathan's parents might be in denial?

"But you're not giving the children what they need!" Her bogus accusation against me hangs off my tongue like a ripe plum as we rise from our chairs. Or: "Now whose being deficient?" I'd lip back—if it wouldn't cost me my livelihood.

I assume it's the stress from such an eventful day when I succumb to a migraine in the middle of my final class. In Miss Alison's and Miss Priscilla's classroom, that now contains the demanding little Tenacia, I gradually realize that a swirling, brown paisley, like the scales of a water moccasin, is engulfing more and more of my field of vision. It's not safe. I could fall over the children as they move in and out of my blind spot.

"Quick, every body on the rug!"

I telescope down to the floor and the curious children cluster in a circle around me. From my knees, I finish leading our song as sparks and spectrums of color shimmer across the ceiling like ribbons of the northern lights or the flashing marquees of Times Square. Ooh, it's trippy, man! Who needs psychedelics when you can just have a migraine?

That night I tell Mark and the boys the whole story.

"The teachers say that Head Start gets extra money for holding onto children with special needs like Nathan. They think that that's why Miss Catalina ignores the teacher's complaints. It's really so unfair to them."

"It's unfair to everybody. A child like that doesn't belong there. It's not safe for any of you," says Mark with annoyance. "Your head's already paying the price."

"I know, babe. I mean, supposedly they screen for these things—oh, but did I tell you that Miss Catalina says he can actually type in full sentences on the computer? I find that amazing."

"What does Nathan write when he types on the computer?" Haskell wonders.

"Interesting question," says Mark and it is indeed. I'm embarrassed that I hadn't thought to ask it.

Even classrooms comprised of "normal" children can be hazardous places.

In fact, my first incident report had not involved Nathan, Oliver, John Christopher, or even Tenacia, but had occurred in the weeks of early fall when I first came to Marble Hill. As a mother I should have known that the air space behind a restless child, even a child seated in your lap, can be a danger zone.

A wiggly kid who's bent forward may impulsively whip his head upright turning his skull into a wrecking ball as it meets your jaw. And this is what happened to me when, trying to help the class to join hands in a circle, I crouched too close behind Jing, a Chinese boy who attended Room One in the afternoon. When the boy laughed, he threw back his rather large, round head. It hit my chin; I got a mouthful of blood and was lucky to escape with all my teeth.

In Miss Gracia's and Miss Felipa's afternoon class at Our Lady of Miracles, I had not been attacked, but was kept busy protecting the other children from a wrathful John Christopher. He was always ready to grab things out of his classmate's hands and push them to the floor. As with Nathan, the family refuses to accept the teachers' recommendation that John Christopher get a professional evaluation.

Martin Luther King Day

On my next visit to St. Anthony's I will not have to worry about getting head-butted in a classroom or even heavily critiqued by Miss Catalina, because it is a special day. With songs, slogans, and adoration for a savior, Martin Luther King Day in the Bronx is a kind of second Christmas. On the morning of the holiday assembly I arrive early enough to review my notes for the show over breakfast. At my new harbor of fast food on Castle Hill Avenue, the scrambled egg combo I order comes with a patty of hash browns the size and shape of a baby's foot and entitles me to endless refills of coffee.

Unlike at Halloween, the teachers now give me a thorough heads-up as to what numbers each class will present. The compound of St. Anthony's sits on approximately an acre of land and encompasses a cluster of separate buildings. Today I am to meet my teachers and children in a large auditorium at the back of the grammar school, a building half a block from where I teach and just to the right of the great Cathedral.

Backstage with my guitar I peek from the wings as noisy families fill the aisles and administrators boom amplified introductions over the P.A. Born in 1960, I was about the same age as our preschoolers when Dr. King led his historic march over the bridge at Selma. For this occasion I planned songs that would invoke the Civil Rights era, such as "We shall Overcome" and the old union anthem "I Shall Not Be Moved."

Instead, the teachers prepared simple, babyish carols, setting new words to old nursery chestnuts such as "The Bear Went Over The Mountain" and "Twinkle, Twinkle, Little Star" —such as "We're-Black-and-White-and-all-are-free-for-Martin-Lu-ther-King" as sung to the tune of "Mary Had a Little Lamb." That encore was rehearsed by all the classrooms.

I am not especially nervous as the program begins. My musical contribution is almost shamefully simple, and I am confident that nobody will accuse me of falling short of my job description, as happened last October. Still, for some reason, I feel hollow and unlike myself.

I will not understand why that should be until the echo of the final applause has dissipated, and back at the preschool building I must crawl onto the cold bathroom floor of the staffroom. Hidden behind the solid, wooden door I loosen my collar and close my eyes. Once again, trails and auras of a migraine trickle before my vision, accompanying the slamming pressure in my head and nausea that I know to expect.

"Your headaches always seem to come on Friday." At home Mark tries to sleuth out what it is about my mornings at St. Anthony's that brings me to my knees. "What happens on Fridays that's different from the rest of the week?"

"Why is this night different from all other nights?" My mind jumps to the four questions of the Passover Seder. It occurs to me that I have, in fact, altered one element of my routine in the time since the headaches began.

"I've started eating fast food breakfast."

This unscintillating detail hardly seems worth mentioning and yet Mark jumps up to pace.

"I'm getting a hunch," he tells me.

Having a Ball

For a week in February all city public schools and Head Start centers close down for a wintry vacation. In the time away from fast food chains, long commutes and work in general, I note that my headaches disappear.

For some time Mark has been shored up at the Bobst Library, researching jobs and sending out resumes. He's even suited up and left the apartment with his briefcase for a couple of job interviews. At home all week I've been so busy with the boys that I've barely seen him.

The last day of vacation is no different. On Sunday afternoon I crowd onto the bleachers at the new YMHA on 14th Street with my neighbor Beverly to watch Haskell and her son Curtis chase a basketball up and down the court. Our sons have joined a league of seven-year-olds. The ball floats haplessly between the opposing squads, often rolling out of bounds to the shrill blast of a coach's whistle.

From behind the wall of mobile partitions that divides the gymnasium, we hear the cheers and smacking reports from a racket ball tournament on the opposite side. Then, from a tiny gap in the partitions, a stray racket ball zooms toward me, smashing into my eye like a meteor. I see a flash and then my eye socket starts to burn, cranking out torrents of water. I cover my face as goopy tears roll down my arms.

"Oh, my God, are you alright?" Beverly and others around me descend with concern. I feel their hands on my shoulders and smoothing my hair. One of them says, "Somebody should get a doctor." I hear another say, "Good thing she wasn't wearing glasses. She could have lost an eye."

"Can you see?" I'm asked. But I can't remove my drenched hands from my face. And this is just how Beverly guides me, hunched over and blinded, to the medical station.

"Watch, they'll offer you a free membership just to keep you quiet," she whispers, and squeezes my arm.

At first I am too tender to let anyone examine me. After a few minutes in the nurse's chair, I begin to see again. Or at least I can open my eye for a split second before I must clamp it shut against what feels like a salty stab of florescent light. Still, with every passing minute I can open it for longer and longer intervals.

"You're a little pale," observes the nurse.

"Probably in a mild shock," agrees Beverly—and this is true. I have low blood pressure and my vitals plunge at the slightest distress; certainly after sustaining a cannon ball.

The nurse suggests that I lie down, while Beverly heads to the gym to pick up the boys. By the time she returns with them, I have enough vision to see that Haskell and Curtis are hanging back, hovering behind Beverly, regarding me with alarm.

"Do I look that bad?" I ask Beverly as she helps me into my coat and winds a scarf around my neck. "Am I that scary?"

"What, more trouble?"

At home Mark jokes that he's afraid to let me out of his sight. Later that night he helps me craft a letter to the administrators of the Y informing them of what happened and recommending that they take greater precautions to protect their guests and members.

A week later a tepid apology arrives by mail with no offers of compensation or any gifts of membership. "So sorry. People sitting on our bleachers get struck in the eye with speeding racket balls. Oh well. Better luck next time, shit happens." It might as well have been penned by Miss Antonette, and referring to bounced paychecks.

In reality she isn't quite that inhuman. When I return to work on Monday morning she is so consumed with trying to comfort a little girl in Room One that she barely notices my bruised face.

As I encounter them in the hallway the child recognizes me and tries desperately to tell me something. "But the bad people took my bathing suit through the window," she wails.

"Come on, Gabby, go and wash your hands for breakfast." Ms. Antonette gently prods the child in the direction of her classroom. "Her home got robbed," she confides in a whisper to me.

At the end of the morning I sit visiting with Miss Antonette while Mr. Felix finishes mopping the staffroom. Mr. Felix—doesn't he belong at St. Anthony's?

I learn from Miss Antonette that the two janitors, Mr. Felix and Mr. Justin, have switched centers in some kind of do-si-do. Apparently from time to time

Head Start will switch two employees, giving them the "opportunity" to work at a different center. Sometimes these changes work to the advantage of a teacher or janitor, bringing them closer to home and shortening their commute. Sometimes the change creates burdens.

In either event, the reassignments are mandatory. She says that switches like this are as random as the weather, but I feel certain that Miss Catalina had her malevolent hand in this one. She always looks so pained when she sticks her nose into the staffroom and finds high spirits and laughter. I recall how she'd narrow her eyes when she came upon the Felix and Priscilla show. Wouldn't it be just like her to cast asunder that dynamic duo?

I wave to Mr. Felix, and he waves back, with a double-take. He's probably seen the black eye I tried so hard to cover with make-up foundation this morning, and he seems a bit embarrassed.

The classes today were difficult. Not all the children had patience for the turn-taking required for the game we played, and I emerge from the classroom in a daze.

"A penny for your thoughts, Miss Leah," Miss Antonette asks as I collapse in her office before the cooks wheel out their dollies of lunch trays.

"Oh, I guess I was noticing that some of the children are much more respectful and cooperative than others," I say. To this she nods thoughtfully.

"Some of that is because the families of these children are from different cultures."

"Am I allowed to ask where the families of the better behaved children are from?"

"Why not?" she replies. "I can tell you that Mexican and also Chinese families raise their kids with tremendous respect for parents, for grandparents, and teachers. We see this here in the classroom all the time. Some other cultures..." She smiles. "We do find we have more difficulties with those children."

In Miss Gracia's and Miss Felipa's room at Our Lady of Miracles, little Lily Fuentes sits in the middle of the floor and lights up the whole room with her smiles and laughter. When I walk in after winter break with my black eye she cries out, "Pikachu, Pikachu!"

Clearly, she recognizes this character on the big red and yellow shopping bag that my sons brought home from the Pokémon store, which I now use to carry my school supplies. Lily never addressed me by name before and now I am "Pikachu." I can see we've made a connection.

Happily, Head Start is not prissy about letting me sing theme songs from popular children's television shows. Some private schools discourage use of music from T.V. and other media in the classroom. But I see no harm; in fact I believe this kind of music can be valuable. Singing a song that everybody recognizes from popular culture teaches kids an active relationship to the music that they've heard, that even a dumb, catchy jingle from TV is theirs to sing along with, perhaps even to make up their own lyrics to as I do with the boys at home.

Thanks to the relaxed policy at Head Start, I am able to oblige the children's requests and we can sing the theme songs from Scooby Doo, Sesame Street, Blues Clues, and Clifford the Big Red Dog. Kids love dancing to the ominous theme from Spiderman, and they will willingly sing along with the syrupy "I love you, you love me" from Barney when we say our goodbyes. Inspired by Lily, I bring the Pokémon theme song to my other classes. It has all the elements of a stirring bluegrass anthem. I keep reminding myself to try it at home with the banjo.

In the afternoon I return from my lunch nook to find the office full of mothers. Another community workshop is in session. Today the subject is domestic abuse.

Brenda Keenan smiles as I appear in the doorway, but a woman I don't recognize addresses the group.

"Ladies," she says, "You know, sex should be something pleasurable." She tells the women that something is wrong if sex is forced upon them roughly or if they feel coerced, and informs them of services—telephone hot lines, shelters, and counseling, and urges the women never to suffer in silence.

One mother recalls being molested as a child when a friend of her family crept through her bedroom window. She hasn't felt able to speak up because to this day she is afraid of the violent fallout that would result from her confession.

I hover outside the office as some women turn around to regard me with curiosity. What can they make of my attending a workshop on domestic abuse with a fresh black eye?

I begin to realize that even those who have heard my story about the racket ball probably don't believe it.

"Is everything alright at home?" At the end of the workshop, Brenda Keenan comes up beside me. "Is your husband still out of work?" She links her arm in mine. "Be careful, Leah. It's very easy for unemployed men to fall apart."

By the end of the day, all the furtive glances from teachers and mothers attending the workshop practically convince me that the accident in the Y gymnasium never happened—and that Mark is, in fact, responsible for my shiner.

I am relieved that within two days my black eye subsides, and I can shed the dark glasses I started hiding behind. By Friday morning in the staffroom nobody notices anything. But I notice Miss Priscilla, in the wake of her dynamic duo. Now Mr. Justin reads quietly where my puppet show used to be.

"I see you've met our new janitor," she says, sliding past me. "Don't worry, Justin. We're not that embarrassing. Are we?" She teases Mr. Justin who smiles and shakes his head, continuing to read his paperback.

Miss Priscilla jokes and smiles bravely, but the disappointment in her large, round eyes tells a different story. "Yes, I am a broken-hearted person," she says at last, pledging a dramatic hand to her heart when somebody mentions Mr. Felix. "But tomorrow I'll go to Macy's and forget all about it."

And then she changes the subject. "Oh, look at that pretty wool! Are you a knitter, Miss Leah?" Over the vacation I began knitting a sweater and she caught sight of the needles poking out from the top of my bag.

"Well," I tell her, "I'm a clumsy knitter. My boys distract me and I miss a lot of stitches."

"Did you know that Miss Julissa also knits? Oh, she makes such beautiful sweaters and blankets for the troops and sends them overseas! Show us what you are making, Miss Leah."

I'm not ready to oblige. What I haven't told her is that my dyslexia wreaks havoc on my ability to count stitches. I'm self-taught and my rows will not be neat and impressive like the ones in Miss Julissa's blankets. The last time I tried to knit a sock, Mark told me that it looked like it had a thumb.

Before lunch I open the door to Miss Salomé's classroom and am happy to find that we Miss Regina remains with us.

Immediately she waves me to come over. With a jerk of her head she draws my attention to where a kind of spooky child, Ophelia, crawls across the floor making cat noises.

"She pulls out her eyebrows, every single hair," Miss Regina whispers through the side of her mouth. I would later learn that this behavior is symptomatic of Trichotillomania, a hair-pulling disorder that may be triggered by depression or stress.

But at the time I didn't counter Miss Regina when she concluded: "She don't belong here. What's going on I don't know, but this I could tell you... she got issues that aren't being addressed."

Laryngitis On Rye

With sick days and personal days at their disposal it's amazing how fragile staff can become—and without them how very hardy we consultants have to be.

After missing a whole work week to jury duty, I am determined that nothing else keep me from my billable appointed rounds. In past months I had intrepidly managed blizzards of frozen, horizontal rain and long subway delays. I am bionic. I have sung and made merry through pending colds, allergies, cramps, migraines and any number of garden-variety sore throats. In the end it wasn't anything I "had," but rather what I lost that threatened to bring me down.

One Highbridge Tuesday morning my poor chafed vocal cords give out entirely. I wake up with a case of laryngitis so severe that I can barely think words, much less speak them. I feel like acres of fiberglass insulation are pushed between my throat and windpipes. How am I going to pull off my six classes when I can't even whisper prompts to a teacher? I'll come up with something. I'll have to! Staying at home today would cost me almost two hundred dollars so I am on my 6:50 subway train from the Astor Place station, the same as every Tuesday morning.

As my Number 4 Train rockets through the dark tunnels up to 161st street I anxiously try to wring some kind of shtick or gimmick from my affliction that can carry the day. Mercifully I don't have to squirm for long. Inspiration strikes me on the line at the deli where I wait to buy my egg salad sandwich. When it is my turn, I have no voice to place an order so I pantomime my desires to the guy behind the counter. I point to the basin of egg salad, miming spreading it with one hand onto the other. For a flourish I lick my lips and the aproned deli worker cracks up. When he reaches for the white bread I begin shaking my head, gesturing "no" as if my very life depends on it and exaggeratedly mouthing, "rye-rye-rye bread!"

My silent ardor elicits giggles from the customers in back of me. It dawns on me that I may be able to spin this egg salad into gold once I'm up the hill. For if I can make a line of tired office workers laugh before they've had their morning coffee, then surely I can bring the children into the game. All my life I've been told that breakfast is the most important meal of the day, and never has it been more so than now.

OPEN SHUT THEM

As hoped, miming everybody's favorite songs turns out to be a winner. The teachers are supportive, and the children are up for all the guessing games and charades I can throw at them. And if my voice is useless, thankfully my fingers are not. With the guitar ringing out to guide them the children are actually singing out boldly, and I find that activities such as "Open Shut Them" adapt surprisingly well to being led by a mute.

Next I try omitting the words altogether, and perform only the gestures, encouraging the children to do the same. The class loves the precision we achieve when we all clap our hands together, and smack our thighs while only mouthing the words. This is the version of "Open Shut Them" that I now call "The Quiet One." Once your class is familiar with "Open Shut Them," try this variation.

Open Shut Them

Public Domain

To complete the first two classes I have had to hang, minute-to-minute by my wits, but once I coast into the safe bay of Miss Magdalena's room I know that I can finally relax. As soon as she recognizes the problem, my resourceful friend grabs her tambourine and knows exactly what to do. I hold down the chords while in her lovely contralto she leads us through "*La Bamba,*" "*Des Colores*" "*Eres Tu*" and now that she's learned it from me, "*Mi Cuerpo Hace Musica.*"

Having perfected my mimed version of Old MacDonald in the previous class, I was just taking over the action when disaster strikes. The classroom door groans open to admit Miss Bilkis like a draft of cold air. For a few minutes she stands in the back of the room, her face inscrutable behind the windshield of her oversized glasses, her folded arms supported by the shelf of her gargantuan bust —but my heart had already sunk. Even though the children are laughing and having fun guessing the animals I pantomime for them, the old bulldog simply cannot manage the mental leap needed to account for the game we were playing, and why.

"What ch'oo doing?" she finally interrupts. I point at my throat and Miss Magdalena steps in bravely.

"Miss Leah has lost her voice so we're having a different kind of music class today," she explains. The stubborn woman shakes her head, "No."

"She has to sing," she announces flatly. And then to me in a snide tone: "You have to sing. How you gonna give them music if you don't sing?"

In the face of her mule-like stupidity it is probably a good thing that I don't have a voice. If I had a voice I might call her a gorilla in a cardigan or a knuckle-dragging primitive and tell her that she deserves her own panorama beside the other phases of "early man" on display at the Museum of Natural History.

Between her and Miss Catalina, I am fed up with having anti-epiphanal administrators skulking around the hallways and barging in to sabotage whatever life and ingenuity I bring to their classrooms. Without my voice I am safely muzzled, no need to apologize for my private thoughts, no matter how vicious.

I do have to contend with Miss Magdalena, who gazes at me helplessly. There is nothing else to do except to strain something out to satisfy the doltish supervisor, with her oversized specs that give her face all the emotional range of the cab of a garbage truck. I choose the ABC's hoping the kids can chime in and overpower me. Unfortunately, the children have picked up on the tension in the room and are subdued.

It is almost the end of my first set of classes so I won't have to croak for much longer. Still, by the time Miss. Bilkis lets herself out of the classroom, all the golden magic spun that morning has reverted back into just half an egg salad sandwich. I have no idea how I will get through the afternoon, but at least there would be something to eat for lunch.

There is an empty chair to inquire about at Our Lady of Miracles. Once I regain my voice I remember to ask Miss Magdalena why I haven't seen Nabid in her classroom. She nods slowly to my question.

"Pilar!" she calls indicating that the other should lead the class. She takes me to the corner to whisper that there has been a terrible accident; in their kitchen at home Nabid's mother had spilled boiling water from the microwave over his neck and shoulders, burning him so badly that he remains in the hospital. With a sad face Miss Magdalena tells me that it is unknown whether he will return to school at all this year. We clasp our hands and she brings them to her lips, shaking her head. It will be hard to go back to the group knowing that it no longer includes the shining eyes of one of the sweetest children I've ever met. His lovely smile; would we ever see it again?

Broken Guitar

"Gimme a blueberry muffin, toasted wi'd butter and tell Siro don't burn it!"

Trusting Mark's hypothesis about fast food and migraines, on Fridays I now eat my breakfast at the Castle Hill Diner, an old-fashioned dining car that sits across the street from St. Anthony's Cathedral. It is restful here. Shored up in my cozy booth, I can hypnotize myself watching the flow of traffic outside the window as two young Greek waitresses, Lena and Laurie—sisters—serve me. I hear other orders relayed to the kitchen as I spread out my usual picnic of coffee, ideas for my classes, and my newspaper.

My new surroundings are quiet and pleasant but, in spite of all the coffee I've consumed, I'm still tired. And worse yet, I'm simply not in the mood for it all today. I want to put my head down on the tabletop and close my eyes. But I can't be late for my first two classes on the second floor of the nursery school. Gadzooks! When did the time slip out from under me like a surfboard bucking me backwards into the deep? One minute I am sitting at my leisure, and then suddenly I must throw myself together like the Jews fleeing Egypt.

I hurriedly call for my check and throw everything—my notes, my newspaper—into the plastic bag that holds my school supplies. I wave to the girls as I push my way through the heavy glass door. But in my haste I have not settled my guitar case properly on my shoulder. As I struggle with the door, the case slips off my shoulder. Before I can wheel around to break its fall, my guitar slides down my back and hits the floor with a loud, terrible crack like a human bone snapping in two. In my shock I drop the plastic bag I was pinching in my fingers spilling everything that it held; my notes, silk scarves and stuffed animals land face down in a puddle of orange juice. My *New York Post* flops out, scattering itself everywhere as Sally Brompton's voice resounds from the horoscope page: "Today be especially careful with your personal property!"

All morning as I teach my classes the crack on the top of my guitar stares back at me.

Oh, my poor green guitar. Will it have to be repaired? How much will it cost? Will I have to buy a new one?

But even the terrible fresh gash gets sidelined as I find other patients at home must be stabilized. It is no sharp crack like the guitar hitting the floor but rather a dull blow and such a *deja vu* when Mark shows me the batch of our recently written checks flagged for uncollected funds and the same pox of overdraft notices spring to the cheeks of our account. Clearly another over-drawn, humiliating weekend lies ahead. But this time it is all too obvious who the culprit might be. This time we know who stole the tarts.

"Yeah, yeah, yeah, I know. Just send on all the paperwork. This is really bad." When I reach her on Monday morning, Brenda Keenan is just as fed up and as vexed as we are. "We'll take care of it as soon as we can" she promises. "I honestly don't know why this keeps happening, Leah. We're terribly sorry."

Newspaper headlines back then were indeed full of lawsuits against abusive priests and long-hidden accounts of clerical pedophilia. Could it be that the coffers of the Archdiocese where truly tapped out and that they had to dig into the Music consultant's last pay period to settle their latest molestation charges?

Or was it entirely something else?

Whatever the case, this time I am not planning to say a word about it to

Miss Antonette. We have been getting along, and I don't want to have to start resenting her all over again. But Mark, Brenda Keenan and I were all left with the same fishy feeling.

With my bank account, my guitar, and my life in general feeling splintered in spite of the cost, I return to upper Broadway for the comfort of a hot lunch. Although I was there for breakfast, I am in need of another hit of my Nicky and The Land and The Sea Restaurant where I can always be sure of a big hug just for walking through his door.

Back in the staffroom I find a subdued Mr. Felix hunched over a sketchbook with a Rapidograph pen. When I admire the skulls, roses, and intricate paisleys he draws without taking his eyes from the page, he tells me that he is studying to become a tattoo artist. Clearly he misses Miss Priscilla and all the lively companionship back at St. Anthony's. His days of sitting alone in his blue jump-suit at Marble Hill will be numbered; he wants out.

I am barely able to face the top of my guitar. That morning had seemed like a perfect time to just leave it zipped in its case like a body bag and to debut a new children's game I had learned from Ananda. She calls it "Whiz" and it involves timing a group of kids as they pass an object hand-to-hand around a circle. The idea is to do it again and again, the process getting smoother with each repetition so that the thing goes faster and faster creating a new "personal best" for the group every time. Whiz! As with many of my Ananda-derived activities, the children and teachers in both rooms enjoy it so much that I decide to make it the centerpiece of all my classes for the rest of the week. After we rehearse for the Extravaganzas of course...we will have Whiz for dessert, with some Go Bananas and Stuffed Animal Tally Ho on the side.

WHIZ

This is Ananda's variation on a passing game I grew up with called HOT POTATO. To play WHIZ, sit in a circle with a group of children on the floor. Show the children an object, such as a small doll or stuffed animal. Almost anything can be used so long as it's safe for children—neither sharp and pointy, nor too heavy. Ananda reccommends not using a ball, as children will want to throw a ball. Tell everybody that we're going to play a new game called WHIZ. Explain that the object

---

of the game is to pass the doll, bear, pillow, from one child to the next and send it all the way around the circle. Next, show them a timepiece with a second hand. It could be your wristwatch or a clock on the wall. Explain that you're going to say "Ready, set, go" and you're going to use the clock to tell how long it takes for the object to get passed around the circle. Tell the group to go as fast as they can. Say, "Make it go WHIZ, WHIZ, WHIZ around the circle and back to me!"

Passing the object to their neighbor is not as easy as it sounds. Some kids will become shy or stunned when the object is thrust into their hand or appears in their lap. Others will become excited and throw the object carelessly out of order or out of the circle all together—so don't be surprised if it takes a couple of trial rounds before your object can complete the circle. When the group first achieves this, hold up your "hot potato" for all to see and cheer "Yeah, we did it! Now let's see how long it took us." If you lost track of the clock then just make it up; who's to know? Let's say you're clocking your first run around the circle at 35 seconds. If the group is enjoying themselves than ask them to try it again. Challenge them with, "Let's see if we can do it even faster!" Your group may be excited to learn how many seconds they can shave off their "personal best" once everybody gets the hang of it.

Still having fun? Try taking WHIZ to the next level by presenting new ways to pass the object. For example, you might ask the kids to sit with their legs bent in front of them and pass the object under their knees. Try having the kids pass the object behind their back, or with their eyes closed for a real challenge!

GO BANANAS

This variation evolved as I discovered that a plastic banana from the classroom kitchen made an excellent object for WHIZ. Acquire two bananas and you're ready to go. As with WHIZ, sit your class in a circle with you on the floor. Only this time say that "Go Bananas" is the name of the game, and hold up your two bananas—one in each hand for all to see. Tell the gang that when you say, "Ready, set, go" you're going to pass both bananas, one to the right and one to the left, at the same time. At some point in their journey both bananas are going to arrive at the same child, let's say this child's name is Brian. As this occurs have lucky Brian show off his bananas while you lead a chant of "Brian's gone Bananas! Brian's gone bananas!" or "Malika's gone Bananas!" One or two rounds of this may suffice for some groups. For others, you may have to engineer a way for everybody to "go bananas!"

STUFFED ANIMAL TALLY HO!

Ananda also advised me to visit other preschools where I might get inspired by watching different teachers. From a preschool in my own neighborhood I picked up this lively stuffed animal chase, which—if well timed—can produce more excitement than "WHIZ" and "Go Bananas" put together!

This is another activity for a circle of children on the floor with you. With Tally Ho the main event happens to be two stuffed animals that are going to chase each other. It could be a dog and a cat or a cat and a mouse, but any pair will do so long as you can construct a compelling little scenario so everybody knows who's chasing who and why. You might invite the children to make up the story with you. You could ask them why the dog wants to chase the cat, or talk about how the cat wants to catch the bird. You should be holding the animal that's going to do the chasing. The second animal should begin it's journey on the opposite side of the circle from you, preferably in the hands of a second teacher or at least a child who understands the instruction. With the usual send off, "On Your mark, get set, GO!" both animals are passed from hand to hand in the same direction. The adventure is to see if animal one can encroach on animal two before completing its round. This game can be played even if two stuffed animals can't be found. In one class where there was only a squirrel to work with, a small brown bean bag became the "acorn" that ran away from the hungry squirrel.

On Tuesday as my bus whines upward, I look to the left and try to follow the savage drop of the woods that seems to melt beneath us as we rise. Through the bare branches I notice a small row of houses which I've never seen before, perched like eagles on the side of the bluff. Who lived there? Were they abandoned, which would not be atypical in Plankety Plank, or were these places now shelter to squatters, or animals or some kind of Highbridge hobbits?

By the afternoon, In Miss Magdalena's and Miss Pilar's room I am troubled by the fresh bruising on Roberto's temples. We are all on the floor, giggling through the clumsy excitement of our first round of Whiz! in the circle, Roberto sits just two heads away from me. Clearly, a blow to the head caused the purple and yellow tattoos above his laughing eyes. I'm not sure what to do.

Although employed at Head Start, I am not yet required to undergo the procedure to become a "mandated reporter" as I would be for my subsequent jobs. As part of that training I would be made to examine ghoulish diagrams like those of the marks left by an adult's hand crushing a child's gullet and quizzed on my ability to spot these and other telltale signs of abuse.

"What's up with Roberto?" I take the excuse of having to retrieve one of my plastic bananas from where it's been flung from our circle to confer with Miss Pilar. She tells me that this bruise is nothing—last fall they saw Roberto come to school with a black eye. Now I remember that, not so long ago, I came to this classroom sporting a black eye, which, in my case, was not the result of abuse at home. So what kind of story was written on the side of this child's head? Possibly the bruises, as well as his black eye, were only the expected products of the rough and tumble life of any little boy. Or were they the result of some criminal neglect, or the calling card of his stepfather's knuckles?

I'm concerned, but I don't harbor illusions of stepping into the fray like a hero. I don't know this community, but I do know that even good intentions can sometimes backfire. I worry that Roberto's parents might withdraw him from Head Start if they feel overly scrutinized. I certainly don't want to make anything worse for this kid. For all the good done by A.C.S. and other agencies, I have also heard horror stories, tales of botched interventions that lead to children getting placed in foster care that's at least as bad as the environment from which they were removed.

Ideally, this would be an occasion to enlist the expertise of a supervisor, but the teachers regard involving Miss Bilkis as a lost cause. "Oh, she's aware of him," they tell me. "But what do she care? She don't want no paper work. She don't want no headaches." This isn't the first time I've heard the teachers render this kind of judgment.

As I fetch the plastic banana from beneath a chair, Miss Pilar turns back to Roberto who is sitting with the others, eagerly awaiting another round of the game.

"What's happened to you, Roberto?" she asks him. "Is somebody hitting you at your house?" Miss Pilar cups his chin in her hands tilting his face toward her so she can examine it.

"Tell the truth, Poppy. Don't be afraid," urges Miss Magdalena.

But Roberto has nothing to say, and wants to keep playing Whiz.

Blood Money

By Friday morning at the Castle Hill Diner, in spite of Laurie and Lena's blunt reprimands, Siro, the cook, continues to have a heavy hand with his griddle. The 'toasted' blueberry muffin I order arrives looking like a plated charcoal briquette. I send it back with one of the sisters telling her, "I think this steak is overdone." Without my asking, she brings me a slice of apple pie fresh from the glass display stand. I'm not fancy. Beneath a garland of Ready Whip its slimy filling and cardboard crust taste delicious, more than compensating for my botched first choice. The waitress returns to refresh my coffee and lingers to see me devouring mouthfuls of her pie with apparent satisfaction.

"See, everything's okay here so long as he don't have nothing to do wit' it," she remarks. I can't tell if she's making a joke.

As this is the morning that the children present their Spring Assembly I don't have to go trooping all the way back to the preschool as I normally would. Once I finish my breakfast I can proceed directly to the Auditorium, where just last month we had our Martin Luther King Day program, and wait backstage for my classes to arrive.

For their show, the teachers prepared the usual little verses about bunnies and birdies and flowers for the children, not so much to sing as to incant. As a finale, a tuneless "You Are My Sunshine," chorused by all, overpowers my lone and now fractured guitar. I watch parents squint into camcorders, recording the event as younger siblings wiggle and chatter and babies cry. My workload is light today. After performing, the children rejoin their families and return home. Before my weekend begins, I must stop by the preschool and complete my paperwork.

"You are my sunshine," I hum to myself as I zip away my guitar unnoticed in the hubbub of the reuniting families. The last time I was here I had the first symptoms of a migraine bearing down on me and still faced a string of classes. Today I have no headache, and I am not responsible for any more music. Perhaps it really is the beginning of spring! I feel lighthearted, even giddy, with the sun breaking through the clouds outside and this unexpected bonus of a shorter day. With all families leaving, there are no children for me to help shepherd back around the corner. For this reason, when the violence breaks out I have already left the building.

At the main office as I pull a blank consultant's form and exit report from the file cabinet, the angry crowd pours in from the hallway. Families stream past the front desk and descend upon Miss Catalina's cubicle with children screaming and everybody yelling at once. One of the panicked secretaries sends me to the staffroom to enlist Mr. Justin for help. He is at his usual station, reading. He clearly hears the commotion from down the hall but, when I make my request ,he does not respond. His nose behind the paperback, he slowly shakes his head. "They'll say I touched 'em," he says deliberately. "They'll say I manhandled 'em and then who gets in big trouble? Me. No sir, no thank you. I'll be right here. I'm sitting this one out."

Returning to the office, I watch the proceedings from the edge of the crowd. Above the mayhem soars Miss Catalina's hysterical voice as I'd never heard it before, repeating in her stilted accent: "I wheel handle this! I wheel handle this! I am the sup-er-vis-or!" Her desperate call for order is so thoroughly overpowered by the mob that I almost feel badly for her.

"Aye Carumba! Can you believe what's going on?" Back in the staffroom Miss Priscilla's bulbous eyes are as round as dinner plates. According to her it all began when one child found a dollar bill on the auditorium floor. Another child claimed it as his own, and in no time a dispute broke out between the parents. Apparently one mother rode over the other mother's foot with the wheels of her stroller. As their stunned children looked on, the brawl escalated: the two women flogged each other with umbrellas.

"It was over a dollar!" repeated Miss Priscilla looking incredulous. "It's just blood money, you know? All this over a stinking dollar bill!" she said, shaking her head sadly.

Since I can do nothing to alleviate this disturbing situation, I decide to go home. I expect that it will take special effort to round up Mark and the boys, and I don't want us to be late for a party that an old friend is hosting for me on the Upper West Side. It will be the evening of my forty-third birthday.

Spring Has Sprung, The Grass Has Ris

I Wonder Where The Flowers Is?

Tunneling between subway station and classroom, I have only fleeting contact with the natural world. Still, the first caress of spring is unmistakable. It first hits my nose—that blast of salt, both hopeful and nostalgic, from New York's countless waterways. Nutty minerals rise from the unbuckling earth beneath melting snow. As pea-green leaves unfurl, even the pollution smells sweet. Small but defiant purple and yellow crocuses appear in tree pits of the sidewalks. Robins and sparrows swoop and chatter. Dogs feel the change. They smile and wag their tales. In Tompkins Square Park squirrels give frenzied chase to one another through the still bare branches, sometimes dropping right out of the trees in their thrall of mating and attraction. Even in the dull interiors of Marble Hill Head Start, love is in the air where things are clearly deepening between Miss Antonette and her Lone Star heart surgeon. In a saccharine voice she coos on the phone and I overhear that she will be flying to Texas for the week of spring vacation.

Already the children's cubbies are less choked with all the bulky winter wear that they stuffed there for months. Spring even appears in their artwork. In an afternoon class in Room Two a child who is usually withdrawn hands me a painting. "Well, thank you, Sean," I say holding it up to study.

"This is me walking in the flowers," he explains. "Smell it, Miss Leah!"

"Okay," I sniff.

"Do you see, it smells like juice!" he cries.

"Okay," I nod.

"Yes, Miss Leah. The strawberries smell sweet, and the feet will smell good if the socks are clean."

Almost immediately, another damp piece of paper arrives in my hands.

"Look! I made eyebrows, a bunny, and quicker," announces another young artist.

Even reluctant Highbridge begins to yield to brighter days. As I was hired in the fall, I had never before seen the harsh confrontations of Plankety Plank softened by spring buds and blossoms on the steep lines of the hill. And yet it's still winter upstairs in the drafty office of Our Lady of Miracles Two. Shivering at our desks from across the narrow room, Miss Inez and I commiserate as usual. But I haven't seen Miss Lucy all morning. The week before she had not looked well and it wouldn't surprise me to learn that our shadowy chill had put her over the edge with a flu.

Sadly, I learn that our clammy little office is not the problem. Over the weekend Miss Lucy lost her daughter to cancer. I hear it from Miss Magdalena when I'm there for my last class. "It's a terrible thing to loose your baby. There's nothing worse," she sighs.

Instantly my eyes brim, and I must look away. On my way home I am still thinking about poor Miss Lucy when the Number 4 Train gets taken out of service. A loudspeaker informs us passengers to leave our train at 149th Street. A disabled train is blocking the tracks, requiring that we transfer to a whole different line by walking through the tunnel that leads to the Number 2 Train. Naturally, this happens on a day when the first train is particularly crowded.

At the next station we displaced commuters fill the stairs and passageways. But when we arrive on the 2 Train's platform we find it already choked with bodies, from end to end. Confusion, mayhem: What are we to do if this subway line suffers its own set of delays? Gingerly we insert ourselves, further bloating the crowd that had been there to begin with.

I don't like crowds. Suddenly I've had enough of being squeezed tighter and tighter, feeling shoes and jackets and breath and flesh pressing in on me from every direction. I decide that remaining below is simply too hazardous. Time to bail out to the street. I'll cut my losses and wait out the congestion on the Grand Concourse. I'll call the *Pukulan* school and tell them that I'll be late. It shouldn't create a problem. Surely Sam and Karen Duffy won't mind looking after my boys.

I about-face, attempting to wend my way back toward the exit sign—except that I can't move. Apparently the Number 4 Trains are still dumping their passengers like landfill. At that moment yet another wave of arrivals streams in, pouring itself onto our mass of bodies and sending toes balancing ever closer to the edge of the tracks. A surge from the crowd could easily skim any number of us into the path of an oncoming train. I am stuck here, crushed, can't escape to the street or move an inch to either side. On my back my guitar bears down, almost tipping me forward.

I am trapped in a great crowd that is fast outgrowing our confined space. We recognize the danger. Somehow, the more there are of us, the quieter we become. The walls close in around us and everybody tries to breathe and not panic. It is so quiet that the click from a scruffy teenage boy who stands a few shoulders to my right thumbing his cigarette lighter on and off can be heard plainly. Like the cocking of a pistol in the crawling silence, it echoes off the arch of ceramic tiles that looms above us. Through the bramble of limbs I have a view of the tiny flame jumping up and disappearing under his thumb as he pans the crowd in either direction, daring us to respond with a testy sneer.

The platform hosts a sea of flammable down jackets in all directions. If anyone were to snap, or if this psychopath should lose control of his cigarette lighter, then there will be a subway fire and we are all every last one of us going to die, right here and now. There will be a stampede. The bulk of the charging throng will block the exits, and we will be trapped on the platform and smoked like a rack of bacon. Perishing hideously beside my guitar and my bag of juggling balls is a distinct possibility. Miss Lucy and her daughter come to mind again—and strangely, I am at peace. I feel spectacular relief that my own darlings, Haskell and Simon, are not with me here. Trapped in an imperiling, squeezing crowd, I am happy that my boys are at their *Pukulan* class, belting each other in the gut and flipping each other over on the mats. They are safe. If I die beneath 149th Street, my children will live.

This thought sustains me until the empty trains start showing up, one after the other like lifeboats. I am among the bodies that wedges inside, grateful to fill the car. In the prayer I make standing as the train bucks and urges me homeward, I hear Miss Magdalena's words: "There's nothing worse than losing your baby." Again my tears fall for Miss Lucy. I would rather burn in the tunnel than go through what she endured.

On Friday morning I gather that Laurie is the shier and quieter of the two sisters who wait on me at the Castle Hill Diner. I can't be sure who it is when one of them plunks herself down on the other seat of my booth to ask, "Wanna see my pride and joy?"

"Okay." I shrug expecting to look at a picture of nieces and nephews or perhaps a littler of kittens. From her apron pocket the waitress flashes a photograph of two bottles of dishwashing liquid, the brand names of "Pride" and

"Joy" boldly displayed.

"Ha ha ha, bet you didn't see that coming!" she laughs, standing up again.

"Very funny," I tell her. This is a gag that would go over with Miss Priscilla. "I wish I had a copy for the girls in the staffroom" I say and return the picture to her.

"Dat's my Pride and Joy!" she whoops again and bounces off with it toward the kitchen, already barking orders mawkishly at Siro the cook. So this one must be Lena.

At school I am informed of a change in policy. As a result of last week's riot in the auditorium, there will be no more school-wide assemblies held at St. Anthony's. All further programs—Earth Day, Cinco de Mayo, even the Extravaganzas—will be conducted by each class separately, in each classroom. Only the families of the children in each class will attend. No more attempts to unite the entire Head Start community under one roof. The center simply cannot afford to host another violent outbreak—over a dollar bill, or anything else.

As if I am somehow implicated, Miss Catalina now frequently lets herself into the classrooms as I work, keeping taps on everyone with the air of a lofty parole officer. In addition to making me uptight, her increased surveillance presents me with another layer of difficulty: Often Miss Catalina initiates long conversations with the teachers in a phony stage whisper, and their buzzing and murmuring creates a static that undermines my focus with the kids. When I catch her eye, she will make the disingenuous gesture of cupping a hand to her mouth and continues talking as if her raised hand in any way diminishes the volume of her voice or the distraction that it causes. Other times she simply remains at the back of the room fixing me with a goony smile that never augurs well.

"You should really be down at the children's level as you work. We'd like to see you sitting in your chair," she announces one Friday.

Anyone familiar with how I work knows that I fly up and down from my seat all the time. It is just my style, who I am in the classroom. Yes, we sit and sing. But I also hold it as my sacred duty to break up the children's mostly sedentary school day with as much physical activity as I can pack into our sessions. Music and Movement—both words form the title of my position there.

"We're rehearsing the Extravaganza," I counter. "We're practicing their dance number so I must be on my feet."

"Well Miss Leah, we do find..." (always the ever-indicting "we," I note)   "... that you tend to over-stimulate the children. Are you not aware that some of our teachers complain about you?"

Her arrow meets my heart.

"Actually, I did not know that."

I spoke the truth. Last week Miss Ascension, the Peruvian teacher who come back to replace Miss Regina, apparently thought enough of me to bring an authentic "*pollo de juvio,*" a rain stick, all the way from South America for me because she remembered that I had demonstrated the drum, the banjo, and other instruments for her class.

So, who would complain about me? Miss Salomé, as hyperactive as any child, was always the first one on the floor when it was time to boogie. And I mentally inventoried the others: Miss Cresi and Miss Julissa in Room Four, Miss Alison and Miss Priscilla in Room Six; these women were all my friends! I simply don't believe her. And it wouldn't be wise to say it, but the only complaints I'd heard from the teachers were about Miss Catalina.

"Please Miss Catalina, tell me who complains about me?" I face her with my racing heart practically amplified by the sound hole of my guitar.

She closes her eyes for a moment, then smiles.

"There's no need to get defensive, Miss Leah. The general impression is that you do not lead the room with the authority and structure that young children require. When you are disorganized it sets a tone that makes the children wild and you see, that creates a problem for our teachers." She smiles again, all teeth.

The wicked Witch of Oz had her winged monkeys, and Miss Catalina had words such as "disorganized", "unprepared," and how could I forget that not long ago I was also "deficient"? The old school mistress knows how to yank my chain.

From my back pocket I seize the wad of folded notes and my lesson plan, scrawled just that morning at the Castle Hill Diner. With my hand beginning to shake, I thrust them forward but she steps aside to clear her throat. "Ohh, well. I'm sure you have many ideas for us...." she says inconclusively.

"Then you're welcome to read my exit reports." I blurt. "You'll find an explanation for everything you see me doing there."

It feels like clashing swords with a demon. First I am "deficient" for not beginning the Extravaganzas six months early. Now I am "disorganized," and supposed to work from my chair. Even through the stress it occurs to me that Miss Catalina herself may have been disciplined by the center's sponsors after the chaos at the assembly and for the mob scene that followed. Who knows? Perhaps even threats and sharp words had been bandied about by Florence Galway—whom I knew, firsthand, is most adept at finding scapegoats when they are needed. Can all this faultfinding be Miss Catalina's way of passing the latest round of accusations down the bureaucratic food chain? Why else does she have it in for me? I don't want to carry this aggravation home for the weekend, but I fear that I'm already tangled in her web. With her "disorganized" and her "unprepared," this spider has managed to bite. My anger springs like blood from the fang marks she leaves.

After my final class I walk out the door to begin the long-coveted week of spring vacation and, in my distraction, practically stride right into traffic. Am I losing my mind? Flooded with rage, I board a train on the elevated platform with no knowledge of having entered the subway system or having climbed the stairs.

The train closes its door and still I'm back at St. Anthony's, arguing my case in the classroom. I wasn't "disorganized" or "unprepared" as Miss Catalina charged. Hardly. How about: I was resourceful and passionate about bringing the children a valuable experience? Why is she out to get me? Whispering to teachers through my classes and then accusing me of not managing the room; all this baggage from a supervisor who is supposed to help me!

Just south of Whitlock Avenue where the tracks sink below street level the persistent lawyering in my head is replaced by Haskell's innocent voice: "But Mommy, why does Miss Catalina hate you?" I slump forward and cover my ears. I don't want to think about it anymore, but not even the wail of my train entering the tunnel can obliterate his question.

Over Spring Vacation one rainy day I take the boys to play at a neighbor's spacious loft. There are lots of great things for the boys to do here: bean bag chairs to wrestle on, pillows to throw.

Later the kids come up with a game that involves hitting each other over the head with two long and brightly colored, transparent plastic tubes. These hollow tubes are light as air and make a great toy for the children because they can bonk each other as hard as they like, but nobody gets hurt.

"What are they?" I ask my host. He tells me that they are gels for florescent tube lighting and that I can find them at any electrical supply store along Canal Street. They come in a variety of colors and cost only a few dollars. Upon learning this I am now lighting up and blinking all different colors myself, imagining the wonderful things I could do with these colorful, child-friendly tubes in the classrooms.

The first obvious application is to use the tubes as bars for playing limbo. I adapt my second idea from an activity I'd watched Karen Duffy lead.

DUCK AND JUMP

With the children scattered over the mats in front of her at the "One With Heart" Dojo, I've see Karen Duffy wield a baton the size of a broom handle. Crying out "Duck!" she swings the long stick just slightly below the average height of her students, forcing them to bend down in order not to be struck as it sweeps past.

Next she cries "Jump!" while sliding the stick in an arc on the floor, forcing the group to jump as the bar glides under their feet. The leader then continues calling out "Duck" or "Jump" in an unpredictable sequence so that the children must remain alert, never knowing if they will be made to "duck" or "jump" on the next command.

This is an excellent fitness activity for school-aged children as well an exciting party game. For fun you can even mix it up, calling out "duck" as you sweep the tube along the floor or "jump" as you swing it in the air. Older children may want to take turns being the leader and wielding the tube. Again thanks to the hallow plastic gels nobody gets decapitated.

DUCK AND JUMP WITH PRESCHOOLERS

With young children the fun begins right away, as you demonstrate how to duck and how to jump. The children will enjoy watching you do this. Bring them to their feet so that everyone can practice these new skills together. Before introducing the tube, try a preliminary round of the game, calling out "Duck" and "Jump" while demonstrating the correct response to each of these commands for and with the group. As always, an additional teacher or two would be invaluable for maintaining the cohesion of such a lively and relatively sophisticated activity.

Children will be intrigued when the teacher first introduces the tube and holds it out for them to touch. Assure them that no one gets hurt with a light plastic tube. This is a chance for the teacher to be funny and hit yourself over the head to prove your point. Boink!

Even after plenty of demonstrations and practice runs, many children will not be able to duck and jump where and when they belong in the game. Try simplifying things at first. For example, sweep the tube above the children's heads so that only the teacher has to stoop. The children will still find it exciting. Beware, however, that young children may also still be learning how to hop and jump and may not be ready to execute these skills on command.

Many children will try earnestly but mistake the timing so that their jumping feet land directly on the tube with a crunching sound that dents the plastic. I've played with my tubes until they're quite scuffed up and treat myself to a shiny new one only if the plastic crimps or tears, leaving a sharp edge. Be sure to slide the tube slowly along the floor and encourage any of the more hesitant hoofers to simply step over the bar when it arrives at their shoes. As a safety measure, instruct the children to remain where they are and wait for the tube to come to them. Discourage the children from chasing the tube and possibly causing collisions.

As with many activities involving new skills, practice makes perfect. Leave a colored gel in the classroom closet and break out "Duck and Jump" on rainy days. Over time there will be noticeable improvement in the groups' coordination.

The next week I bring the game to Marble Hill where it becomes an instant success in both classrooms. By Tuesday my new orange gel is at work, amusing the children of Highbridge, at least until the inevitable occurs. In my second class of the afternoon the children are yelping with delight, bending and attempting to jump as the sliding tube pursues their sneakers when Miss Bilkis enters the room. Immediately her jowls tremble at the sight of all the ebullient chaos.

"This is an outside toy!"

We knew to expect this kind of criticism and, behind her back, Miss Gracia and Miss Felipa roll their eyes.

Here We Go Gathering Nuts in May

"So, how's your pride and joy?"

On Friday morning I joke with the waitress at the Castle Hill Diner, thinking that I'm talking to Lena only to have Laurie correct me.

"Oh, you must be thinking of my sister. That's her thing."

Lena has left for Greece and won't be back for another month. After setting me up with coffee and apple pie, Laurie does just what her sister did last week and slides into the booth to sit across from me.

"I'm thinking of becoming a teacher," she announces with a yawn, spreading her fingers on the tabletop to examine her manicure.

"Laurie, think carefully. It's a lot more work than it seems. And sometimes the adults are more difficult than the kids."

It just comes out of me. I think of Miss Catalina, she of the mind games—as well as a host of other occupational indignities, bouncing paychecks, and blows to the back of the head among them. With her sensuous good looks and rather feline self-absorption, Laurie strikes me as a candidate for a future in cosmetology.

"What about working at a beauty parlor or being a hostess at a nice restaurant?" I feel a little guilty for coming on like some antiquated, sexist old relative, but don't feel that my advice has squelched any heroic pedagogical zeal in my waitress. Listening, Laurie only nods lethargically. She flips her lustrous ponytail, cracks her chewing gum, and manages to look particularly unteacherly.

In my first class of the morning, little Anita covers her ears as she always does when I take out my guitar. I overlook her gesture as best I can—still, her unrelenting protest does not make an easy beginning for the day. Nathan, the autistic boy who once struck me in this room, no longer attends Head Start. But across the hall in my second class, Oliver has a meltdown. He knocks over a chair and wails through the entire session. Above the uproar of Miss Natalia trying to bring him under control, I can barely be heard leading the class in song. Luckily, I escape before Miss Catalina could decide to make one of her surprise attacks and dub me "unprepared." Closing my eyes over the bathroom sink on my ten-minute break, I no longer chastise myself for being negative about Laurie's teaching aspirations.

As I prepare to open the door for my third class I'm jolted to remember that I won't be seeing Miss Regina there anymore. While I'm fond of Miss Ascension, the returning assistant teacher, I am still jonesing for my feisty old friend whom she has replaced. Nobody seems to know where Miss Regina has been reassigned. They tell me only that she could be anywhere in the pool of substitute teachers that are scattered like dandelion seeds among the five boroughs. I miss the funny things she said and her mischievous smile. Now when Miss Salomé becomes strident and ridiculous, there will be nobody to catch my eye and wink.

After this challenging morning I grieve over the loss of two of this center's more puckish characters, first Mr. Felix and now Miss Regina. What will become of me if Miss Priscilla ever gets transferred? Before I can get too depressed, I will find solace from a most unlikely source.

It happens over lunch in the staffroom when a determined Miss Salomé comes after Mr. Justin wielding a clipboard. "Do you have anything to contribute to our newsletter?" With her pencil in the air she accosts him with her scorching cheer. As always, Mr. Justin's keeps his eyes on the pages of his book. Finally he sighs.

"What do you want to know?" he asks wearily.

"Oh, tell us something in-ter-esting about yourself" she chirps, "some hobby that you have perhaps, maybe something about your family?"

For several minutes the two of them remain suspended. Mr. Justin doesn't move while Miss Salomé zooms in on him like a pointing hound that has treed a woodland animal. At last he clears his throat. "Tell 'em I ain't won the lottery yet and that's why I'm still here." My unfolded copy of the New York Post conceals my giggles. Even without Mr. Felix and Miss Regina, the staffroom Punch and Judy show lives on.

I doubt that this tidbit of soft-spoken snark will complete the interview but he is saved from her further questions by the arrival of two uniformed janitors that I have never seen before. Both African-American men burst into the staffroom with loud, resonant voices and high fives for Mr. Justin. "Aye, Look who it is! Look who's still here!" they tease clasping hands and smacking one another on the back. For a few minutes the three men reminisce about bygone days when they worked at other centers.

I have never seen Mr. Justin so animated and happy as he is with these guys updating each other on the lives of old friends and recalling sports victories from some past association. As they leave, one of the men pauses on the threshold, pointing his finger back toward the staffroom. "East Tremont, the varsity field!" He shouts his parting words and Mr. Justin laughs quietly and shakes his head "Yeah, ... we had an eleven man team for 7 yard rush," he says, dreamily returning to his paperback.

Through the whole encounter Miss. Salomé has been carrying on her own shouted conversation with another teacher, oblivious to Mr. Justin having told his real story.

Because I too have not yet won the lottery, I am the next one to get Shanghaied by Miss Salomé and her newsletter, while I'm eating my "too fishy for the children" Friday salmon filets and trying to read the paper. Suddenly with my mouth full of waxy potatoes, I'm supposed to deliver an uplifting paragraph. I'm not feeling nearly as eloquent as Mr. Justin managed to be. The simple truth is that my life doesn't feel very newsworthy at the moment. Mark's temp assignment ended last week, and he's back to the numbing business of arranging job interviews and sending out resumes.

When I'm not at Head Start, I can be found rushing off to teach private guitar students, performing at kiddie parties or pushing my amplifier in a shopping cart to Hospital Audience gigs. I'm a perpetual motion machine, but all these activities don't come close to paying our household expenses. And standing before me is Miss Salomé, like some bossy fourth grader with her clipboard, positively gyrating with self-importance.

Is there no rest for the weary? But Hi-Ya! As they have on other occasions, Haskell and Simon pop up in my heart to defend their mother—this time with the *Pukulan* lesssons they've been taking. Now I have it. The bulletin about me will read that after school, Miss Leah's two sons study a form of Indonesian Kung fu at a Dojo called One with Heart. This form of martial art incorporates strikes and movements learned from jungle animals such as the tiger, cranes, monkeys, and snakes.

"Better be nice to your boys Miss Leah, you don't want to get flipped onto your back!" And "Oh, Ha ha ha, thank you Miss Leah!" She's happy with the silly scoop I provide and scratches away at her clipboard. I make a break for Castle Hill Avenue to spend the remainder of my lunch hour in peace.

IF YOU'RE HAPPY AND YOU KNOW IT, SAY HI-YA!

Pukulan again inspires me to add more spice to "If You're Happy and You Know It." Now I insert what will become the explosively popular "Hi-Ya!" to the verses. Within the half hour I have the children of Room Six making a Karate chop in the air to cries of "Hi-Ya!" and they're thrilled! Their eyes dance with this bite of mischief and aggression. After "If you're happy and you know it, clap your hands, stamp your feet, and wave 'Hello!'" I have them jump up and use that same hand to slice the air in front of them as they cry out, "Hi-Ya!" and squeal with delight.

For the rest of the year they will not let me finish the song without including this verse.

HI  **YA!**

I leave St. Anthony's energized and proud for having brought "If you're happy and you know it" to the next level. Sitting on the train, I am happy and I know it.

Mutiny

At St. Anthony's, unpredictable Nathan has been placed elsewhere. But by late April the teachers in Room One face another challenge. Diego, a pale Hispanic child, who had always been cooperative and high-functioning, deteriorates after his father abandoned the family. Teachers now must stop him from lashing out at the rest of us. From the time I open the door to when I leave, he growls and thrashes under their restraining arms.

"How's it going, Diego?" I ask as I pass him by to get to the front of the room. I hope to connect with something of the boy he used to be; the boy who used to try to snatch my costume jewelry, who liked music sessions. I meet his dark brown eyes but his expression looks frozen, or perhaps heart-broken beyond endurance.

Diego isn't the only changeling I face.

Before every class begins, I stand in the quiet hallways and cherish my last moment of stillness. As soon as I turn the knob and open the door, the spotlight pours on me and my numerous responsibilities begin. When the teacher has good control over her flock I find the children sitting in rows, listening to a storybook while they anticipate my arrival. If the teachers are indifferent, and the room I enter is in chaos, then I risk being sacked like a quarterback. The children may rush me crying, "Miss Leah. Miss Leah!", throwing their arms around my legs and hitting the strings of my guitar, almost knocking me over. I am reminded of a summer camp counselor who'd actually had her shoulder dislocated by an overly amorous group hug from the campers who cherished her.

At these moments, of course, the first thing I do is to send out an S.O.S. to the teachers. I used to depend on their quick response to classroom emergencies but as I feared, now that they have to work harder rehearsing the Extravaganzas when I come, some teachers who had always been my allies no longer cooperate with me.

At Marble Hill Miss Lucia and Miss Blanca remain supportive. However in Room One the usually upbeat Ms. Nicole shows me her dark side. Now when I ask for her help with a child she goes on strike, becoming sarcastic and contrary. "No, Mommy. I'm not going to do that for you. You on your own!" she snaps, her double chin held high.

In her room we were rehearsing Harry Belafonte's "The Banana Boat Song," as well as a traditional Bahamian number to represent the Caribbean Islands. For their costumes we plan to decorate the children with pictures of assorted fruit dangling from grass skirts that would be cut from the cloth of the ever-present butcher paper. Ms. Evangeline and Ms. Nicole have created cardboard stencils, circles for the oranges, as well as shapes for bananas, apples, and purple triangles to represent bunches of grapes. Ms. Evangeline dozes through our rehearsal as usual, but Ms. Nicole cooperates as we practice our songs and the little hula dances that accompany them. I hope that things are improving between us, but her hostility returns by the end of my afternoon class in her room.

"Here, I can't finish all this. You do it." She thrusts the stencils and a stack of construction paper into my hands. She seems to feel the Extravaganza is something I am imposing on her, and does not perceive the burden from on high that I struggle to figure out myself. "If you want them done by your show, then you can take them home with you," she continues.

Later, riding the subway home, I resent the additional plastic bag of Ms. Nicole's supplies that I squeeze onto my lap. The teachers aren't supposed to load me up with their "prep" work. Is she daring me to put in a complaint, part of a war I am not anxious to begin? Instead, I leave Mark with the boys, and late that night I step out with my sister, Naomi, and her friend Tony for a scissors party. We spread our project over a table at a neighborhood café where we cut out apples and oranges and drink wine. It might not be the wisest combination but then nobody loses a finger or even sustains a paper cut. The show must go on! Children in Ms. Nicole's class didn't have to know that the construction paper fruit salad dangling from their costumes was fermented in sangria.

In my second class at Our Lady of Miracles, Miss Felipa—another dissenter—also becomes uncooperative. At the beginning of the year she was always helpful and ready to mold her full lips and pretty South American features into a warm smile when I appeared. But slowly, over the year, she becomes belligerent and fed up in the classroom. Perhaps it has something to do with Miss Gracia's pregnancy. The less work Miss Gracia was able to perform, the more Miss Felipa remained in her chair when the kids acted up, ignoring my appeals for help and studying her fingernails.

One day when I have the children dancing in a circle, I need another teacher to help me keep order. She stands up reluctantly after my third request for assistance. Even then, she brings only one hand to our circle. With her other hand she cups a cell phone to her ear as she continues her conversation through our Hokey Pokey.

"You put your cell phone in, you put your cell phone out"... well, that was a new one!

'When You Assume...'

How many times had I heard the clever old adage, "When you assume, you make an *ass* out of *u* and *me*" and still didn't learn? How can I be surprised when Miss Antonette manages to annoy me again? The pressure of the upcoming Extravaganza brings out the worst in both of us. Last week I sat in her office discussing how to pep up what feels like a lackluster program.

"Oh, that's cute. You should do that." She liked my idea of making fans from tassels and Hawaiian-themed party plates, which I could staple onto tongue depressors for the children to dance with. In a party goods store I can easily find simple plastic *leis* for decorating our little *kanis* and *wahinis* (boys and girls in Hawaiian). While there are plenty of 99 Cent stores in Marble Hill, the cost of outfitting four classes can easily multiply into a budget-buster for my pocket.

To my question of, "Who will pay for these items?," Miss Antonette wrinkles her nose and waves dismissively. What does that mean? "Shall I bring you the receipt?' I ask, by way of clarifying the matter. And to this I believe she says "yes."

A week later Miss Antonette smiles to see the colorful fans I've made that sparkle in the hands of the children. She likes the dance, but she doesn't want to pay the fiddler. After the morning classes, when I present her with the receipt for $16.40, she shakes her head, "No."

"I can do nothing for you," she says as coyly as she had the first time my paycheck from Head Start bounced. She says that she never agreed to reimburse any of my expenses. She has no idea why I think she would.

As with so much else at Head Start, I find I am left to my own devices.

A New Circle Game

In late May the weather begins to flash tempestuous previews of the summer ahead. On Tuesday morning I awake to rumbles of thunder. After lunch I remain in my hideaway backstage and curl up with a textbook that I pull from the stack I find leaning in a dark corner. The book happens to be a general introduction to music for grade school children. At the end of a chapter on rhythm, I get intrigued by instructions for an African game that involves singing while passing blocks around a circle.

Although the game is intended for older children, I like the idea of sitting my Head Starters in a circle, each with a wooden building block before him to pass to the child beside him on the beat of a song. As with Whiz! and other new skills that we try as a group, we'll never do it perfectly—but playing this game together can be a valuable challenge and one that the gang will enjoy.

THE AFRICAN BLOCK CIRCLE GAME

Sit the children on the floor in a circle. In front of each child put a small wooden block such as one of the small squares from the set of classroom building blocks. If blocks are not available, other objects can be used, as they don't have to be of identical size and shape for this version of the game. Begin by having the group sing a song that everybody knows, or teach them one especially for this purpose. The book had notated a short African chant, but any song with a strong 2/4 pulse will suffice.

One, two, one, two. One! On the first beat the children reach out and pick up the block that's in front of them. Two! On the second beat have them place the block in their hand in front of their neighbor to the left (it could be to the right, so long as everybody is passing in the same direction). Now the block that they first held is in front of their neighbor and everybody finds that a new block has landed in front of them. One! On the next beat everybody picks up her new block. Two! Down it goes in front of her neighbor and until the song is finished. If singing a song together as you pass blocks proves too complicated, try passing the blocks around the circle to a beat from recorded music.

THE AFRICAN BLOCK CIRCLE GAME WITH STICKERS

Trying to coordinate a circle of preschoolers passing blocks in the same direction on a beat becomes a sort of jolly mess. Some children understand and can pass and receive their block on time, but sooner or later blocks pile up in front of the more confused children, creating a logjam.

So I enlist the teachers, and perhaps a handful of my block-passing standouts from the group. The rest of the group watches as I take a sticker—maybe just a colored shape, or a popular figure like SpongeBob—and pop it onto the bottom of one of the blocks.

In a small circle as the other children watch in suspense, the elite group plays a short round of the same game, passing the blocks until the song ends. After the blocks are passed for the last time, everybody turns over his block to see who comes up empty and who ends up with the sticker. Even the children who watch passively enjoy the suspense and are willing to sit for subsequent rounds and to sing along with us as we play.

This version of The African Block Game can be used as an elimination game for classrooms or parties where the person who uncovers the sticker at the end of each round becomes "out." The game continues with the participants shrinking by one with every round until the single person left without the sticker becomes the winner.

For a second variation to be played with young children, each child receives his own individual sticker (no two alike) to put on the bottom of his block at the beginning of a round. The blocks inevitably get jumbled up. When the music stops everybody turns over his blocks and hold them up. This way, everybody sees where his special block with its sticker ended up. Or did anybody get his own block again?

THE WALKING GAME

For yet another variation, have the circle of players remove one shoe and place it in front of him. Run the activity just as with the small blocks, only now the children enjoy the excitement of watching all the different shoes appear in front of them as, step-by-step, these shoes "walk" around the circle. When the music ends the children enjoy seeing where their respective shoes landed. If it happens that the children end up with their own, then you can congratulate the group: their shoes "walked home."

Peek-a-Boo!

On Friday morning as usual I pace the still sparsely populated uptown platform at Astor Place. In echoing stillness I walk all the way to a pair of lonely green dumpsters at the far end of the station where I about-face to continue walking my beat of the jaundiced underworld. But moving down the platform, I spot a new arrival, a pixieish woman with short brown hair and glasses who now stands waiting. Like me, she holds a bag with toys and dolls poking out of the top. As I draw closer, we smile at each other.

Her name is Kathy Cohen, and she's just a little older than I. She explains that she's leaving her career as a publicist to go back to school to gain credentials needed to work with autistic children. She's been particularly stirred by child-directed models of learning and play pioneered by the late Dr. Stanley Greenspan, a child psychiatrist of whom I'd never heard. I introduce myself and tell her what my own bag of toys and the guitar on my back are doing on the platform at this hour.

Kathy has warm brown eyes and an engaging hoarse voice. By the time the Number 6 Train thunders into view, we have become fast friends, robustly exchanging our educational shop-talk. The subway doors open and we step into the car, still clucking like hens about case studies, certifications, and difficult supervisors, both hers and mine.

As we near Grand Central Station, Kathy tells me that she's giving a paper that day on 'object permanence,' the dawning awareness in children that objects continue to exist, even when the children can't see them.

"Oh, so that's what you call it," I say with a chuckle. Kathy's paper focuses on this phenomenon's earliest expression in babies and toddlers, but I encounter a more sophisticated level with my preschoolers everyday: I notice that my students become dumbfounded when they encounter me anywhere other than in their classroom, where they think I belong. The fact that I carry on a separate existence, that I have a home, that I walk to and from school just as they do, is a radical revelation to them.

"I saw you, Miss Leah! Miss Leah, I saw you!" They'll point at me and shout. "Miss Leah, I saw you in the play yard" or "I saw you on the sidewalk!" I hear it several times a day. The children cry out their discovery again and again, and I think: "Hold the presses. Somebody must call the *Times*!"

I describe this to Kathy, and dig into my bag for the book I plan as a surprise for the children, a treat for their diligent Extravaganza rehearsals. Its title is *Peek-a-Boo* and every page includes a little curtain or flap to lift or a tab to pull that uncovers different faces, animals or objects, *peak a boo*! Now you see 'em, now you don't!

Kathy looks at the book and her face loses color. In a voice so quiet that I can barely hear her above the roar of the train she asks "Leah, is there any way

I could borrow this book, even just for today? Your book is exactly what I need to demonstrate this concept, it could be the *pièce de résistance* of my whole presentation."

We are pulling into the 42nd Street station where Kathy changes trains, so I have only seconds to decide.

"Oh, sure. Take it for the week." I hand it to her and she hurriedly tucks it into her shoulder bag as the doors slide open.

"Oh my God, thank you so much!" Behind her glasses her eyes melt with gratitude.

"Good luck today," I wish her.

"I'll get it back to you next week" she pledges breathlessly. "We'll meet on the platform, same time, same place!" and she joins the mass of people exiting the train.

In the Sisterhood of Object Permanence, we will see each other again.

So, peek-a-boo! Suddenly my book is gone and my bag lighter. Yet I don't mind having sacrificed it for the good cause of highlighting my new friend's dissertation. With my luck, reading *Peek-a-Boo* in the classrooms at St. Anthony's will only land me in the dunce chair. I may be told, "These children have already had their story time," and, of course, "why wasn't I using my class time to rehearse for the Extravaganza?"

In my defense, our songs and dances are shaping up nicely. For our rendition of "*Mi Cuerpo Hace Musica*," I implement my mother's winning idea of creating ponchos out of the broad sheets of butcher paper. At school we cut circular head holes into yard long strips of the stuff and drape them over our performers. During the week the clever Miss Julissa, the teacher who knitted things, paints the bold stripes and zigzags of a real woven Mexican poncho onto the costumes and *Olé!*—we have ourselves a variety show.

In fact, allegedly "deficient," "disorganized" as I am, all my classes are more than ready for the big day. I've found my young performers more apt to cooperate when they have something to look forward to after the focused and repetitive work of a rehearsal. Still, for months now, Miss Catalina has turned the classrooms into a battleground where any fun supplies and novelties must be smuggled in to the children before she seizes them and levels her charges. I am beginning to feel like a spy. What I need is a many-pocketed trench coat for concealing my goodies, like a watch thief.

Rules, Rules, Rules

On the first truly balmy Tuesday at Our Lady of Miracles the warm temperature makes me forget about the item in our handbook that requires both consultants and staff to cover their knees. Overlooking this demand, I sport a pair of culottes that day, something akin to a long and loose-fitting skirt. It's nothing that can be called "an outside toy," but as soon as Miss Bilkis spots my bended knees, she makes me cover myself in a long royal blue Head Start bib smock that falls to my shins.

All day teachers giggle as I appear in their classrooms swallowed in the long, stiff apron that fits me like a drop cloth. Meanwhile, in my second class of the morning, Miss Felipa slouches in her chair, with the hot pink strap of a thong peeking from the rolls of fat that spill over the waist of her tight blue jeans. That is okay, that is not inappropriate. But heaven forbid the children should catch a fleeting glimpse of Miss Leah's scaly kneecaps! Don't do this. Don't do that—it is everywhere I go!

In a few short weeks school will end and I will face a summer of being unemployed and penniless. I am beginning to think it can't come fast enough.

Witch Tag

Against the odds, I still bring in light sticks to play with and simple sponge-ball magic tricks to reward my little Vaudevillians for their good behavior. But just as often it is the children who provide treats and surprises to break the monotony.

As a child, I liked to tease myself by asking my mother to play certain records in her collection that I found scary and forboding, like the low bassoon dance from the Nutcracker Suite or the percussive, implacable cycles of Ravel's "Bolero." Hearing the opening strains of these pieces, I would dash from the record player to hide under the livingroom furniture, away from the creeping pursuit of the music. This was fun because, while it elicited genuine licks of fear from my pulse, I knew that I was safe, tucked under my father's easy chair.

The school children are just like I was. They love to be chased and to flirt with danger when they are sure that there is no real consequence. At Highbridge one sunny Tuesday Ms. Magdalena and Ms. Madelyn take our class out to the schoolyard to hold Music and Movement in the open air. Outside the children show me their original game of "Witch Tag," where the pursuing "It" has to crook her fingers and cackle like a witch as she chases the others. I love the game and try to broaden their clever "Witch Tag" into "Monster Tag," which can encompass ghosts, dinosaurs and zombies, giving us opportunities to frighten each other with yet other movements. But of all the "bad guys" that stalk the children, none is as beloved as My Giant Robot.

Simon's Giant Robot

When he was little, anything that frightened Simon or made him angry was referred to his Giant Robot. "My Giant Robot will get you!" he would shriek to Haskell, who had provoked him. But sometimes that Giant Robot couldn't be trusted. Once or twice it was implicated in the case of broken dishes or other small accidents: "My Giant Robot did it."

I imitated Simon's Giant Robot at school just by lurching around the room after them, in a kind of variation on our "Zombie Tag." But for some classes I taped an empty cereal box to my back like an oxygen tank and let the children drop in pretend coins to "activate" me. In another popular variation I offered the children my arm and have them revolve it to "wind me up." Once "wound" to satisfaction, I would lurch to life and mechanically chase the squealing class until I "ran out of gas" —at which point it would be somebody else's turn to wind me up.

But "Why in the very temple of delight veiled melancholy has her sovereign shrine!" I agree with the poet Keats that even in the classroom, pleasure and delight seem to occasion as many problems as pain. My greatest fans are the first to become petulant and act out if I am not quick to deliver their longingly-anticipated fix of a particular song or game. Sometimes they're craving "The Giant Robot," or it could be a frolicking round of "Duck and Jump" or my routine where we pretend to bake, and then burn, a cake together. Activities that have an element of surprise like "Open, Shut Them" can go sour when kids can't wait through the set-up and want me to rush straight to the punch line. Then, just like the pretend cake we're baking, the activity itself burns and seems to fill the room with smoke and chaos. Sorry, *My Giant Robot did it.*

Lady Luck

Not content to be just a nursery school teacher, I join an emerging girl band, Lady Luck. I am not on the guitar or the banjo with this group, but instead I slap my old half-size upright bass that has leaned dustily in our bedroom corner for years, a relic from my troubadour life before Mark and the children—before ALL of the children. Between epic laundry folding and the dish washing that erodes my fingerprints, I arrange bass lines for the set list of Lady Luck and join in for their Thursday night gigs at a local bar.

But sadly, I'm not having luck with the ladies. While it feels good to play something other than "Five Little Monkeys Jumping on the Bed" and "Old MacDonald," I must leave hurriedly at the end of our second set. I can't linger drinking after-hours as my twenty-something, devil-may-care bandmates do. They are not expected at Castle Hill early the next morning, and do not have to be asleep at a reasonable hour or turn into a pumpkin.

Alas, the gap between these lassies and me extends even beyond our disparate bedtimes. I've tried doing "the hang," bonding over sandwiches and beers, but we're not connecting. When we are together, the Lady Luckers continuously photograph each other with their cell phones and pass around the results for giggles. I don't blame them. Perhaps if I were young, pretty and leggy as they are, this pastime would hold great appeal. But by my age it's irksome.

"Ooh, look at those legs! I have the best view, ha ha. You have to turn around." The girls are on the make, and anything that moves is fair game. They're compulsively cruising everything on wheels; mischievously professing interest in both sexes. What am I to tell them? That at this point a good night's sleep is sexy? And wait 'til you're my age when you'll know exactly what I'm talking about? Yeah, this routine is a real hit with the younger set.

One night at Rockwood Music Hall when the lead singer fails to include me as she's introducing the band, I decide to opt out and this chapter ends without so much as a backward catcall. I figure something's got to be wrong when I have to admit to feeling less out-of-place on Friday mornings, seeing Kathy Cohen in the subway and joking in the staffroom with Mr. Justin, Miss Priscilla, and the others, than I did the night before on stage with my bandmates. The crew at work are, after all, weary people of my own age with bunions and kidney stones, children, and even grandchildren to keep track of.

I don't miss feeling like an old fart on a bar stool with Lady Luck. But quitting the band reignites a restlessness in me. I don't want to exist solely to satisfy three- and four- year-olds who demand their predictable classroom favorites. I want creative collaborators who can hold a conversation and not turn every environment into a meat market as the Lucky Ladies did. I want to dole out harmonies and arrange the original songs that still come to me. I want to find a place for my bluegrass fingers and the fiddle tunes that I love. But who am I, at the end of the day, when no supervisors are cracking the whip and no administrators are signing the paychecks? How does my set list read then? What are the real songs and dances of my heart and who will play them with me?

Field Day at the Mall

On Friday morning Kathy Cohen waits for me at the Astor Place station. In the middle of all the "basic black" that New Yorkers wear, her light colors set her apart on the platform. I admire her spring jacket with its shimmer of pastels. She makes me laugh, describing how she has to shave it like a beard when the cotton pills up. I tell her that I have sheets that do that at home and she says that I should try going after them with a razor.

I ask how her paper on Object Permanence went over and she says that she aced it.

"So how did they like *Peek-a-Boo*?"

She smiled sheepishly. "Don't be mad at me."

She tells me that her thesis advisor wants to hang onto the book and that, in fact, the department wants to continue using it to teach.

"Wow!" I tell her. I had brought *Peek-a-Boo* on a whim to entertain my preschoolers. Now it was entertaining the dissertation committee at City College. Peek-a-boo! Apparently, we never outgrow it.

I tell Kathy that the long-term loan is fine. Even if she'd returned it to me, I cannot use it today. At St. Anthony's I find buses idling in front of the school.

Surprise! A field trip is scheduled today and all six classes at St. Anthony's will be taken to an indoor play space at a mall in suburban New Jersey. As with the autumn apple-picking trip, Head Start has forgotten about my music classes. Just like last time, there is no particular role for me other than to support the teachers. Will today be harder than ususal? I have no idea what to expect, but if I want to get paid for my time, then it's New Jersey or bust!

Once on the bus to which I'm assigned, I recognize little Cresi, the child at whose birthday party I entertained around Christmas. Last month she acquired a pair of pink, plastic glasses. Tears stream from the bottom of her smudgy lenses. The girl is frantic because the administrators won't let her ride on the same bus with her mother, who teaches another class. Cresi is a fragile child, even at the best of times. Being bussed from her school to a strange place while separated from her mother is traumatic. Normally, every class rides in a bus with their own teachers. But couldn't an exception be made in this unique circumstance to alleviate the distress of a staff child?

I feel the sadistic handiwork of Miss Catalina in this inflexibility. Once her class has boarded the bus, Cresi won't let me out of her sight. Will today be harder than usual? As Cresi sits beside me and clamps my wrist in the grip of her astonishingly cold, small fingers, I am left with no doubt.

"Bend down, Miss Leah. I need to tell you a secret. In your ear." I bend down to her and she whispers "Miss Leah, you make me happy."

At the mall I keep busy fishing kids out of the pits of colored plastic balls they slide into and walking them to and from the bathroom. Most of the kids adapt quickly and enjoy the unfamiliar surroundings. Oliver, however, becomes over-stimulated. At every opportunity he dashes for the exits and fire doors. Time and again, Miss Natalia hauls him back wailing, her own strong, ragged voice penetrating the mayhem like a laser.

As the other children play in bouncy houses and navigate the padded, plastic jungle of the play space, Oliver weeps and continuously tries to escape. Even at lunchtime as we get taken to a shabby, windowless "party room" and are served half slices of a surprisingly sumptuous pizza, Miss Natalia doesn't have a moment to sit and eat. She watches Oliver, runs after him or tries to calm him down. I wonder if, at home, his parents are as diligent as she.

Throughout the day, Miss Natalia never appears to tire. But once we're back in the staffroom she all but breaks down. "Aye, first I watching Oliver but now we have babysitter and you know, babysitter crazy too." Apparently an aid accompanied us to help supervise Oliver—although the only person I'd seen with him was Miss Natalia. "I tell Miss Catalina" she goes on, "Please, you know next time we make a trip, to please don't bring Oliver. He doesn't enjoy it, I tell her, you know...I tell her...just, PLEASE!" Seeing Miss Natalia look so desperate makes me remember how the day began with Cresi's tears on the bus. Most of the kids and teachers have had fun at the mall, but clearly it hasn't been a holiday for everyone.

THE EXTRAVAGANZA, Marble Hill

After all these months, I come face-to-face at last with this mother of all culminating events, the first of the three musical Extravaganzas. As I arrive at the Land & the Sea restaurant, I find I'm not the only one with the jitters. As Nicky brings my coffee his emotional blue eyes are wide with fear. In his strong accent he says that he has been to the doctor to get some kind of test: blood, thyroid, pancreas. Interpreting his broken English, I am sure only that his news doesn't sound good.

As he hurries off to wait on other customers, I am grateful that I have concerns of my own to distract me. I have notes to go over and prompts to memorize. Remembering the humiliating day at Our Lady of Miracles when I was made to cover my knees, I proactively draped myself, for this occasion, in an ankle-length polka-dotted gown with a large, silly bow at my back. I've used it for calling square dances, and now the gown should be perfect for taking the stage as master of ceremonies.

Nervously, I run over the shows in my mind as I finish my blueberry muffin and drink my coffee. When I'm done, Nicky is not in the dining room. I organize my things but will not leave until I have said goodbye to him. Today is the last day that I am scheduled to work at the Head Start Center at Marble Hill. Especially today, after what he's told me, there is no good way to let him know that this is to be our final Monday morning together. No one at work, not Miss Antonette or Brenda Keenan, has said anything about my returning next year—so it is quite possible that nothing will ever call me to this far-away subway stop and bring me through the doors of his restaurant again. Under my coffee cup I slide a juicy tip. When he returns from the kitchen, I choose to say nothing at all. But today Nicky gets two hugs.

Outside the strong morning sun twinkles and dives behind the steel beams that hold the elevated tracks. On the short walk to school for the last time, I think of Nicky. Will he be all right? Or must he undergo chemotherapy and lose his hair, just as mine is coming back? Waiting for the light to change on Broadway, I run my fingers through the fluff at the top of my head. For the first time all year my curlicues are long enough for me to have pinned a flower there.

At this center there will be two performances, one for the two morning classes and another one for the afternoon. As families arrive they are directed to Miss Lucia's and Miss Blanca's room, which is the larger of the two classrooms. There aren't enough chairs. Parents and siblings sprawl everywhere, overtaking the tables and the floor. Once they settle, I wend through and over them to the front of the room, sending a wink toward the barely cracked classroom door to my right. Just behind it in the hall the children are waiting in line with Miss Antonette, ready to enter on the cue of my turning on the CD player.

The room quiets down and I welcome everybody to the center and introduce myself. I thank them for the honor of letting me get to know their kids and explain the "Head Starters, Who We Are!" theme of our performance. Because our opening number will be "Black and White" by The Three Dog Night, I have brought in one of those large, circular cookies that is frosted half chocolate and half vanilla and called "a black and white." I flip on the boom box and the children file in, just as we planned.

As the song begins, I hold up the cookie for all to see. Impulsively, I take a bite and it brings down the house. Everybody starts laughing, and the room relaxes. The children look natural and we have a great show, straight through to taking our bows to whistles and spirited applause.

The afternoon performance goes much the same way. This time Nioka, Kaleem, and Habib are in my chorus line. To my relief, on this occasion even obstreperous Undine behaves herself. For our island Hula dance everybody wears the plastic *leis*, and I strum a ukulele. The children sway, the construction paper fruit stencils swing back and forth against their butcher paper costumes—such a victory lap after all the adversity.

To my embarrassment, Destiny's parents present me with a bouquet of flowers. Rambunctious Jing, who almost knocked out my teeth last fall, also hands me a present—a magic-markered rendition of my guitar, complete with all six strings and twenty-two frets clearly delineated where they belong on the neck. His mother assures me that he made it all by himself. "It for you, special!" she says, beaming with pride.

"You did it!" As the families reunite with their performers, Miss Antonette throws her arms around me, full of giggles. She knows that the visiting administrators are pleased with the center, and I feel that I have helped her to shine.

With the shows behind us even the contrary Miss Nicole comes in for a hug—her bright, woodpecker's laugh restored as she pats my back. And then I get a warm, humid embrace from Miss Evangeline, a peck from Miss Blanca and a high five from Mr. Felix, who whispers, "Don't let that crazy bird at St. Anthony's forget about me now!" The hardest goodbye of all is of course Miss Lucia. We've traded photographs and so many stories that she feels like an old friend.

"Regards to your family," we both say and, "Girlfriend, try to rest your voice this summer," I affectionately scold—knowing that she never will.

Before leaving, I stick my head into Miss Antonette's office. So much flashes through my mind as she looks up from her desk to smile and wrinkle her nose.

"Ah, Miss Leah!" she sighs, and rises from her chair. For a while we stand reminiscing. We remember when the lunatic was hurling objects out his window, "and peeing!" she reminds me, shaking her head. I ask her if she has seen the overly chatty assessment counselor, Miss Fernanda, and she rolls her eyes. And what of her wayward little brother, I ask? She says that he's applied to a community college. She hopes that this will at least get him out of her mother's house. And her courtship with the Texas heart surgeon? I've saved this line of inquiry for last, and she grins broadly. As of her last trip to Dallas he is actually now her fiancé she says, and we clutch each other and squeal. So, will they be dancing to "The first cut is the deepest" at their wedding? I prod her and she laughs. Certainly her DJs mix would include the eighties music she so loves.

"The eighties, Miss Leah. That was my time!" I can see her tilting back in her chair and gushing this as hits from The Romantics and Culture Club wailed from the CD player on her shelf. I had other memories in this office as well. "I can do nothing for you." She had sounded so harsh and thoughtless after the Archdiocese had bounced my paycheck. And then she'd repeated the statement when she refused to pay me for the art supplies I purchased, which helped make the Extravaganzas so successful.

There were times when I wanted to smack her, but now all was forgiven. In the afterglow of the strong performances at the end of our last day, I feel close to her. I remember how, early on in my tenure, she'd playfully swatted my guitar case as I left for the day, saying, "I see you came to us prepared to work." So I had delivered on that promise. I had done good work here in her classrooms. Today the children and I had made her proud. Before I leave we hug again. Now we can be proud together.

THE EXTRAVAGANZA, Our Lady of Miracles

Early summer up the hill is actually beautiful. Flowering bushes push through chain-link fences and conceal the loops of barbed wire that crown some of the lower facades. Tree branches, which bore only snagged plastic bags all winter, are now splendid with waving leaves. Their gentle shadows and the dappled light they throw distract my eye from the usual trash and graffiti. As my bus overtakes the crest of Ogden Avenue, only the mausoleum-like projects remain untouched by the seasonal finery.

"Oh, it's you down there!"

At Our Lady of Miracles Mr. Brock arrives to find me in my polka dots, sprawled on the floor beside his supply cabinet frantically regluing flyaway feathers to a stack of butcher paper costumes.

"I'm sorry, do you mind? I didn't know where else to work." I jabber.

"Not at all, Leah."

"Gosh, I hope they'll dry in time," I say, getting up and dusting my knees. The husky, barrel-chested art teacher ducks into his apron and smiles. Shyly he asks if I will be coming back next year. I don't know what to say. I've been too busy with the end of this year to even think about returning. I collect my stack of costumes and screw on the top to his bottle of Elmer's Glue. I thank him for the use of his floor, hoping that he will understand I'm also saying, "Thank you for your helpfulness, thank you for your gentle presence in this place so far away from my home. Have a good summer, have a good life." As with Nicky yesterday, I choose not to say a real goodbye.

There will be two performances today, like there were at Marble Hill: one for the morning classes and then a second for the afternoon groups. Head Start does not have use of the auditorium downstairs, so the shows will take place in Miss Felipa's and Miss Gracia's classroom. It's a tight fit, as it had been at Marble Hill, as the families of all three of the morning classes arrive. They quickly overflow the seating, and some fathers must hover at the periphery of the room.

"Oh my public, how they love me!" The wise-ass voice of Bugs Bunny reverberates in my mind as I face the sea of camcorders and recording devices held by the parents. I've never been so well documented in all my life, and feel nervous as I make my introductions. Although Highbridge is the neighborhood with the most severe poverty of the three centers where I work, it is the uncontested leader for expensive gadgetry, per capita. The children here seem as accustomed to being filmed as movie stars.

In front of the cameras our Banana Boat sails, our percussive Native American chant is powerful—but what really carries the day is when Miss Gracia's and Miss Felipa's class performs a number of which I have no prior knowledge. Apparently on their own time they have prepared a little dance to accompany the disco hit from the seventies, "YMCA." As the boom box plays this number, teachers tie bandannas to the children's elbows. Upon the last note they fall to their knees with fists raised in the air. The defining moment of our program earns foot stamping from the audience and thunderous applause.

Afterwards, I am flooded with congratulations from parents. I receive credit for this winning finale, even though I had nothing to do with it. No need to explain. I graciously accept their praise, which seems to balance out my having been blamed for crimes I had not committed, over the course of the year.

I'm astonished that such a racy number had passed muster with the powers that be. "YMCA," with its innuendo of under-aged gay hook-ups as a performance piece at the Catholic Our Lady of Miracles Elementary School, where we were made to cover our knees? Really? I would have expected Miss Bilkis to reject it as an "outside toy" for sure—a way-out there toy. And on this of all days, where is the old bridge troll? I look around, but surprisingly, she is nowhere to be found.

When I still don't see her by the end of our show I descend the stairway on the other side of the school, planning to check in with her. But Miss Bilkis is not in her office. Instead I find a young Filipino woman sitting at her desk, beneath the framed picture of Mother Theresa and Lady Diana. As she rises to greet me, I am impressed by how pretty this young woman is, every bit as svelte and comely as Miss Bilkis is not. After we introduce ourselves, she tells me that Miss Bilkis is retiring from Head Start and that she, Miss Daphne, will be the new site supervisor at Our Lady of Miracles, starting in the fall. She is surprised that I have not heard about this change of guards before and I am surprised to be hearing it, period.

"Leave it to old poker face to not let on," I think to myself. "Well, congratulations...and welcome," I tell Miss Daphne, and we both laugh. Before I leave, she asks if I have heard the news about Florence Galway.

"No, what's up?" I turn around.

"Did you not see it? It was all over the papers," she begins.

Florence Galway has been accused of embezzlement, padding her salary from eighty thousand up to two hundred fifty thousand dollars. She and the finance director, who was also siphoning money, were both asked to resign.

"Yes Miss Leah, she's utterly disgraced herself—stealing resources intended for some of the poorest children in the city. The New York Times says they're putting her in the Hall of Shame."

Florence Galway's thievery might have affected more than the children. Perhaps this explained the mystery as to why my paycheck had bounced twice.

"But wait, there's more," continues Miss Daphne. "Did you hear about the retaining wall that collapsed onto the West Side Highway earlier this month? Well, guess what? That was right near her apartment building. I think she had to be evacuated. Talk about instant karma, huh!"

I can't believe it. First I must process that Miss Bilkis will be gone. Whether or not I ever work here again, there will be no more bulldog to come frowning into the classrooms, no more "this is an outside toy" to contend with. Not a bad thing—an improvement, if anything—but it heralds the end of an era. For so many months now, dealing with Miss Bilkis has been right up there with death and taxes. When first I arrived and caught sight of the old eyesore, she'd stunned me. Now suddenly vanished, she stuns me all over again.

And then there is item number two: Florence Galway, the Wicked Witch who complained frivolously about me and threatened my job last fall, now charged with embezzling thousands of dollars from the charitable agency she was paid to oversee. Instant Karma; what comes around goes around. Her reputation destroyed, her home shaken, that's right, lady—don't mess with the funding for children at Head Start. And for that matter, don't mess with me!

I'm so absorbed in this real life revenge fantasy that I barely realize Miss Daphne is still speaking. "Will you be staying on with us?" she asks brightly.

For the second time today I don't know how to answer this question.

"I suppose I should be asking you that," I counter.

She smiles and again we laugh. She tells me that she will speak to Brenda Keenan, and that they will let me know.

Back in the office on our side of the building I find myself alone. They're all upstairs: Miss Lucy, Miss Inez, Miss Magdalena and the other teachers. As I zip away my guitar, I hear their happy voices, talking to parents and laughing. What to do? I'm not good at ending things and saying goodbye. With this bunch it's almost too much for me. I'll cry. I'll sob like a child. With the bright commotion still resounding from the classroom, I creep downstairs holding my bags and guitar. With my free hand gathering the bottom of my gown like Scarlet O'Hara, I burst from the cool hallway into daylight.

THE EXTRAVAGANZA, Castle Hill

On the Thursday night before the final show I have trouble sleeping. The first two Extravaganzas have gone without a hitch. But up ahead is St. Anthony's, the center of migraines and mind games, my toughest day of the week for so many reasons—anything can happen. What if Miss Catalina sets a trap for me? What if some of the families resume their tussle from the spring assembly and I get blamed for the melée? Tossing and turning from my strange world of anxiety, I sleep fitfully. In the only dream I can remember, Lena, my waitress at the Castle Hill Diner, is back from Greece. She looks different; instead of her long brown ponytail in my dream she wears her hair in a short blond bob.

Later that morning at the Castle Hill Diner, I find that Lena is indeed back from Greece. I know immediately that this is Lena and not her sister, Laurie, because she now wears her hair in the short, blond bob that I saw in my dream.

"Miss Lena, I saw you!"

I want to repeat it again and again. I feel just like the kids at school who must call out when they see me somewhere unexpectedly. I tell the newly blond Lena about how her hair-do entered my dream and she smiles.

"Oh, you must be a psychic person."

She tells Laurie that I'm a psychic, and the two sisters want me to read their fortunes. This evidence, from my strangely prescient dream, of more in life than subway tunnels and four-lane highways to connect us makes me feel magic in the air.

And then there was Florence Galway's apartment building, crumbling beneath the weight of her own evil. Since none of the neighbors were hurt, I could almost hear myself reading it as a bedtime story to the boys. Leave it to a neighborhood called Castle Hill to produce such a fairy-tale ending.

I don't tell the sisters that it's my last day of coming to their diner, at least for the summer, and possibly forever. I prefer to finish our party in high spirits. "I'll see you in my dreams!" we laugh as they follow me to the door. "Girls, thank you for the apple pie all these weeks." To myself I say: "Thank you for the mirth. Lena, Laurie, both of you. After this morning I will remember you as my pride and joy!"

For the Extravaganzas at St. Anthony's, a cavernous multi-purpose room at the back of the preschool has been adorned with banners painted by the children and cutouts of flowers. In the first show I'm surprised that Anita bursts into tears upon learning that today is our final music class. After months of watching her clamp hands over her ears as I enter the room, I hardly felt she cared.

All the children behave today. Oliver, Cresi, Diego—even our more fragile students and tough customers cause no disturbance and respond well to the teachers.

Most importantly, the parents behave. Six times that day, mothers, fathers, and grandparents pour in to occupy the rows of folding chairs. Six times I tell them I am the music consultant Leah Wells, and I thank them for the honor of working with their children. It is not untrue and yet by the sixth repetition, I begin to glaze over.

Final Curtain

As the room empties after the final performance, I pull the stillness around me like a blanket. I feel in a trance; at first I don't realize that I'm being watched. In true Miss Catalina fashion, she says nothing. But as I stoop to pull strips of masking tape from the floor, poking them with a pair of scissors, she hovers over me with an intensity that almost makes my ears ring. What am I going to hear from her now? That I'm "disorganized" and "deficient?" I am too exhausted to worry about it.

"I was hoping you would join us for the finale," I finally say, to break the uncomfortable silence. "Why didn't you get up and sing 'This Land Is Your Land' with us?"

"No. I never sing." She dismisses my question and hurriedly changes the subject. "Have you heard that the renovation of our center at Monsignor Boyle is complete? You know there could be five days of work for you this fall, Miss Leah. You may find you are a very tired lady, Miss Leah." She keeps laughing. Gradually I realize that this is her way of praising me. This is her way of letting me know that not only can I keep my job, but she is offering me more work, as much as I can take, and possibly even more than that.

"Your sons will say, 'Where did our mother go?'" she chides me, her voice even sillier and higher than usual. "Where did she go? Now she is always with Head Start in the Bronx."

All I can think, as she awkwardly laughs and laughs, is: "Why does Miss Catalina hate you?" As I have so many times before, I hear Haskell ask his adroit question. Only now, for the first time, she provides an answer.

"When I was a little girl in my country," she says, "did you know that I had a choirmaster who couldn't stand me? He separated me and forbade me from singing with the other children. He said that if I sang in his class it would ruin the music—not just for him, but for everybody else, you see."

I did see.

I put down my scissors to face her.

"Well that's not right," I say. "That's not right at all. You know that we would never treat any of our kids that way."

Miss Catalina nods her head and turns to look out the window. Girlishly, she rocks backward onto the heels of her loafers and stares at the traffic passing on Metropolitan Avenue.

"It happened so long ago," she says quietly, "but I can still feel the pain as if it were yesterday."

Exit Report

Life got easier. On the homefront, Mark found work and our household finances improved. I continued to teach at Head Start for years and found that even pulling off the Extravaganzas became smoother with practice. Using my increasingly time-tested songs and activities, I became more comfortable and adept with groups of children—I've been able to deliver five days of classes at as many different centers. A veteran consultant now, I have insights about what tends to work and what doesn't work well in music classes for the very young.

On Another Note details my relationships with staff members at the Head Start centers, and upon these adult relationships pivots the success of a program for children. My years in the business have taught me that team spirit between those in charge means everything. A visiting consultant can work easily with groups of children when qualified administrators, supervisors, and teachers set the tone. By "qualified," I do not mean they've merely earned degrees and certificates; I mean people sensitive to the emotional and cognitive growth of children. With devoted professionals I, as a visiting contributor, can provide the richest experience for children because my needs are met as well.

For example, I should never have been expected to lead five classes consecutively, as I was at St. Anthony's. How could my fifth class approach the caliber of my first or second? Such overscheduling exacerbates the natural burnout rate in this field. I much preferred the pace at Our Lady of Miracles: three classes in the morning, and three after lunch. I had much more to give the children.

Regular classroom teachers put in longer hours than mine, I realize, but their school days encompass an ebb and flow of energy, including quiet naps and meals. For a visiting consultant there is no such downtime. From the time the classroom door opens until the moment it shuts behind her, a consultant must implement and structure her program—making her a busy MC indeed.

My mission has become getting children out of their seats and moving, in contrast to their sedentary school day. In order to do this safely and effectively with preschoolers, support from classroom teachers is essential. To prevent chaos and collisions, teachers must supervise the children as I lead musical activities. I cannot perform both functions at once: I cannot sing and discipline with the same voice.

This is especially true for classes that include children with special needs. I favor the diverse classroom approach, especially for young children. But I cannot overstate the degree to which teachers must be trained to handle a range of students.

Too often, teachers perceive my sessions in their classroom as their break time. Either they come and go, leaving me unassisted with rooms of preschoolers. Or they talk among themselves, creating a distraction in the classroom and diffusing the energy. Sometimes administrators will actually delegate a specialist's visit as teacher's "prep time," thus institutionalizing this gap in teamwork.

Music is ceremony. We need a group's respectful focus. We need some agreed-upon rules and we need to know who is in charge. What music teacher wants to sing alone? A song by itself is like a deflated balloon. It needs air and voices and clapping hands to make it fly.

Appendix

BOOKS

Music and Games for Children:

Classroom Music Games and Activities by Julie Eisenhauer
(2014, Lorenz Educational Press)

Games That Sing: 25 Activities to Keep Children on Their Toes
by Loyan Beausoleil and Leah Wells (2011, Heritage Music Press)

101 Rhythm Instrument Activities for Young Children by Abigail Flesch Connors
(2004, Gryphon House)

Experiences in Movement, Birth to Age 8 (2004, Delmar Learning)

One, Two Three, Echo Me! Ready-to-Use Games and Activities to Help Children Sing in Tune by Loretta Mitchell (2003, Heritage Music Press)

Little Hands Fingerplays and Action Songs: Seasonal Rhymes and Creative Play for 2- to 6-year-Olds by Emily Stetson and Vicky Congdon
(2002 Vanwell Publishing, Ltd,)

Wiggle, Giggle and Shake: 200 Ways to Move and Learn (2001, Gryphon House)

101 More Music Games for Children by Jerry Storms and Cecilia Hurd
(2001, Hunter House)

101 Music Games for Children by Jerry Storms and Cecilia Hurd
(1995, Hunter House)

The Library of Children's Song Classics (Amsco, 1993)

American Folk Songs for Children (Oak Publications, 1948)

About Head Start:

The High-Performing Preschool: Story Acting in Head Start Classrooms by Gillian Dowley McNamee (2015, University of Chicago Press)

Head Start: The Inside Story of America's Most Successful Educational Experiment by Edward Zigler & Susan Muenchow (1992, Basic Books)

WEBSITES

Music and Games for Children:

http://pbskids.org/games/music
http://www.sfskids.org
http://www.nyphilkids.org

Preschool Music Curriculum and Teacher Training:

http://musicfactory.com.sg
https://www.musictogether.com/teach
http://www.musikgarten.org
http://www.thelearninggroove.com
http://musicrhapsody.com

Acknowledgments

Starting at home, I thank my husband Mark Wells and sons Haskell and Simon for graciously living in the shadows of string basses and banjo cases—and for their quirky innovations and suggestions that proved invaluable in my classrooms, and in this book.

Speaking of classrooms, certain colleagues shaped my approach to preschool education and provided unforgettable tips. Thank you Loyan Beausoleil, Karen Booth, Eileen Doster, and Amy Greenberg.

My musician comrades who trekked with me to many a preschool, hospital, and private birthday party gig include Sean Mahony, who provided the musical notation for this book; Daniel Mackler, Paul Helou, Henry Hample, John King, Robin Greenstein, Clarence Ferrari, and Roy Goldberg, who have all contributed recorded music, original songs, many good tunes and support over the years.

Lisa Cupolo, a truly gifted writer and editor, worked on an early version of my manuscript. Her enthusiasm and belief encouraged me to go forward with this project.

Once I had a working draft, other editors and specialists put in a great deal of time and care. Thanks to Elspeth Macdonald; Ruth Formanek, Ph.D.; Elaine Marshack, D.S.W., and my parents Aaron Rosenblatt, D.S.W., and Judith Rosenblatt. My father still corrects my grammar, and my mother so tenderly brought songs and love of music into my life.

As I developed this book, I appreciated the special input of friends like Anoush Bagdoyan, Judi Baller-Fabian, Tony Brescia, Tank Burt, Jaime Lubin, Kate McNamara McKeon, Patricia McNamara, Christopher Reardon, Carl Schnedeker, Paul and Nancy Schulkind, and Maren Swenson Waxenberg.

New friend and neighbor Gabe Turow, Ed. M., Ed.D. wrote our Foreword and introduced us to renowned preschool educator Judith Burton.

My talented second cousin, Anne Finkelstein of AJJ Design helped significantly with book design and production.

Our worthy publicist Sue Havlish of Nashville kept us going and got us out into the world. Where would we be without her?

A very special copyeditor left her creative mark upon my writing. Nancy Burke's guidance and suggestions were essential to this book. I regret that she is not here to help celebrate its publication. I will never forget her.

Finally, I had a teammate throughout the process of delivering this book from its beginnings (in a Spiderman backpack full of scraps and notes) to the book you're holding today. My sister, Naomi Rosenblatt, editor, and publisher worked at each phase with me. Together we organized material and searched for its best expression, we researched, networked, and envisioned. This project flew with us to the Bahamas, and bussed out to a motel on the beach in Montauk. To the ocean and to Naomi, thank you.

Author Bio

Leah Wells, a veteran children's music educator and performing musician, is the founder of the How Do You Do Music™ children's book series and the Restless Room Books™, both published by HelioTot, an imprint of Heliotrope Books. She is also the co-author of *Games That Sing: 25 Activities to Keep Children on Their Toes* (2011, Heritage Music Press), and a 2005 nominee for an Editorial Award of Excellence by the Parenting Publications of America (PPA). In January 2012 Leah's article *The Politically Correct Preschool and its Discontents: One Teacher's Story* was the Winter Exclusive Web Feature for the Canadian Education Association (CEA) Journal. Leah lives in New York City with her family.

CPSIA information can be obtained
at www.ICGtesting.com
Printed in the USA
FFOW02n1248241115
18794FF